本土

CHINESE ARTISTS IN A TIME OF TURBULENCE AND TRANSFORMATION

CAO FEI
HAO LIANG
HU XIANGQIAN
LIU CHUANG
LIU SHIYUAN
LIU WEI
LIU XIAODONG
QIU ZHIJIE
TAO HUI
XU QU
XU ZHEN
YANG FUDONG

This catalogue accompanies
the exhibition «Bentu», jointly presented
by the Louis Vuitton Foundation, Paris,
and the Ullens Center for Contemporary Art, Beijing.
The exhibition opens at
the Louis Vuitton Foundation
on 27 January 2016.

© Éditions Hazan, Paris, 2016
www.editions-hazan.fr

© Fondation Louis Vuitton, Paris, 2016
www.fondationlouisvuitton.fr

ISBN: 978 0 300 22238 8

BENTU

Distributed
by
Yale University Press,
New Haven
and London

HAZAN

FONDATION LOUIS VUITTON

CHINESE ARTISTS
AT THE FONDATION LOUIS VUITTON

CHIEF CURATOR
Suzanne Pagé

EXHIBITION «BENTU»

CURATORS
Laurence Bossé & Philip Tinari
with Claire Staebler

ARCHITECTURE
Cécile Degos

COORDINATION IN BEIJING
Winnie Hu
Christina You
Yang Zi
Felicia Chen
Lotus Zhang
Dai Weiping

COLLECTION: SELECTED CHINESE WORKS

Françoise Cohen
Nathalie Ogé

ARCHITECTURE
Jean-François Bodin
assisted by Hélène Roncerel

PRODUCTION
AND COORDINATION
Elodie Berthelot
Elise Blanc
Lucille Enel
Benjamin Baudet

ARTER
Renaud Sabari
Lisa Delmas
Manon Darphin
Coralie Goyard

LIGHTING
Laurent Escaffre – Ingélux

GRAPHIC DESIGN
Yan Stive

GENERAL COUNSEL
Pascale Hérivaux

CHIEF FINANCIAL OFFICER
Jean-Christian Séguret

DIRECTOR
OF COMMUNICATIONS
Isabella Capece
with Jean-François Quemin,
Clémentine Proby, Patricia Buffa

PUBLIC RELATIONS
Roya Nasser, Leslie Compan,
Brunswick Arts

CATALOGUE FOR THE EXHIBITION «BENTU»

EDITING
Suzanne Pagé, Laurence Bossé,
Philip Tinari, Claire Staebler

COORDINATING EDITOR
Annie Pérez

GRAPHIC DESIGN
Frédéric Teschner
with Lisa Sturacci

HEAD OF PUBLISHING
Raphaël Chamak

ÉDITIONS HAZAN

DIRECTOR OF PARTNERSHIPS
AND RELATIONSHIPS
WITH MUSEUMS
Jérôme Gille

EDITOR
Chloé de Lustrac with the
collaboration of Marion Lacroix

COPY EDITOR
Bernard Wooding

TRANSLATION FROM
FRENCH TO ENGLISH
Charles Penwarden
John Tittensor

ENGLISH/CHINESE VERSION
mot.tiff inside
Sacha Vichnevski, Hu Xiaoli Violette,
Catherine Wang, Jim Wu,
James Buxton, Hu Xiaoli Violette,
Joshua Sigal and with the invaluable
contribution of Timothy A. Frisk

PRODUCTION
Claire Hostalier

TABLE
OF
CONTENTS

BENTU
CHINESE
ARTISTS
IN
A
TIME
OF
TURBULENCE
AND
TRANSFORMATION

PREFACE
SUZANNE PAGÉ

The Fondation Louis Vuitton is opening this year of 2016 with China and its artists. At both the inception and the heart of this six-month season is the exhibition *BENTU*. It occupies the pool-level galleries, while the other galleries will be dedicated to a selection of Chinese works from our collection.

THE EXHIBITION
The *BENTU* exhibition, the first part of this survey of the Chinese scene, takes a deliberately limited selection of artists. This is no panorama. Such surveys have already been offered to remarkable effect, notably in Paris at the Musée National d'Art Moderne in 2003 and at Lyon's Musée d'Art Contemporain in 2004 – with all the inevitable limitations when you are dealing with a country whose population is now around 1.4 billion. Ten years later, we thought it was a good time to take a fresh look at the creators of this "soil" whose economic, political and cultural forces are a constant source of interest in our thoughts and our media.

The aim of this exhibition is to highlight some singular artists whose work is symptomatic of the current Chinese scene. They challenge the *clichés* and expectations based on assumptions and presuppositions that our frequent visits to studios in Beijing and Shanghai and exchanges with our various partners showed us to be just that.

The exhibition presents a limited selection of twelve artists, representing a diverse range of generations and approaches, living in continental China. Like artists everywhere, they work in multiple expressive modes, moving between them with remarkable fluency. The same goes for the boldness with which they handle techniques and tools, whether from local tradition or the latest technologies, which some artists audaciously combine. Generally speaking, what immediately struck us here is the exceptional ease with which these artist move through "turbulence and transformation". "Chaos is inspiring," says *Xu Qu*. This can be seen, first of all, in their ability to travel the world and always feel at home, the better, now, to come back to their "soil" (*Bentu*). Also noteworthy is the way their works reflect the constant mutations of society and its new parameters, as these impact the economy, ecology, urbanism and, on an unprecedented scale, relations between town and country. We were also impressed by the emergence of strong individuals triumphing over the mass, their powerful singularities echoing the constantly accelerating evolution of society.

See, for example, that free and happy woman dancing, oblivious to those around her, in the video by Hu Xiangqian which resonantly introduces this exhibition. Or again, the way Liu Shiyuan affirms her independence by preserving in the exhibition space her "room of one's own", insulated with carpet tiles bearing motifs from all around the world.

Familiarity with these artists and their work made us aware of the huge discrepancies that inspired their ideas and work – disparities that have developed on a scale and at a speed unknown elsewhere. In particular, while some, such as Cao Fei, feel the urgent need to grasp and act on the global flow of events and exchanges, others simultaneously reappropriate the heritage they are now allowed to revisit. These approaches, which may seem surprising, have their own coherence, if we bear in mind the particular articulation of traditional and contemporary in the work of these artists and the dialectical interpretation necessary in the Chinese situation. This is expressed in the title, *BENTU*, which pinpoints a notion central to the thinking of artists, critics and researchers working in China today.

In the first room is a spectacular piece by Xu Zhen, a multifaceted artist prominent on the national and international scenes, aware of living and working in a society where cultures come together and even compete. Here his stunning conflation juxtaposes two casts of sculptures from the Louvre, one Hellenistic and the other from 19th-century France, in a provocative appropriation of Western culture combined with a brilliant aesthetic neutralisation achieved simply by the serial effect, which removes any sense of signature or reverence. The same irony can be found in the gymnastic exercises to which the artist reduces religious rituals in his video installation. This distance is indeed shared by many other artists here.

In an approach close to calligraphy, which he first practised on his own body in the performances for which he became famous, Qiu Zhijie now makes spectacular maps portraying the transformations of his country, China, comparing it to its past.

With the monumental paintings by Liu Wei showing visual transcriptions of the city, we have another, more urban kind of mapping, in a manner clearly based on the latest computer technologies. For this exhibition he has conceived a new project inspired by Gehry's architecture. According to the artist, the materials he used – plexiglas, glass, mirrors, metal – refer to his own surroundings in Beijing, the aim being to play on the viewer's spatial perception.

Whereas Hao Liang goes back to the pure tradition of silk painting, based on in-depth archive research, in order to revive the memory of a centuries-old garden, conceived in the tradition of the Literati and now transformed into a theme park, Liu Xiaodong offers a portrait of the inhabitants of his childhood village, to which he returned after various national and international journeys. Aware, no doubt, of the heritage of Maoist posters, he positions himself within the humanist tradition of realist painting, here to focus on minorities struggling with the great rural exodus.

A similar social awareness is evident in the austere, welldocumented new installation by Yang Fudong, responding to the tragic disappearance of a certain kind of landscape. Its aridity is tempered by the humanity of the large figures that punctuate the demonstration.

This engagement and vigilance is also manifest in the projection by Liu Chuang, its demonstration of "natural" pollution calling for an oblique reading. Likewise we must look beyond their appearance to see the "abstract" compositions by Xu Qu for what they really are, namely, enlargements of various international currencies whose mobility symbolizes financial flux in the world, including the ones that relate to art. Also highly revealing, young artist Tao Hui has a good knowledge of the international scene, yet roots the short fantastic stories presented here in a cryptic memory drawn from a very personal local imaginary world, in an oscillation symptomatic of *Bentu*.

Most of the artists in the exhibition belong to the thirty-something generation, but with two major deviations (28 and 51 years old), which is necessarily significant in a country where the rotation of generations and their successive waves follow on in a fascinating acceleration.

The two curators, Laurence Bossé and Phil Tinari, have made a precise analysis of the title and the works, and explained their choices and the exhibition sequence.

SELECTED WORKS FROM THE COLLECTION
We thought it would be useful, in order to support and illuminate this approach to this very complex Chinese scene, to spread it across all of the Foundation's galleries. That is why the second stage of this

event dedicated to China continues through the Foundation's Collection itself. Most of the artists shown here belong to an earlier generation, but we can note that four of them also appear in *BENTU*: Cao Fei, Yang Fudong, Tao Hui and Xu Zhen.

This hanging of the Collection begins on level 2 in galleries 10/11 with a set of works whose mood is mainly contemplative. For example, *Tree* by Ai Weiwei stands in Gehry's great vessel connecting the sky and earth. This piece was made with techniques traditionally used in temple construction. Two works by Huang Yong Ping reflect his twin roots in Eastern and Western culture, with an admixture of his own particular magic. In one, a giant bottle rack reminiscent of Marcel Duchamp serves as a support for mannequin arms holding symbols, relating both to "Buddha with a thousand arms" and the goddess Guanyin, but also banal everyday objects. The other revisits the legend of Saint Giles, here given a supernatural, magical quality by the use of gold. Finally, a monumental Buddha head introduces us to the work of Zhang Huan, who is also present in a self-portrait as Buddha. The assimilation is very explicit.

The work of Zhang Huan then continues in **gallery 9**, centring on a form of history painting. His two spectacular panoramas here evoke, respectively, a military parade on Tiananmen Square, and the construction of a big canal after the reforms driven by Mao Zedong and built by myriad peasants. They are done in ash from the incense burned in temples.

The Foundation commissioned Yan Pei Ming to complete his landscape of an Acropolis seemingly damaged by a flight of crows. This diptych evoking "modern times" is done, symptomatically, in a new midnight blue colour. Here we see a column of people – refugees? pilgrims?

protesters? – advancing under stormy skies towards an uncertain future.

At the centre of the same gallery, Xu Zhen creates a striking, strangely Situationist compilation of cultures fusing emblems of Eastern and Western heritage. Placing an overturned *Winged Victory of Samothrace* on an iconic bodhisattva, the artist annuls aura and memory just when he seems to be magnifying them.

Further on, in **gallery 8**, he evinces the same ironic distance in his Pop-style enlargement of the goddess of compassion, Guanyin, one of the most venerated deities in China.

Level 1 (gallery 5) gives access to a very different, emotional and floating atmosphere, with dreamlike, mysterious installations by Yang Fudong[1]: the first is paradisiac, the theatre of bucolic scenes in a luxuriant traditional garden. Also without a narrative framework, the other consists of translucent, coloured screens that immerse us in a factitious, timeless world where five young woman inhabit a light, sophisticated dream, drawing heavily, as always, on the style of movie glamour from the 1930s to the Nouvelle Vague.

Another major figure, but from another generation, Cao Fei invents a complete parallel world in the digital domain of Second Life (**gallery 6**), installing her own avatar, China Tracy, in *RMB City*, a combination of worlds where symbols of Chinese culture (bicycle, panda, bust of Mao, etc.) mix with an unchecked proliferation of architecture, in a flux of circulation.

Gallery 7 is set aside for a bi-faceted work – painting and sculpture – by Zhang Xiaogang, an artist famous for his monochrome portraits of impassive figures with unnerving charm. Here, the greatly enlarged faces of five children represent the social dreams of their parents, dressed as adults in keeping with their designated status: worker, peasant,

1.
From June to September 2016, all five parts of Yang Fudong's project *Seven Intellectuals in a Bamboo Forest* (2003–2007) will be shown in galleries 1 and 2.

soldier, student, shopkeeper.
A glacial aesthetic underscores
the incongruity of the half-naked
figures and heightens the strangeness
of the scene.

Works by two artists are shown
in **interstitial spaces** on the edge
of the galleries. One of them,
Zhou Tao, attests to a deep-rooted
ancestral practice, while the other,
Tao Hui, is showing a video shot
recently in Iran that has universal
emotional resonance. Here we find
the complexity and oscillation
characteristic of the exhibition *BENTU*.

On the ground floor, finally, **gallery
4** sees a British artist of West Indian
descent, Isaac Julien, who is acutely
aware of immigration and diaspora
issues, pay homage to Chinese
culture – its legends, its cinema,
its calligraphy, its music and its poetry.
His installation consists of sequences
shot in Shanghai and in the province
of Quangxi with four major figures
in the contemporary Chinese arts: the
actors Maggie Cheung and Zhao Tao,
the artist Yang Fudong, and master
calligrapher Fong Fagen. He started
with a tragic event when Chinese
workers were swept away by the tide.
Referring to a sixteenth-century
legend relating the saving of Chinese
sailors by the goddess Mazu, the artist
pulls the viewer into an immersive,
dreamlike flux of images and sounds,
which constitutes a moving
introduction to a certain kind
of Chinese sensibility.

Thus, the significant group of artists
from the Collection shown here
confirms the strong personalities
of the protagonists of this scene,
whose members evince both great
originality and real plasticity in the
face of contradictory opportunities.
These qualities are evident, too,
in the four artists whose respective
works in the two exhibitions show
major differences of tone and
resonance.

The exhibition "BENTU, Chinese artists in a time of turbulence and transformation" is the result of a collaboration between the Foundation and the Ullens Centre in Beijing (UCCA). Its director, Phil Tinari, a man of deep local knowledge, guided our research in the field in Beijing and Shanghai. He co-curated this show with Laurence Bossé, curator at the Foundation. After numerous visits and discussions, they made their selections based on new criteria that were themselves a response to a particularly rich and shifting and profoundly other Chinese scene. At their side, Claire Staebler, strongly present throughout the elaboration of the project, played a decisive role.

We wish to extend our amicable thanks to the artists of the exhibition "BENTU" and their unshakeable confidence in the implementation of the project. Through them, we also express our gratitude to the studio teams and their galleries, who were all strongly committed to making the project a success.

Our gratitude goes to the catalogue authors for sharing their illuminating insights into the current situation in China, and into each artist in the exhibition. It also goes to the very talented graphic designer Frédéric Teschner, and to Annie Pérez, our indispensable editorial coordinator.

We are especially grateful to Cécile Degos for setting up the exhibition display, and more generally to Elodie Berthelot and her team, and to Renaud Sabari and his collaborators at Arter for their precious engagement.

This project could not have come about without the decisiveness of Bernard Arnault and the constant support of Jean-Paul Claverie. It has benefited from the benevolent determination and engaged, friendly support of Myriam and Guy Ullens, the founders of UCCA in Beijing.

S.P.

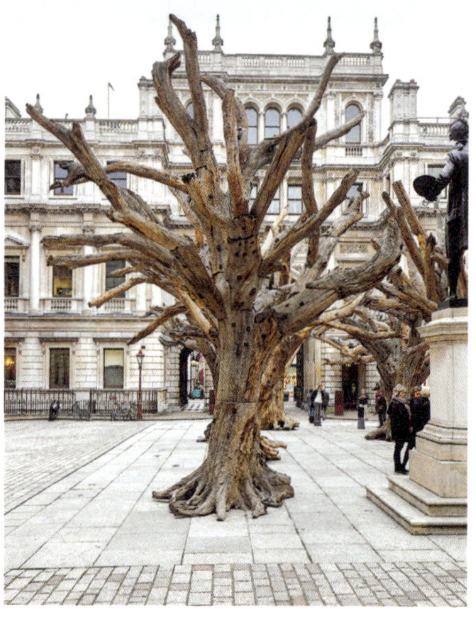

1

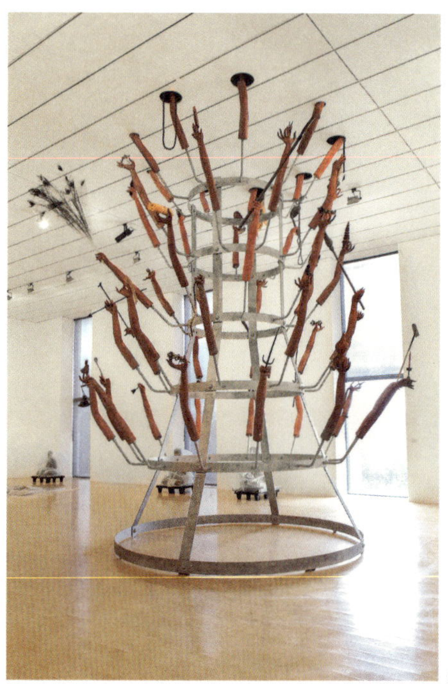

3

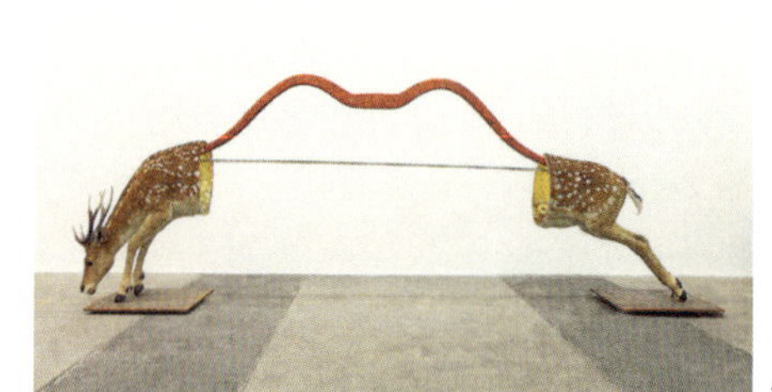

2

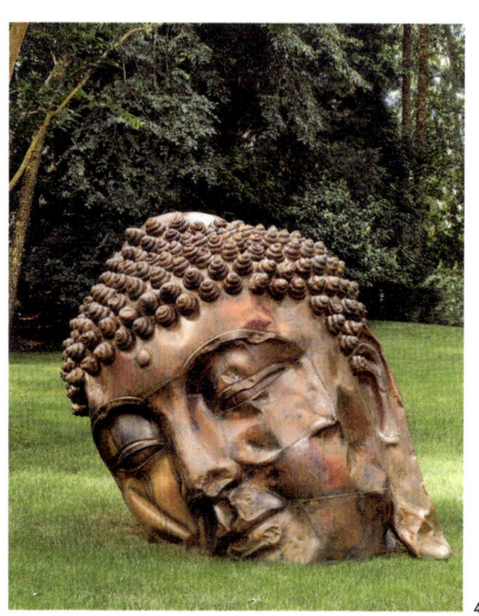

4

THE
COLLECTION,
A CHOICE
OF CHINESE
WORKS

GALLERY
10/11

AI WEIWEI
Born in Beijing
in 1957
Lives and works
in Beijing

1
Tree
2010
Tree sections
530 × 560 × 660 cm

HUANG YONG
PING
Born in Xiamen
in 1954
Lives and works
in Paris

2
L'Arc de Saint-Gilles
2015
Wood, iron, fiberglass,
dog hair, gold leaf
156 × 448 × 70 cm

3
*Cinquante bras
de Bouddha*
1997–2013
Metal, plastic, polyester,
various objects
477 × 404 × 415 cm

ZHANG HUAN
Born in Anyang
in 1965
Lives and works
in Beijing

4
Long Island Buddha
2010–2011
Copper
172 × 277 × 177 cm

ZHANG HUAN

5
Great Leap Forward
2007
Ash on linen
286 × 1080 cm

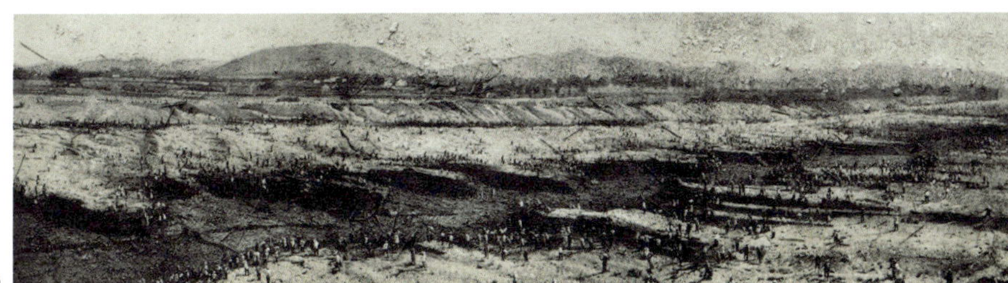
5

6
Sudden Awakening
2006
Ash and steel
70 × 78 × 100 cm

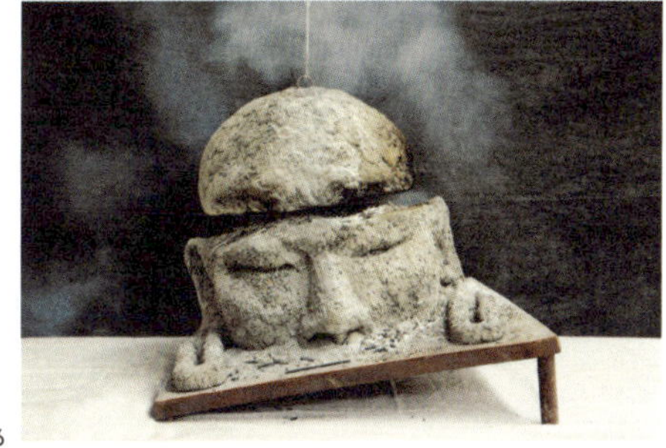
6

XU ZHEN
Born in Shanghaï
in 1977
Lives and works
in Shanghaï

7
*Eternity – Tianlongshan
Grottoes Bodhisattva,
Winged Victory
of Samothrace*
2013
Fiberglass, steel, concrete
626 × 460 × 230 cm

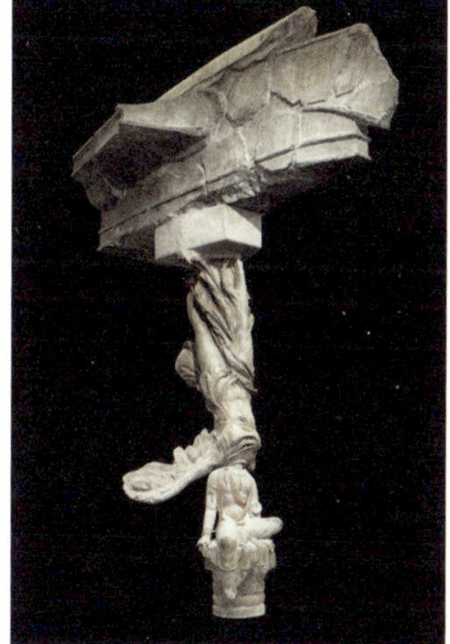
7

YAN PEI-MING
Born in Shanghaï
in 1960
Lives and works
in Dijon and
Ivry-sur-Seine

8
*All Crows Under the Sun
Are Black!*
2012
Oil on canvas
280 × 400 cm

9
Les Temps Modernes
2015
Oil on canvas
Diptych: 280 × 400 cm
(each panel)

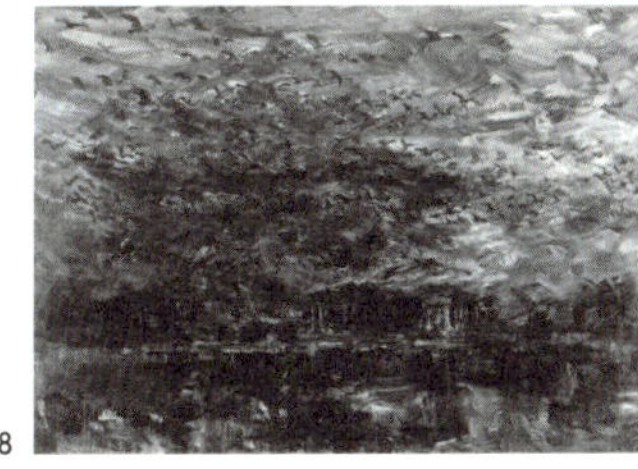
8

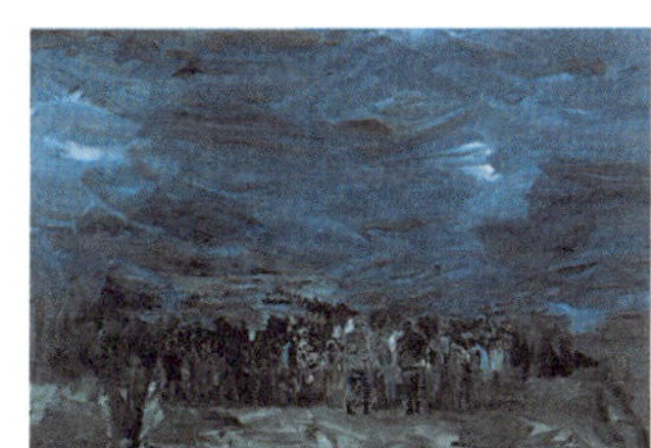
9

XU ZHEN

10
New
2014
Painted stainless steel
130 × 110 × 402 cm

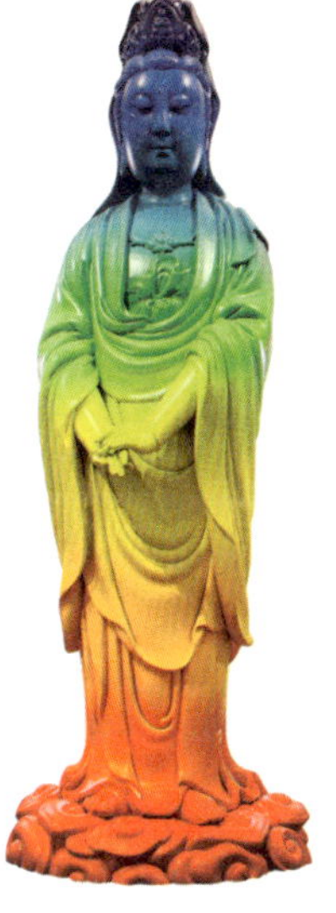
10

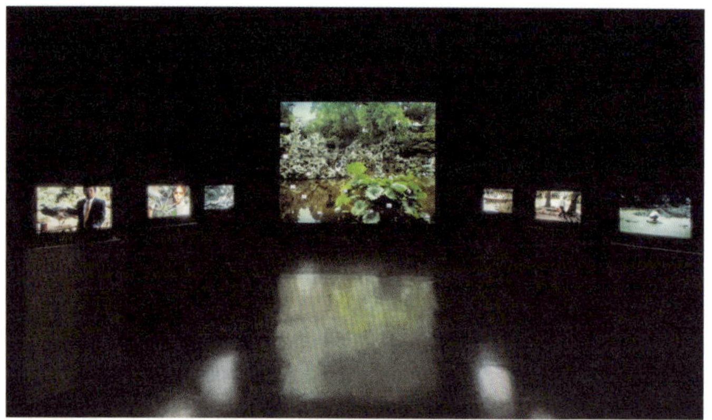

11

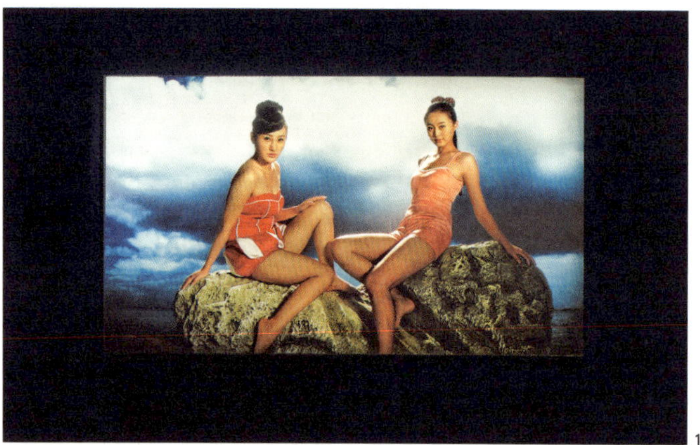

12

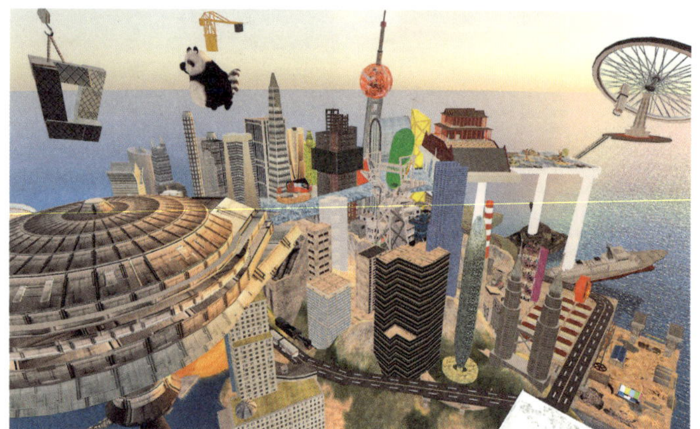

13

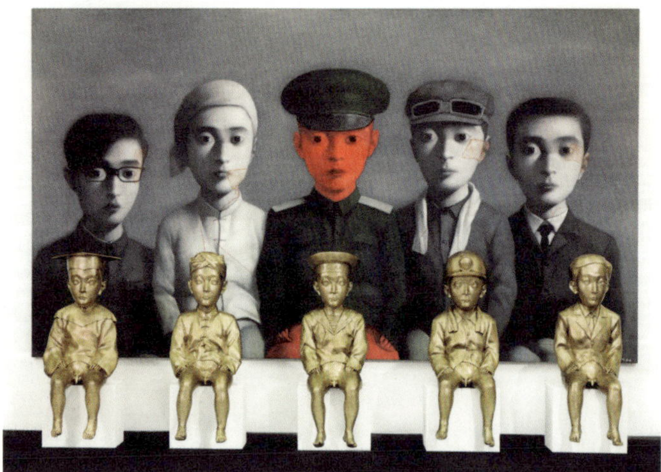

14

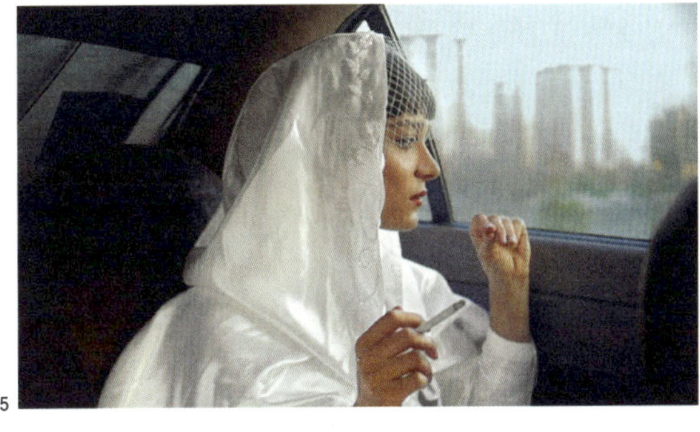

TAO HUI
Born in Chongqing
in 1987
Lives and works
in Beijing

15
The Dusk of Teheran
2014
Video, colour, sound
4'

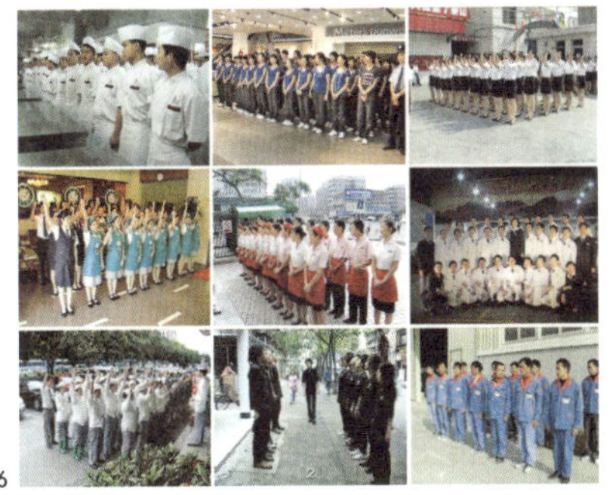

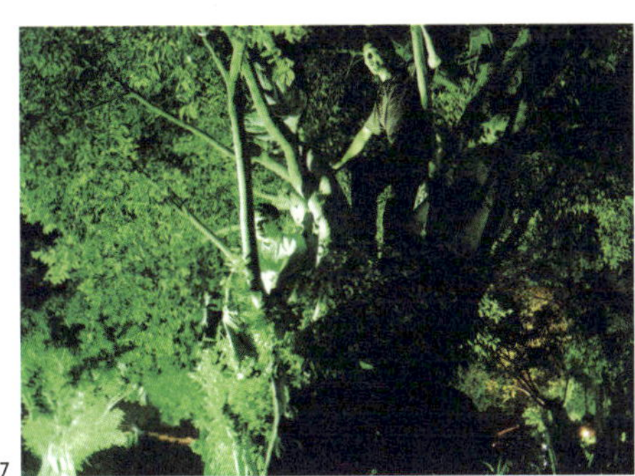

ZHOU TAO
Born in Changsha
in 1976
Lives and works
in Guangzhou

16
One Two Three Four
2008
Video, colour, sound
3'33''

17
*Chick speaks to duck,
pig speaks to dog*
2005
Video, colour, sound
6'

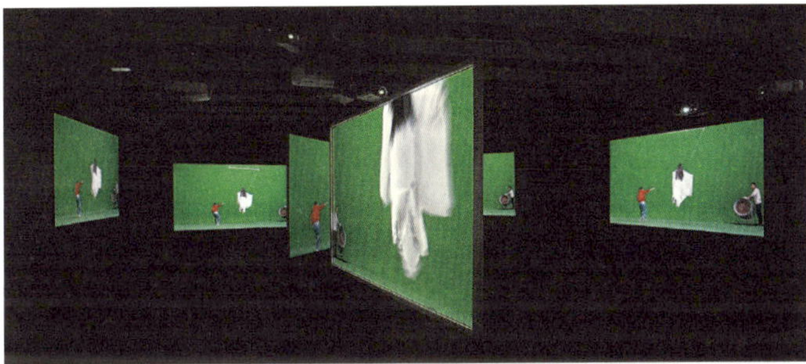

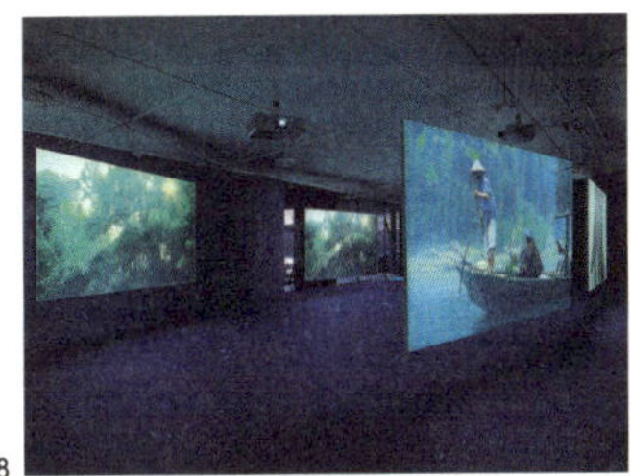

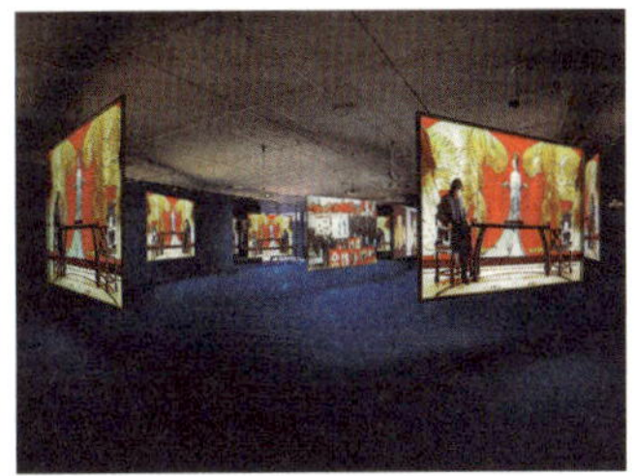

**GALLERY
4**

ISAAC JULIEN
Born in London
in 1960
Lives and works
in London

18
Ten Thousand Waves
2010
Video installation,
colour, sound
49'42''

**GALLERY
1 ET 2**
(from June 2016)

YANG FUDONG

19
*Seven Intellectuals
in the Bamboo Forest,*
Parts I–V
5 films (35 mm)
transferred to DVD,
black and white, sound
Variable duration

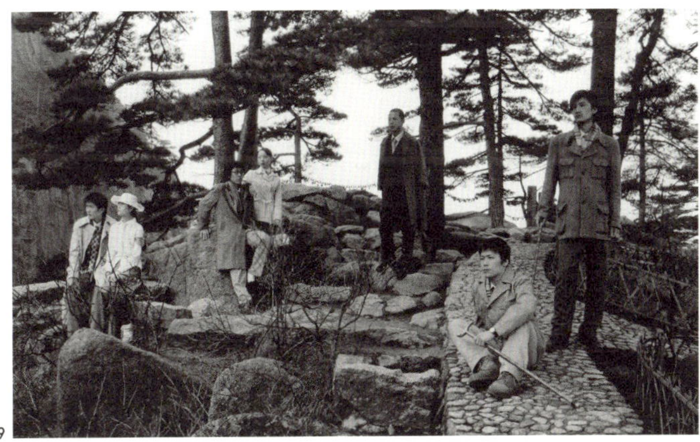

19

INTRODUCTION
LAURENCE BOSSÉ

To go to China today and meet the artists who live and work there – to discover their work and their projects – is to find our curiosity whetted by a host of approaches as surprising and fascinating as they are, at first glance, disconcerting.

This exhibition follows in the wake of several others, most of them group shows. It brings together twelve artists of different generations; the oldest – Liu Xiaodong, Qiu Zhijie – began their careers in the 1990s, and the younger ones – Tao Hui, Hao Liang and Liu Shiyuan – in the course of the last decade. Each one is presenting one or two recent or hitherto unshown works, some specially created for the occasion. The exhibition embraces various media – painting, sculpture, installation, video – which many Chinese artists are using today, simultaneously or successively and adhering to no particular hierarchy.

The connections we intuit between works that look so different from each other upset our preconceptions. Reflecting very individual personalities, these exhibits have less to do with artistic movements and trends than with correlations between production processes. Addressing current social issues, they are symptomatic of a new intellectual style and of the attitude driving many of today's creators in China.

Over a very short time artists who, for reasons of circumstance or as students, had spent varying periods in other countries – in the West in particular – returned to China extremely well informed about historical and recent developments in contemporary art abroad. This more or less coincided with the emergence in China of an art market that gradually integrated them into the international scene while, along the way, they experienced the information technology revolution.

China's artistic opening-up to the outside world took place in several stages. First came the artists who little by little – beginning in 1978 with Deng Xiaoping's policy of outreach and reform – absorbed certain tenets of modern and then contemporary art; but it was not until the early 2000s that galleries of contemporary art really made their appearance in China, together with institutional collections, the first of them in Beijing and Shanghai. Private foundations and state museums proliferated, at the same time as outside collectors began arriving and auction houses opened.

After the initial excitement of discovering and experimenting with the international production tools and practices that took root thanks to this increased openness, artists adopted a more objective stance and a more critical attitude: they began unearthing and revisiting the indigenous knowledge, philosophies, customs, techniques and skills that they are now combining and incorporating into a revivified cultural corpus.

The issues they have raised can be grouped under the umbrella tag *bentu*, which suggests the notion of origin and is notably deployed by critic and researcher Gao Shiming as "an attempt to re-envision contemporary Chinese art not as an expression of essential national-cultural identity but instead as the outcome of a process of historical return and re-discovery involving cultural dissolution and reconstruction".[1] Thus, in collaboration with Phil Tinari, and after many discussions, we decided to adopt "bentu" as the guiding concept for the exhibition.

With its return to and reinterpretation of the past, this approach is to be found in the work of Qiu Zhijie, Hao Liang and Tao Hui, who are metamorphosing and revitalizing the traditional techniques of calligraphy, cartography and painting on silk. Other artists, among them Liu Xiaodong and Yang Fudong, appropriate new economic and ecological issues and social

1.
Paul Gladston, "Somewhere (and Nowhere) between Modernity and Tradition: Towards a Critique of International and Indigenous Perspectives on the Significance of Contemporary Chinese Art", *Tate Papers* Issue 21.

phenomena, signalling the rapid,
radical changes taking place in cities,
the countryside and peri-urban areas
and bringing a documentary *modus
operandi* to bear on preserving the
traces and emotional power of the
past. Opting for the trite yet effective
communication format of the music
video, Liu Chuang offers a more
alarming docudrama look at
pollution, while Hu Xiangqian's
video-performances bring a touch
of irony to their close scrutiny
of the mores and shortcomings
of Chinese society.

Meanwhile other artists are
calling into question art's connection
with the global economy: Xu Zhen
criticizes the way art functions in
relation to the market and Xu Qu
focuses on financial rigging. Woman
artist Cao Fei points up the way
information technology is impoverishing
personal relationships through their
sheer disembodied proliferation.

Liu Wei's strategy and the
project he has created specially for
this exhibition are emblematic of
his protean experimental output.

All the works here testify to the
force and distinctively rich variety of
the approaches developed by artists
who, in today's China, are tirelessly
reinventing a contemporary art that
is at once global and local.

This exhibition could never have
become a reality without the inspired
collaboration of Phil Tinari, who was
unfailingly backed up by Claire
Staebler.

L.B.

INTRODUCTION

BENTU
ART
FROM
A
CHINA
IN
CONSTANT
CHANGE

PHILIP TINARI

What does China think? In the West we are constantly offered stories of China's incredible rise to wealth and power, but what is the cultural, social and intellectual situation that lies beneath such great change? What are the anxieties, interests and pleasures of life in China today? What kinds of new subjectivities have been produced by the economic transformation that has now been in progress for nearly four decades? What does it mean to be living and working as an artist in China today, in relation to both a national political system and a global audience? What does the displacement of hundreds of millions from the country into the cities, and some of those back again, mean for everyone? What are the hopes and dreams of ordinary people there, and of society more generally? On what are they built?

The word *bentu* literally means "of this earth", a way of talking about a distinctively local set of conditions and possibilities. It carries slightly negative connotations, in contrast to words like *yangqi* "of the ocean", which point to more cosmopolitan identities. It refers to a specifically Chinese way of doing, working and thinking – not as essentialized from the outside but as perceived and questioned from within. Of course, in today's China the local and the international overlap in complex and interlacing ways – contemporary art itself, which has a history in China that dates back precisely to the beginning of the reform era in the late 1970s, is itself a product of this history. The artists and works that follow reflect on this complex positioning in distinctive ways.

Xu Zhen's sculptures (*Eternity – The Soldier of Marathon Announcing Victory, a Wounded Galatian*, 2014) open the exhibition on an irreverent note – combining and repeating in five identical copies two masterworks from the Louvre, the Roman *Dying Gaul* (first–second century AD) and Cortot's *The Soldier of Marathon Announcing Victory* (1834). This work belongs to Xu Zhen's "Eternity" series (2014), which originally juxtaposed key Roman and Greek sculptures with Buddhist statues, literally putting them head to head. In this more recent example, he instead brings a classical masterpiece into gravity-defying contact with a nineteenth-century work on a similar theme, implicitly asking the question of what it means for a Chinese artist to be the one appropriating these images in a sort of reverse Orientalism.

Qiu Zhijie contributes a new addition to his on-going series of maps (« Map of the Third World »), which have previously used his signature ink painting style and bilingual literary wit to explore everything from the history of Western colonialism to the history of the Post-Sense Sensibility art movement with which he was involved in the late 1990s. Here he responds by creating a map of China's current intellectual state, its collective mind, placing various influences, elements, desires and fears into an imagined topography of rivers and mountains.

Yang Fudong, an artist well known to the Fondation Louis Vuitton, shows a monumental piece entitled *Blue Kylin* (2008-2015), which examines in over twelve screens a sad condition of environmental degradation that exists around one of the country's main marble quarries in Shandong province. Returning in 2005 to Shanghai from the filming of one of his Seven Intellectuals films by the coastline of this province, Yang was saddened to pass through regions where landscapes had been utterly destroyed by workers who themselves were risking lives to extract marble from mountains, which was in turn used to create kitschy, ornamental, faux-traditional statuary. *Blue Kylin* is a portrait of the place and the people involved in this mindless endeavour.

Hao Liang is interested in what Mao once called "using the past to serve the present". His *The Virtuous Being* (2015, the Chinese title could be translated literally as "This Gentleman", another name used for bamboo) scroll structures a series of imagined relationships between the artist, past artists and their intellectual inspirations. A noted young ink painter, Hao Liang became interested in Wang Shizhen (1526–1590), a Ming dynasty writer and intellectual who occupied a place in the cultural universe of his day roughly equivalent to Apollinaire at the turn of the twentieth century. One of Wang's key ideas was of a theme park-like garden called Yanshanyuan, itself based on ideas from the Tang dynasty poet Wang Wei (701–761) that had been immortalized in paintings of that era. Early twentieth-century intellectuals actually built a garden to these specifications in Wang's hometown, later left to languish under Communism and finally converted into an amusement park during the 1990s. Hao Liang's scroll explores these connections and transitions between different utopian moments and impulses, always grounded in a deep research.

For Liu Xiaodong, the idea of going home is much more literal. Like many in China's major cities, Liu comes from somewhere else, in his case the very small factory town of Jincheng in Liaoning province, known for its paper mills. In 2010, at the invitation of UCCA and under the curation of Jérôme Sans, he returned to his hometown and spent the summer there painting his childhood friends and surroundings. This incredibly poignant cycle, titled "Hometown Boy", is a meditation not only on the artist and his life journey out of the provinces and towards international fame, but of the persistent disparities and mentalities that divide where people come from and who they

become – of course, not only in China but all over the world. Working in his characteristic method of a humanist realism, and from images made on-site in the town, Liu Xiaodong offers a reflection that is at once specific to a place and universal in its meaning.

Tao Hui, a very young artist who had his first solo show at UCCA only earlier this year and who was featured prominently at the Asia Now fair in Paris last month, is a different kind of storyteller, often using the visual language of popular television. In his *1 Character & 7 Materials* (2015), a sculptural video installation in which the viewer wears a wireless headset to hear a story being told as they watch a series of seemingly unrelated images on the screen, Tao Hui explores a typical if also fantastical plot from a small town like the one in Sichuan where he grew up. In the story, a teacher becomes infatuated with a student, is impregnated by him, and subsequently alienated from the community. In this poetic retelling, inspired by the artist's family experience, the politics of an ordinary Chinese town become comprehensible to the outside.

Xu Qu is another young artist who thinks intelligently about the current state of world affairs, and inevitably, about China's place within it. For his "Currency Wars" paintings, which are mounted on rolling racks to be moved about the exhibition space, the artist pairs two renderings of a detail from a single currency – one crisp and clean, evoking both new money and the feel of what he considers 1960s geometric abstraction, the other intentionally muddled and vague, referring to both used currency and later trends in painting. He hopes to draw a connection between the aesthetics of high art and those of the patterns that surround us, underlying the global economic exchanges of which we are all a part.

Cao Fei has been consistently inspired by China's vibrant Internet culture, which despite persistent efforts at censorship has nonetheless opened up the minds and worlds of hundreds of millions of people there, many of them young. For *Strangers* (2015), she records interactions that she had with people all over the world using a "Russian roulette"-style video chat programme in which one can speak to a randomly assigned partner until deciding to change at will. In these brief interactions we see the artist consistently experimenting with the boundaries of the format, turning the camera back on itself, or onto various toys and avatars. These momentary encounters hint at the immediacy of certain forms of contact, but also the impossibility of substantive interaction in such a highly mediated sphere.

Liu Chuang has for many years been a close observer and interlocutor of many of the European and American artists now closely associated with the "Post-Internet" moniker. His video *BBR1 (No. 1 of Blossom Bud Restrainer)* (2015) is a pseudo-documentary advertisement for a product developed by a government scientific laboratory in Beijing to stop the spread of the poplar blossoms which cover the city in white seed fluff each spring. The trees were themselves planted during another mass campaign during the Mao Zedong era, creating unforeseen consequences. Liu Chuang's video explores the revealing slippages between state propaganda, commercial advertising, digital savvy and the desire for control over nature.

Hu Xiangqian is a performer whose works take their most effective form in videos. His practice is here represented by a pairing of works, the first a simple single take of a woman dancing in a park in downtown Beijing, *The Woman in Front of the Camera* (2015). In her face we see a hard-won happiness after what are presumably years

of political and economic upheaval, and yet we are never sure in what light the artist wishes to portray her. For *Speech at the Edge of the World* (2013), Hu takes the stage at his former high school in the remote Leizhou peninsula of Guangdong province, orating at the assembled students from a stage using the rhetoric of motivational speakers and airport-store business books everywhere. His homily falls flat on an audience of bored students, who are no more taken by this capitalist ideology than by that of the state.

Educated in Denmark, Liu Shiyuan is a sophisticated explorer of the confused but ever-expanding horizon where China's culture encounters the rest of the world's. For *From Happiness to Whatever* (2015) she presents a room covered from floor to ceiling in square swatches of different carpets, their colours and patterns forming a dizzily collaged whole. In this soft space is playing a continuous audio loop, toggling between Chinese and English, between news and storytelling, between advertisement and announcement. One is left in a confused state, where discursive registers are constantly overruled and replaced.

Finally, Liu Wei, one of the key figures in his generation, has distilled from the semi-urban surroundings of his studio on Beijing's far outskirts a material language that draws inspiration and material sustenance from the construction and destruction taking place all around. He has worked with salvaged wooden doors and window frames, discarded books, sheet metal, mirrors and industrial canvas, maintaining a studio staffed with dozens of labourers drawn from the local population. His works for this exhibition represent a further refinement of this sculptural lexicon, where the contrasts between pure, universal geometric forms and the

cheap, locally marked materials
from which they are made set up
a powerful tension that has allegorical
implications for the Chinese situation
more generally.

Taken in total, these works
offer a set of twelve distinct
but interrelated responses to the
unwritten question, What does
it mean to live and work in China
today, when change has become
the only constant? And what new
lessons might this condition hold
for the rest of the world?

THE LONG MARCH TOWARDS CHINESE MODERNITY

PIERRE HASKI

Visitors to the 2000 Shanghai Biennale, the first time the Biennale left the calm waters of tradition for the choppier seas of contemporary art, were greeted as they entered the exhibition hall by a series of nine disconcertingly realistic sculptures. Made by Liang Shuo, a very young artist from Beijing, they represented a family of mingong, or "worker-peasants", inner migrants who come from the Chinese countryside to work on construction sites and in factories in the big cities. At the Biennale, these very un-urban mingong with their ill-fitting clothes and startled eyes were forced on the attention of the visiting Chinese VIPs, who in life would never spare them a glance. They are the "invisible" members of Chinese society.

For this 24 year-old artist selected for a very safe Biennale, this confrontation with the real in a thoroughly official setting was a new experience – that of a new generation of artists whose codes and language refused to stick to the canons decided by others. These were artists engaged with their times and with the fast-changing reality of China.

At the turn of the millennium, China was indeed a country in the starting blocks: the following year, it was admitted into the World Trade Organisation, while Beijing was awarded the 2008 Olympics and Expo 2010 went to Shanghai. These three factors helped propel China into a decade of unprecedented growth, and anchor the country in the process of globalization, the early phases of which it had missed.

For Chinese society, this sudden acceleration had a galvanizing effect on mentalities, ways of life, human relations, cities and their environment, values and the way it related to the world. Artists, writers and filmmakers now found themselves in the front line, expressing, each in their particular way, this tremendous quest for modernity by a dynamic society.

In spite of all the ambiguities and dead ends, China had been waiting for this moment for a long time. A new biography of the Dowager Empress Cixi, who reigned over China for nearly fifty years in the second half of the 19th century and up to her death in 1908, styles her "the concubine who launched modern China".[1] After the fall of the Qing dynasty and the end of the empire, students of the May Fourth Movement rose up in 1919 against the Japanese invasion, but also to push for modernization, for a "new culture". The history of China in the 20th century is the history of a thwarted quest for modernity.

One of the finest films by the great Chinese director Zhang Yimou, made in 1994, is To Live. Its title sounds like a defiant challenge to the upheavals of history. This family saga relates the tormented history of China in the 20th century, both the sufferings inflicted by invaders and the turbulence within. Yu Hua, who helped write the screenplay, continued the saga in an epic novel, Brothers, a searing depiction of the transformation of China since the late 1970s, as mirrored in a fictional little town whose inhabitants are swept up in the whirlwind of the "Chinese-style market economy".[2]

The Cultural Revolution generation did not want to miss its chance "to live", to quote Zhang's simple expression. The director is himself a survivor of that troubled period. He entered the Beijing Film Academy when it reopened in 1978. Like him, millions of Chinese took their lives in hand and "threw themselves into the sea", to borrow the expression used for Party cadres who went into business without really knowing what to do, but with the necessary guangxi (contacts) and appetite.

And the country changed. Beginning with colour. The old monotonous clothes made way for a joyous, anarchic diversity, followed

1.
Jung Chang, *Empress Dowager Cixi: The Concubine Who Launched Modern China*, London: Jonathan Cape, 2013.

2.
Yu Hua, *Brothers* (2005, 2006), translated by Eileen Cheng-yin Chow and Carlos Rojas, New York: Pantheon Books, 2009.

by modern codes. Cities were transformed, slowly at first, then in a hectic frenzy, razing the past and producing a welter of ever-more audacious buildings, with more and more cars where before there had only been bicycles. It could all be pretty brutal. In the early 2000s, like my neighbours in my hutong (traditional street) in Beijing, I was expelled literally overnight, once the character "Shai", which means "demolish", was painted on my door in the night. An artist, Zhang Dali, was there to leave his signature, "AK47", on these ruins of the old world before it disappeared for good.

The greatest change was in the Chinese themselves. Again, it was slow at first, then so fast as to be almost reckless. Sometimes, they got seriously hurt by trying to venture into forbidden territories, and sometimes, too, they found themselves stuck in dead-ends, lacking a compass to lead them towards prosperity and modernity. But, with every setback, even the most dramatic ones, they dusted themselves down and resumed their long march. This time, they would not be deterred. China could not miss this appointment with itself.

Over the last thirty years the definition of a generation has changed in order to reflect the acceleration of time. In a country that likes to classify its people by year of birth, smaller categories had to be created. In the past, it was the political context that determined a shared identity, like the Great Leap Forward of the 1950s. That generation experienced the greatest suffering, as related by Nobel Prize for Literature Mo Yan in a simple short story, "The Iron Child". This describes the famine that drove children like him to eat coal dust so as to fill their stomach.[3] Mo Yan once told me about the time his teenager daughter told him how much she suffered. He asked her if there was something she needed – food for example, like in his adolescence, or something else –

and she replied with all the assurance of a teen that her sufferings were much deeper than her father's had been during the famine.

Nowadays, a generation lasts barely five years, after which the references, codes and dreams all change. The Internet has shot China into the era of social media and immediacy, of shared emotions and new forms of sociability. In his viscerally powerful film A Touch of Sin, Jia Zhangke, the most brilliant filmmaker of the "sixth generation", shows a young couple killing time on Weibo, the Chinese equivalent of Twitter. The young woman reads the litany of (bad) news on a tablet and asks her companion what comments to leave. For each item he produces an insult. Where once there was total, absolute control of information, today there is a real freedom, albeit closely monitored and restricted, and this often generates more cynicism than feelings of revolt.[4]

More than once, I've looked at a podgy "one son" kid in his dad's black Audi – a symbol of higher social status – when he stops at a red light. I have wondered what this child born into a privileged world in a China that hasn't always had it so good will be thinking when he reaches adulthood. I once put the question to Jack Ma, who is no doubt the country's most emblematic entrepreneur. Alibaba, the e-commerce giant that he founded, is now listed on Wall Street's Nasdaq. He explained that what drove him when he started out was seeing his father retire after a life of hard work and get the equivalent of only 20 euros a month. I asked him what values he was trying to inculcate into his young son, who was born into one of China's richest families at a time of great opportunity. He answered that his number one priority was to give his son the same mentality that he had. Only to admit, straight afterwards, that it was impossible to do.

4.
Pierre Haski,
Internet et la Chine,
Paris: Seuil, 2008.

3.
Mo Yan, "Iron Child,"
translated by Howard
Goldblatt, in *The Columbia
Anthology of Modern
Chinese Literature*, New
York: Columbia University
Press, 2007.

One of the authentic revolutions of the "post-revolutionary" era is the emergence of the individual. In a country that, in both its Confucian tradition and its Maoist collectivism, has put the whole before its parts, the individual was taboo. Rapid urbanization – in 2014, 55% of China's population was urban, as against 26% in 1990 – and the biggest and fastest rural exodus in history, together with changes in lifestyle, have brought forth the individual and, even more, individualism. Traditional values have been so badly trashed that the government felt the need to proclaim children's obligation to look after their parents, and this in a country where, a few decades earlier, the writer Lao She could describe the Chinese ideal as having "four generations under one roof".[5] Huo Datong, China's first Lacanian psychoanalyst, who has created a "Chinese school" in Chengdu, considers that what ensures the future of his discipline in this country of 1.3 billion souls is above all the dramatic upheaval in parent-children relationships.

In the Maoist period the Chinese social structure was simple, not to say simplistic. A person belonged in one of the three official categories: worker, peasant or intellectual. In the early 2000s, the Chinese Academy of Social Sciences conducted a three-year study resulting in a new classification for the people of this country still run by the Communist Party. There are now ten categories. Right at the bottom are the new poor, the mingong, these migrants from the countryside that Liang Shuo represented and positioned at the entrance to the Shanghai Biennale. The most surprising feature is that the Academy placed at the top of Chinese social pyramid the category of directors of state companies and the leading cadres of the Party and the state. Between them came this middle class that didn't even exist twenty years ago, but which now represents about five times the total population of France! These are the people calling for cleaner air, greater food security, access to culture and a better education system.

Back in the early 2000s, there were few authentic entrepreneurs in the private sector, compared to the massive state sector and the directors of fake private companies. Fifteen years later, the situation has changed radically. In new technologies and services especially, a new generation of entrepreneurs has developed a dynamic private sector. This new Chinese economic elite, which is behind the explosion of museums and art centres in all the big cities, is challenging the old order – even if, as the French Sinologist Marie-Claire Bergère has shown in her book on the "New State Capitalism", the state and party system still dominate the Chinese economy.[6]

But whatever the limits to all this, one can only be staggered by the speed and extent of Chinese economic development over the last thirty years, and especially since the turn of the century. The phenomena involved are astonishing. I recently did a report on the world capital of socks, which turns out a third of all the socks made in the whole world. I saw a huge factory run by an American multinational, big Chinese companies subcontracting for European and American brands, but also all kinds of small and medium businesses, and even family firms subcontracting for the subcontractors which consisted of a machine in the living room where family members took turns to work. The most amazing thing is that this mono-production grew out of the secret activity of a few peasants who had got hold of old machines from a nearby factory. Then some clever cadre came along and legalized what they were doing, making it the engine of the town's development. Its success can be seen in the cars that drive round its potholed streets.

5.
Abridged English edition in the trilogy titled *The Yellow Storm*, Gollancz, 1951. French edition, *Quatre générations sous un même toit*, translated by Jing-Yi-Xiao and Chantal Chen-Andro, Paris: Mercure de France, 1996.

6.
Marie-Claire Bergère, *Chine, le nouveau capitalisme d'État*, Paris: Fayard, 2013.

In the 2000s, there were
some who thought that China would
simply become the "workshop of
the world", the centre that assembled
and produced products designed
elsewhere. This was to underestimate
the Chinese desire to regain its past
position, over a century and a half
ago, when Zhong Guo – literally, the
"Middle Kingdom" – was the world's
biggest economic power. Today,
China can produce cheap socks and
fly to the moon. It can assemble Apple
iPhones and generate the economic
giants of tomorrow. And if, today,
not many French or Europeans can
name Chinese brands, there is no
doubt that several Chinese "national
champions" will emerge on the
global stage in almost every sector.

This transformation has taken
place at the speed of light, in a mixture
of planning and improvisation that is
hard to imagine for an outsider, and
with little concern for the collateral
damage done by this forced march
towards progress. The environment,
social inequality, human rights,
minority identities, ethics – all have
been bulldozed by the vertiginous
growth of the last thirty years.
Confronted as it now is by a durable
slowing of this growth, China is
seeking new orientations for
a new phase of its development.

In the process, too, China has
sometimes felt disoriented, struggling
to reconcile its quest for modernity
with its ancient roots, which it
long thought hampered its progress.
Artists, writers, filmmakers and
designers are at the heart of this
quest for meaning – that is, when
they are not themselves caught up
in the whirlwind of development.
And yet it is to them, in particular,
that the new urban youth now
look – these young people who,
growing up without yesterday's
ideological constraints, must
invent everything from scratch in
a country that is at once new and
old. A country that sometimes
wonders what path to take.

"MADE IN CHINA–GLOBALIZATION": ART, PRODUCTION AND SOCIAL CHANGE

LU MINGJUN

I

Since joining the World Trade Organization at the beginning of the 21st century, China has achieved incredible economic growth. In its efforts to bridge the growing economic disparities between urban and rural areas, the government accelerated its drive towards urbanization and by the eve of the 2008 Beijing Olympic Games, this tumultuous programme had swept away many of the existing social structures. It was during this period that the centre of the contemporary art scene began its gradual out-of-town migration, pushed by the expanding metropolis, first to the Yuanmingyuan Art Village in the 1990s, then the Songzhuang Art Village and 798 Art Zone, and lastly Caochangdi Art District and Heiqiao Art District.

The contemporary Chinese art scene has always flourished in the fertile ground of the urban periphery, in suburbs and the margins of the countryside. This is familiar territory for Liu Wei, whose deeper understanding of the process stems from experiencing it at first hand and incorporating it into his art. Living in Beijing's Third Ring while working in its Fifth Ring, Liu's daily commute goes from downtown to the suburbs. Everything he hears and sees in these two different areas then become the materials for his art and drive his creativity: discarded furniture, electrical appliances and recycled garbage have marked out his work from the outset. When we look beyond the abstraction, whether physical installations or multimedia work, we see a specific cityscape of image and concept.

It is hard at first to grasp the sense of Liu Wei's statement "I always stand by the people" until we understand that this does not mean he is simply out to please the public. Instead, this most contemporary artist offers up true visual perceptions of, and original reflections on, people's everyday living experience. How this is done can best be seen in his

creative method. For Liu Wei, the cheap materials he finds represent the relationship between classes, bear traces of people's memory and reflect social change. Walking into his large workspace, a cross between a studio and a factory, we can see traditional handcrafts and modern, streamlined production methods working together under a rigorous regime based on the division of labour. Liu has created a role for himself that is equal parts artist, general designer, general dispatcher and manager, even enjoying the "title" of Administrative Director Artist. Of course, while this production method is commonplace in the Western world, we should note that his insistence on scale and speed are not simply driven by the rapid changes in the capital-led art system, but also stand as a clear representation of China's urbanization and social transitioning in a globalized context. From production to formal implementation, this is the clearest proof that Liu's understanding and techniques bear witness to the seismic shifts within his country over the last decade.

Of course, studio output is only a single link in the chain of production. Today, if curator, critic, collector or gallery manager have all started to visit studios or production facilities to learn more about the artists' work, it is only to forge stronger links between the art and audience. Nevertheless, the art system itself is rooted within China's economic, social and cultural structures, and subject to the same stresses and strains brought on by globalization. It must follow then, that the scale and speed of output is a truer reflection of a globalized art world than a Chinese one. MadeIn Company, established by Xu Zhen, shows this with even greater clarity.

For Liu Wei, production itself carries certain ideas and meanings, even if he distances himself from other links in the art production system: distribution and consumption, for example. Although production is dependent on consumption to an extent, his lack of engagement with the consumer end of the process reveals a self-protective wariness. By way of contrast, these elements are included lock, stock and barrel by Xu Zhen's Madeln Company. Xu does not regard studio and factory production simply as a single link in the production chain, but rather as key element of its consumption.

As early as 2009, just after Madeln Company was established, it was widely considered to be commercial in its approach and capitalist in its strategy, in spite of Xu's tireless explanation of its artistic methodology. Until he launched "Xu Zhen" as a brand in 2013, he seemed to place more emphasis on artistic method or linguistic experiment. Yet the re-release of the label reiterated his idea that on entering the marketplace, works were essentially commodities. In this way, he insisted that Madeln Company was a commercial art institution with properly formulated long-term development aims and objectives, and while some charged him with dressing up art as a commercial enterprise, for Xu Zhen, business and art are not rivals in the first place. For him, nothing is more radical and more contemporary than acknowledging the legitimacy of business, especially when many so-called radical, anti-business practices become, in effect, the most marketable ones. Business is not a factor independent of art; it is art. That is exactly where the difference between Madeln Company and ordinary commercial galleries lies. Thus his later ventures, such as Madeln Gallery and PIMO Shop, are not just a means of expanding his business reach or public profile, but represent the development of possible, practical ways of operating an integrated system.

Xu Zhen has said, "In today's world, all objects on exhibition are commodities, and those on sale are art." His is a capitalist mechanism, concerned not only with consumption but also with production, rooted in China but dependent on globalization. But we cannot overlook the sensory impact and cultural evocation his super-landscapes and aesthetics have on visitors. For years now, Xu has been challenging and defying knowledge and experiences we take for granted. Art is not a reflection of reality, it is a real social phenomenon and should create a sense of cultural chaos. This suggests an alternative reading of "Made in China", or rather, "Made in China-Globalization". Shifting from "Made in China" to a "World Factory", his production system, including his works (or products), reflect and critique contemporary culture and politics, and hint at the mutually dependent but tense relationships between contemporary Chinese art and the world art system. This is where the fundamental difference between Western Pop Art and his work lies.

Simple, full of quirky humour and empty: these are typical features of Xu Zhen's works. They also reflect the reality of Chinese culture and society, and are symptomatic of contemporary art. In his "Eternity" series, heads from Chinese and Western sculptures are swapped and juxtaposed, exposing the reality of today's globalized culture, in which such entirely disparate cultures collide under the cover of a super-landscape. Come what may, production or consumption here create another form of culture. In other words, as a culture, this "production-consumption" mechanism is not just for observation. It provides us with new perspectives on reality and redefines the artists' identities and works. Even so, it still exists within the confines of an art world that mirrors not-for-profit organizations flying the anti-consumer banner, yet, just like them, it will nonetheless end up being absorbed and digested by the commercial system.

For now at least, independent artists are not strong enough, culturally or socially, to influence the system. Pauline J. Yao was aware of this as early as 2008 when she wrote in her book *In Production Mode: Contemporary Art in China* that "*in situ* art in China seems to take more account of its location or exhibition spaces than society or a public capable of thinking. It is targeted at initiates."[1] As Liu Wei's practices and works suggest, the true cultural significance of "contemporary" art is neither urban (compared with other "products", urban consumption of contemporary art is very limited) nor rural, but grows in the cracks between the city and the countryside. It is a space where artists can hardly expect to find people outside their universe.

II

Critics have claimed that Liu Wei and Xu Zhen are both representatives of Chinese neoliberalism and historical nihilism, criticizing them for conspiring with capitalism, bourgeois values and reality.[2] However, such views overlook one point: that the real landscape is not a massive installation. Size alone prevents its commercial viability, leaving it uncompromised by capitalist and neoliberal concerns. On the contrary, it reminds us of class and social differentiation brought about by global neoliberalism and state capitalism, the disparity between economic and cultural structures, as well as the mental strain of widespread alienation from the modern world. Thus Liu Wei and Xu Zhen can be seen to be commenting on and resisting the crisis of reality in a realistic way, in opposition to neoliberalism and historical nihilism. Moreover, in the current world, a new landscape of networks, project work, non-materialization and mobility has emerged. Claire Bishop pointed out clearly that, "Even though participatory artists invariably stand against neoliberal capitalism, the values they impute to their work are understood formally (in terms of opposing individualism and the commodity object), without recognizing that so many other aspects of this art practice dovetail even more perfectly with neoliberalism's recent forms".[3] Li Liao's *Consumption* (2013) exemplifies this apparent paradox.

Li Liao was employed by Foxconn (Long Huayuan District in Shenzhen city) as a production-line worker on 9 October 2012. He worked there for 45 days then resigned after completing *Consumption* and making enough from his wages, once his daily living expenses had been paid, to buy one of the iPad minis produced by his own line. During this period, Li Liao immersed himself within the production chain in an attempt to draw back the veil on the prevailing unequal economic system and social structure. But grand concepts and gestures are not Li Liao's aim. When a producer (the object) turns into a consumer (the subject), he is demonstrating the extreme disparity between the two roles and how they crudely invade our daily life rather than narrow the gap between subject and object, or between production and consumption. This in turn hints at a hegemony deeply embedded in our daily life, and the means of resisting it.

As discussed above, the artwork *Consumption* will eventually be taken up by galleries, art museums and fairs, becoming a part of the capital-driven, international art market that the artist opposes. Artists, in turn, will be signed up by galleries to provide "products" for them. But not all artists take the production system, art system and the corresponding social mechanisms as art media, seeing them rather as links in the chain of production or unrealized concepts, and detaching production from practice. Although artworks themselves have to rely on the art system, artists do not necessarily have to attend to the system and its social operation during the act of creation. We could even

3.
Claire Bishop,
Artificial Hells: Participatory Art and the Politics of Spectatorship, New York, Verso, 2012, p. 277.

1.
Pauline J. Yao,
In Production Mode: Contemporary Art in China, Timezone 8, 2008, p. 147.

2.
Su Wei, "Visual Maze of Liu Wei and Xu Zhen: Historical nihilism?", *The Art Newspaper China*, 3 July 2015.

say that artists have intentionally bypassed this link from the very beginning. Moreover, there is no rule that insists on their taking social reality as the starting point of the creative process. Though they keep a watchful eye on society, this need have nothing to do with art production, existing instead more as an experiment on artistic language and on the dissemination and communication of ideas.

Take Yang Fudong, who is more of a classical artist, as an example. He does not question the means of production, because it is a means of expression. Of course, he has requirements with regard to his studio and working conditions, but these are technical issues. In fact, the scant attention he gives the production process extends to the whole system. It makes no difference to him whether his works are widely disseminated; his sole concern is with new ways of narrating his own, self-generated, image-based languages. By filtering the naked truth through his image language, Yang Fudong presents us with objects to watch and perceive. It is through the aesthetic experience of watching that the brutality and detachment of Yang's language is revealed to us. But harsher even than this is the way in which the senses themselves become subsumed and consumed by the global art market, another act of "Made in China-Globalization".

From "Post-Sense Sensibility" to "Total Art", Qiu Zhijie has consistently resorted to the systematic construction of theories, and education, including some studies on the production system. For him, the studio is not the centre of production, nor is the gallery, the museum, the biennale or the fair. All that truly matters are the artist's perceptions and thoughts; physical conditions or the environment should not restrict the creative process. Far from hiding his interest in money, the latter impinges on his thoughts. Arguably, his output is in the

typical "Made in China-Globalization" tradition, even if he pays little heed to it. Faced with the primacy of globalization, Qiu's decomposition, reorganization and constructions, derived from his own knowledge and cognition, aim at a better understanding of China (especially Chinese artists and intellectuals) in a globalized world. Just as he chooses ink painting for his creation, his work also carries features of Western paintings. Although he uses woven bamboo, a traditional folk craft, his model and structure are still based on the idea of installation. And while he deems calligraphy to be the true contemporary art form, in practice his calligraphy operates within different parameters, relationships and recognition structures. Within the genealogy of his language, knowledge and ideas always navigate the space between the old and the new, the Chinese and the Western. What he calls "Total Art" is in fact a philosophical set within "the Great Unity", as shown by his work where both liberalism and communism end up pointing in the same direction: utopia. Ever the optimistic anarchist, he is making plans for his art well into his 60s and 70s.

There remains the question long asked by Westerners: "Where is China in Chinese art?" Those whose curiosity in identity-politics is satisfied by an assortment of symbols, labels and social practices certainly have the right to an opinion. On the other hand, they have surely fallen into the language trap set by this question. This has given rise to Hou Hanru's "Un-Unofficial Art" and Gao Minglu's "Yi Pai", as well as the recent trend for a return to the traditional, or reconstruction of the traditional, as in the passion for ink painting, for example. Here the aim is to build a new subject matter untainted by Western thought – in opposition to it even. In fact, this is a critical reaction to "Made in China-Globalization". Although artists are trying to work

4.
Robin Peckham,
*Asia Post-Internet:
Networks and Pathways
for a Global Art*,
translated by Xi Liu Winkler,
*Journal of Contemporary
Chinese Art Studies*,
Beijing, the China Youth
Publishing House, 2014.

within the context of traditional media or tastes, their ways of thinking have already been Westernized and globalized, something that is especially obvious to young artists like Hao Liang. Although his ink paintings demonstrate his clear identification with tradition, his visual understanding (including his readings of traditional Chinese paintings) and framing are deeply marked by colonial presuppositions of the Sinologist, the China "expert". This is so far removed from traditional Chinese aesthetics that it could be said to be opposed to it – more evidence of "Made in China-Globalization".

III

The Internet, the engine of hyper-globalization, is permeating artistic production and expression, and since the turn of the new century, artists have been exploiting the Internet as a means of expression. Initially used as an instrument, more recently the Internet has developed its own mode of thinking or cognition, embedding itself into the way artists work and into their language. This can be seen in the works of Xu Qu, Liu Shiyuan, Guan Xiao and Lin Ke. Some of these artists have studied abroad or lived in foreign countries for periods, and their familiarity with the Western art system and its operations have allowed them to enter the system without feeling they are compromising their identity. It is arguable, at least on the level of ideas, that they are free from the influence of the "Made in China-Globalization" concept, happy to take it or leave it. But far from preventing them from being active producers, in fact they are highly attentive to modes of production.

This "Art Post-Internet" trend reveals, according to Robin Peckham, how contemporary life is influenced by messages and vocabularies in a state of constant flux in a globalized world dominated by the Internet. In particular, artists are interested in how the traditional "career path" of studio/gallery/wider world will change, and the impact this will have on their work.[4] With the Internet disrupting the old certainties, social reality seems less of a factor to be considered by the artists. Of course, their practices are not totally unrelated to social change. On the contrary, they are simply the product of social turmoil, for the Internet itself is a social reality. If we have to define their production mode, "Made in e-China" might be a more accurate term than "Made in China-Globalization".

Another reason why we still use the word "make" is because international festivals have overwhelmingly replaced the predominance of biennials and galleries since 2007. The combination of the Western financial crisis of 2008 and the continuous growth of China's economy generated massive growth in the Chinese art market and festival scene, and this in turn has influenced the way artists work. Moreover, the Internet and other media have transformed their working practices and rhythm, bringing new features to the artistic landscape for commercial players and consumers alike. Finally, as China has risen to become the second biggest economy in the world, it will no longer be a "world factory" – passively accepting globalization – but an active force, promoting global rebalancing through "The Belt and the Road" (the short name for "the Silk Road Economic Belt" and "the Maritime Silk Road"), and hinting at a new geopolitical, economic and cultural world order. If "Made in China" or "Made in China-Globalization" derived from China's dependency on the globalized system under the post-Cold War pattern since 1990s, the Internet will bring changes to a current system dominated by the WTO. The concept of "Made in e-China" speaks of a rebalancing process, and new forces such as Alibaba and Tencent are reversing the old disparities that dominated China's relationships, while also reducing identification anxieties. In this sense, "Made in E-China" is a kind of comprehensive dis-localization (or de-bentuisation – see the Bentu definitions of Pierre Haski and Philip Tinari) and dis-identification, which promise an unstressed, non-alienated relationship with globalization. Thus, the true substitute for "Made in China-Globalization" may not be "Made in e-China" but "Made in Globalization (-China)": China, restructured as a new protagonist.

During this process, the pressure exerted by the TPP (the US dominated Trans-Pacific Partnership) cannot be ignored, nor the possible dilemmas for China posed by "the Belt and Road". Boris Groys alerts us to another point: "Big communication and information technology corporations control the material basis of the Internet and the means of producing virtual reality: its hardware. In this way, the Internet provides us with an interesting combination of capitalist hardware and communist software. Hundreds of millions of so-called 'content producers' place their content on the Internet without receiving any compensation, with the content produced not so much by the intellectual work of generating ideas as by the manual labour of operating the keyboard. And the profits are appropriated by the corporations controlling the material means of virtual production. As such, it is not 'immaterial', but thoroughly material."

This reminds us once again that we cannot neglect the operative mechanisms of the Internet, nor the logic and the structure of capitalist societies. In this context, "capitalism" no longer refers to the old model, but to a trans-ideological matrix incorporating capitalism and China's socio-political society. Unable to restrain the development of capitalism, gaining new energy from the Internet's vital force, it is lifting art production to a new "exciting point" even as it traps itself in a crisis: the so-called crisis of contemporary art? arart? material."[5]

This reminds us once again that we cannot neglect the operative mechanisms of the Internet, nor the logic and the structure of capitalist societies. In this context, "capitalism" no longer refers to the old model, but to a trans-ideological matrix incorporating capitalism and China's socio-political society. Unable to restrain the development of capitalism, gaining new energy from the Internet's vital force, it is lifting art production to a new "exciting point" even as it traps itself in a crisis: the so-called crisis of contemporary art?

5.
Boris Groys, *Going Public*, translated by Su Wei, Beijing, Gold Wall Press, 2012, p.163–164.

CAO FEI
HAO LIANG
HU XIANGQIAN
LIU CHUANG
LIU SHIYUAN
LIU WEI
LIU XIAODONG
QIU ZHIJIE
TAO HUI
XU QU
XU ZHEN
YANG FUDONG

CAO FEI

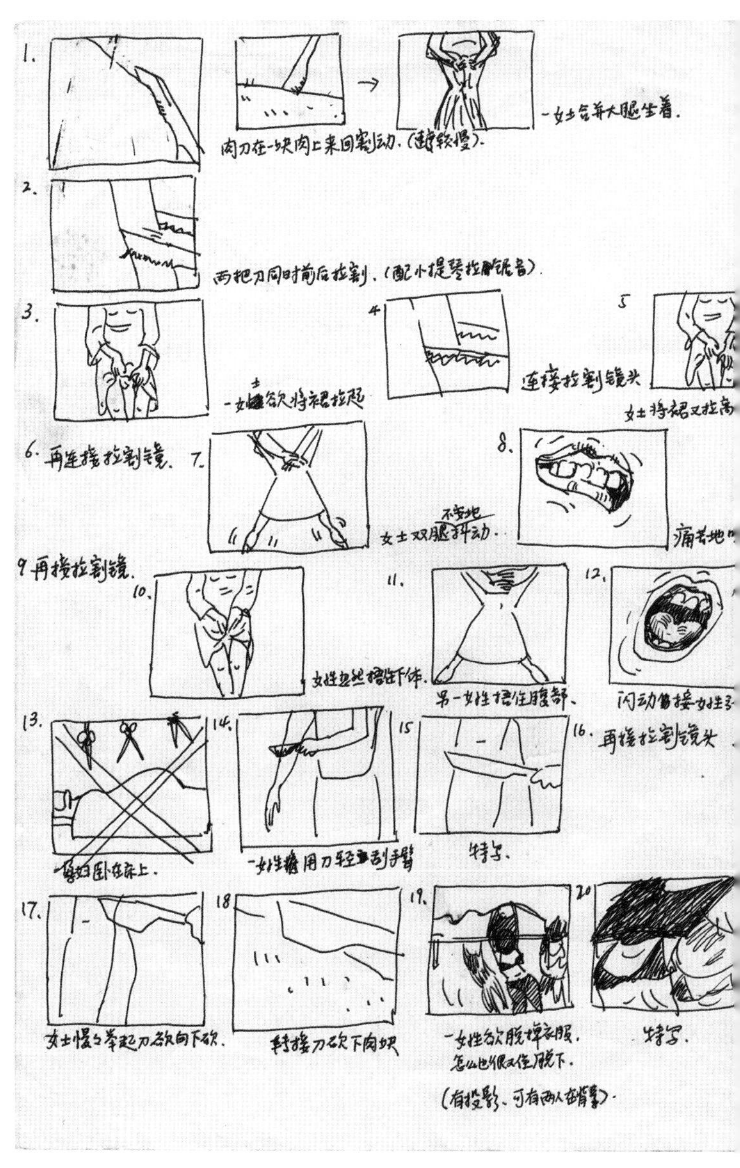

Cao Fei
Storyboard of "Chain Reaction"
2000
Sketch
Courtesy of Artist and
Vitamin Creative Space

WHEN RANDOM CHARACTERS MEET WITH THEIR APPARATUS

NIKITA YINGQIAN CAI

1.
The Chinese version of this short story was provided by the artist herself for the purposes of this article. An English version was published as part of the volume accompanying her solo exhibition at the Vienna Secession in the summer of 2015, *Splendid River* (Vienna: Revolver, 2015), p. 9–14.

"With her child away at boarding school, she spends most of her time at home, tidying up the rooms, mopping the floors, cleaning the windows and dancing to the aerobic shows on TV while the soup brews in the kitchen. Occasionally, she strolls around the neighbourhood garden or the local mall for amusement. Her husband loathes home-cooked meals, and goes out nightly after watching the evening news. She often wakes up in the middle of the night, and finds that her husband has not come home." This passage is from Cao Fei's short story "Building Fifteen" (2003).[1] The story's protagonist is a housewife resigned to her endless domestic labour, punctuated by shopping rituals and popular media. Taken together, these daily chores become a governing network of apparatus (as described convincingly by Giorgio Agamben), not only turning her into a submissive, neurological being, but rendering her hollow outside the apparatus.

Cao Fei was born in Guangzhou in the late 1970s, a time when people in this city and those nearby, a colossal urban area known as the Pearl River Delta (PRD), were becoming affluent. The geographical definition of the PRD is less impactful than the national economic and administrative repartition policy to strengthen economic development, which included Hongkong and Macau in the same map of the pan-PRD. The shared Cantonese culture and the geographic and economic proximity between Guangzhou and Hong Kong provided young people in the area the chance to experience and relate to pop culture, consumerism and an urban lifestyle at an earlier stage than those in the rest of China. Thus, a young generation was created as a side product of the ideological and economic means of the state, and the cultural perception of the Pearl River Delta area evolved and resolved according to the growth of the same generation. This is clear, for example, in Cao Fei's early works, including her oft-cited film *Imbalance 257* (1999), documenting the subversive ways her fellow students passed their time, which pioneers her unique theatrical style and approach. Another of Cao's video pieces is *Rabid Dogs* (2002), which combines video and performance. On viewing these works, you might think the protagonists were showing early signs of some sort of neurological disorder. Cao's early works, which are playful but not necessarily fun, are characterised by their biting absurdity, instantly conveying the artist's prescience and concern about alienated desires and self-objectification in a controlled society. Of course, the angst of today's youth comes wrapped up in a pretty package, fuelled by advanced technologies. Especially after 2000, with the Internet boom and the advent of the virtual economy, techno savvy young people were the quickest to embrace its openness and benefits. *RMB City* (2007–2011) can be seen as Cao's response to this burgeoning but forever young cyberculture. Various virtual projects and communities had been constructed in the online world Second Life, and *RMB City* was acquired by the collections of MoMA, the Walker Art Center, and the Louis Vuitton Foundation as early as 2008. With the new millennium, Cao Fei was embraced by the celebration of new media in the global art world as a representative of the provincial utopia. And her appropriation of easily recognized symbols of global culture and China made her not only a leading figure of the new generation of Chinese artists, but a beacon of global optimism. Looking back on the first decade of the 21st century, one might realize that rapidly evolving technologies and their increasingly widespread use have often resulted in the ephemerality of the medium themselves, which makes the artworks witnesses of their own epoch. In that respect, this age differs from that age of Nam June Paik.

But let's go back to 2003, when Cao Fei was writing "Building Fifteen". She was only 25 years old and had just graduated from the art academy. She had already participated in a few exhibitions, and had plans to produce videos with similarly minded colleagues and friends. For her, marriage was neither a clear concept nor a goal in her life yet. Still, she created a lonely, depressed housewife in her writing, thus ahead of schedule. Perhaps this protagonist had her secret wild youth suppressed, but for Cao Fei, she was more or less a typical housewife who finds herself trapped within a fateful network of apparatus. Ten years later, married and mid-careered female artist Cao Fei put a similar housewife in her well-exhibited film *Haze and Fog* (2013), which plumbs the spiritual malaise accompanying China's rapid urbanization. In a 2014 interview, when discussing how she chose the characters to be placed amid the plastic buildings of *La Town*, Cao Fei said, "I didn't have a script or anything when I started. I just selected characters I thought were interesting. Then I separated them into a lot of categories like men, policemen, businessmen, sex workers, and I started to match them up to create little scenes."[2] The characters in Cao Fei's works are not necessarily the product of closed, predetermined scripts, but have been given different faces and involved as the natural process of life in the varied contexts. Not only did she imagine these characters and create their heroes in the virtual worlds, she also empowers them with her camera and helps these people construct their own utopias in reality. To prepare for the shooting of *Whose Utopia* (2006), she created stages for the workers who are bound to factory assembly lines to perform their dreams as a theatre of emancipation, which redefined the boundaries separating dreams from reality and creatively intervened in the use of time and space. However, Cao Fei's conclusion is not necessarily

2.
Charles Schultz, "CAO FEI with Charles Schultz", *The Brooklyn Rail*, 3 October 2014. http://www.caofei.com/texts.aspx.

optimistic: Since one cannot destroy these apparatuses and their networks, the only thing one can do is to make deviant use of them or build a counter-network in a heterotopia.

In her new work *Strangers* (2015), Cao Fei takes clips of her own video chats with strangers from Omegle, a website for random chatting. The images are dim and of poor quality. Most of the time, the chat is silent and dull. The chatters are not communicative subjects but passive respondents to Cao Fei impromptu scripts, and the scenes are voyeuristic mini shows directed by her. These almost unidentifiable faces appear only for a few minutes. Bored to death, they do not attempt to have any meaningful communication. It seems that the youngsters who used to be crazy about cosplay (short for costume play), hip-hop and online games[3] have now removed their masks and handed over their control of excitement to the random choices of the internet and its technology. Technology, created by subjects who emerge from "the relentless fight between living beings and apparatuses", according to Agamben,[4] has shaped its own subjects and then uprooted them. Having looked at the world with the eyes and minds of a desperate housewife and those of an innocent child, what answers will Cao Fei bring us this time?

3.
Cao Fei has worked in all three of these areas: *Cosplayers* (2004), *Hip Hop: New York* (2006), *Hip Hop: Fukuoka* (2005), *Hip Hop: Guangzhou* (2003) and *RMB City* (2007–2011).

4.
Giorgio Agamben, *What is an Apparatus? and Other Essays*, translated by David Kishik and Stefan Pedatella, Stanford University Press, Stanford. ISBN (paper edition): 9780804762304. http://www.sup.org/books/title/?id=1745. Giorgio Agamben writes: "I will call an apparatus literally anything that has in some way the capacity to capture, orient, determine, intercept, model, control, or secure the gestures, behaviors, opinions, or discourses of living beings."

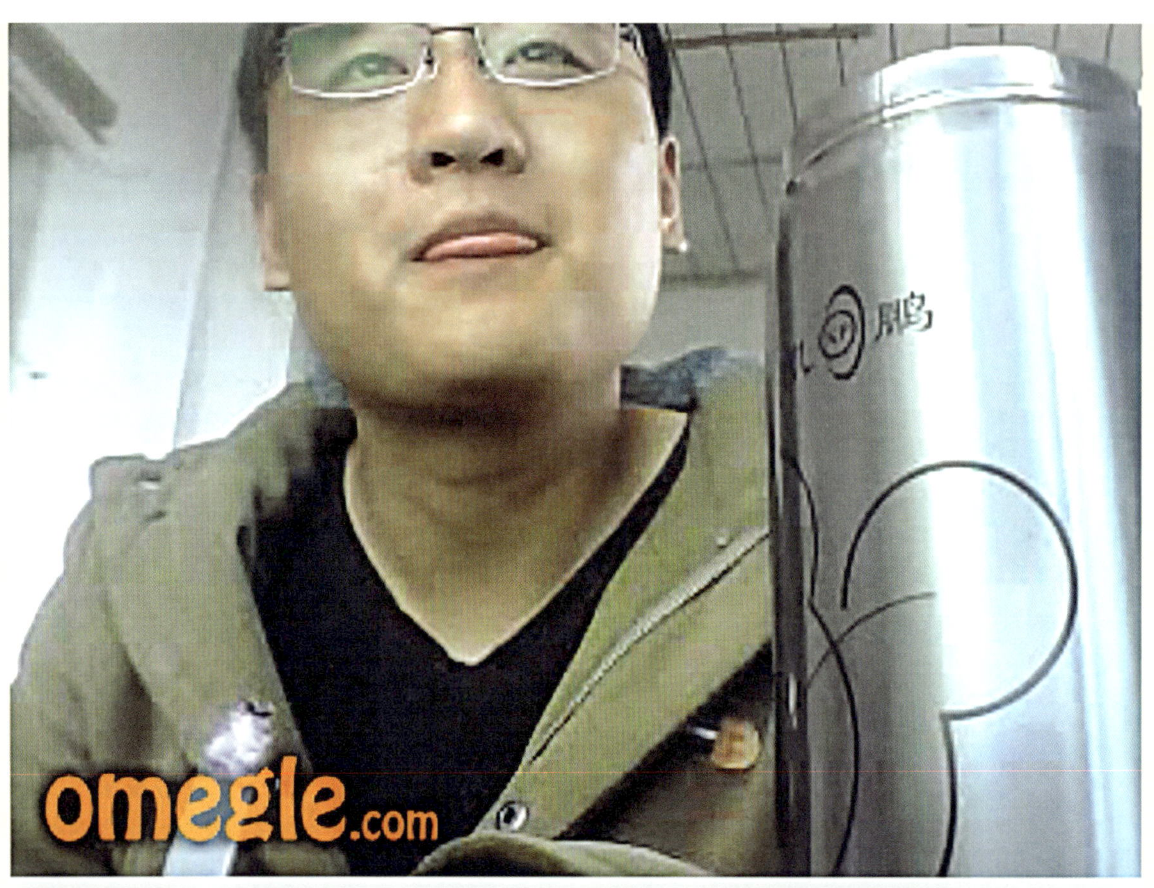

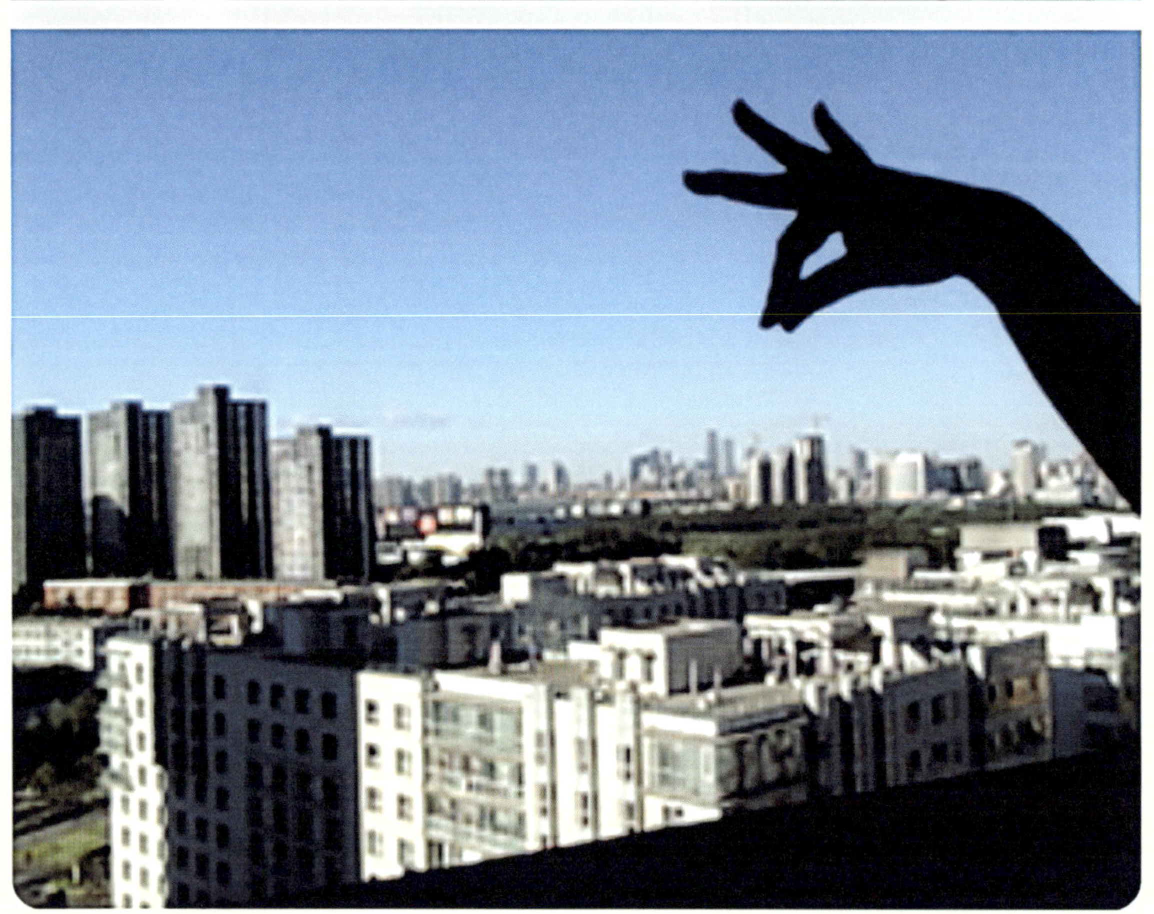

Cao Fei
Strangers: City
2015
Video
4′18′′

now chatting with a random
er. Say hi!

th speak the same language.
"English" from the menu in the
to disable.)

ger: ∘ ∘

op
sc

Send
Enter

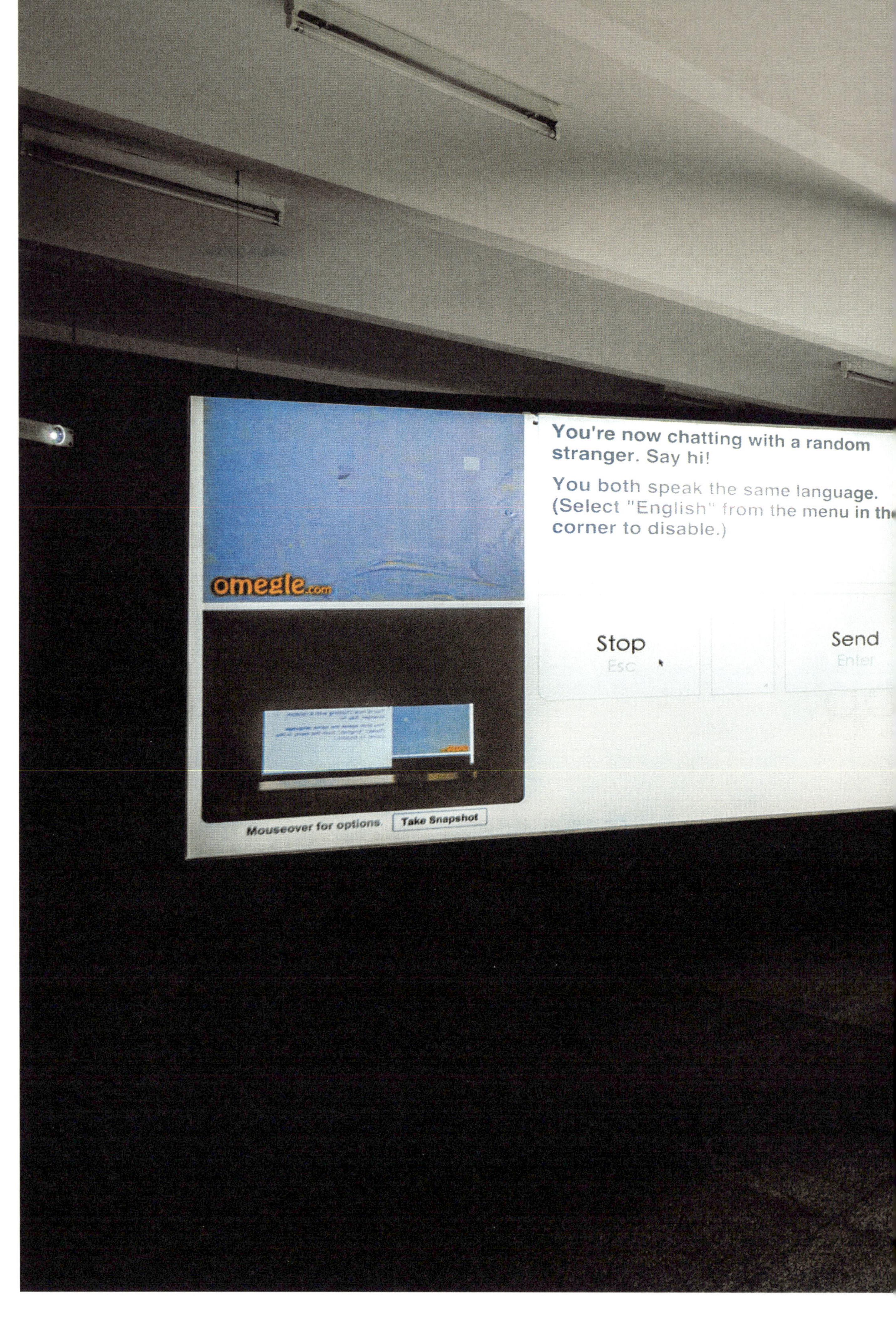
omegle.com
You're now chatting with a random stranger. Say hi!
You both speak the same language. (Select "English" from the menu in the corner to disable.)
Stop
Esc
Send
Enter
Mouseover for options.
Take Snapshot

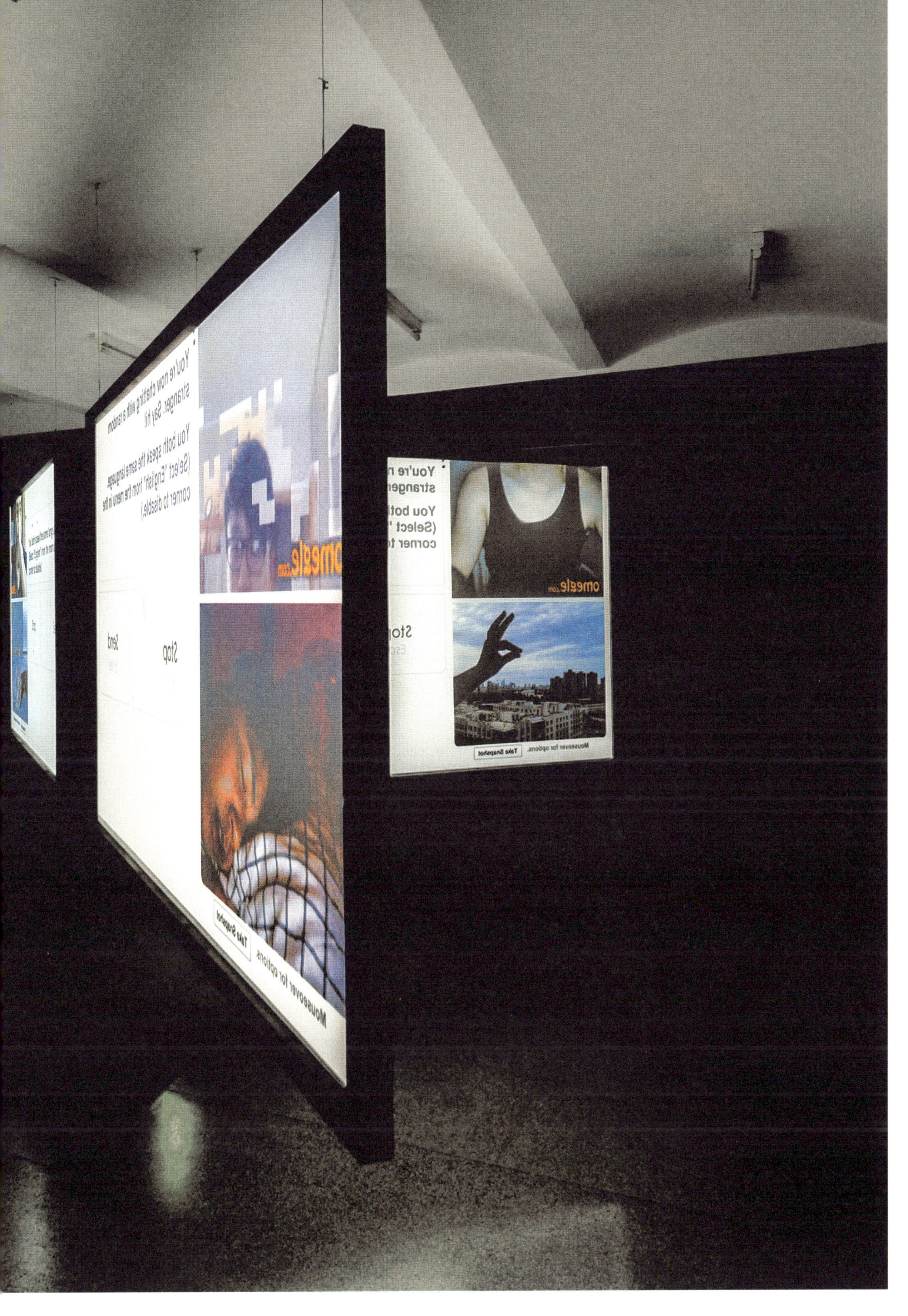

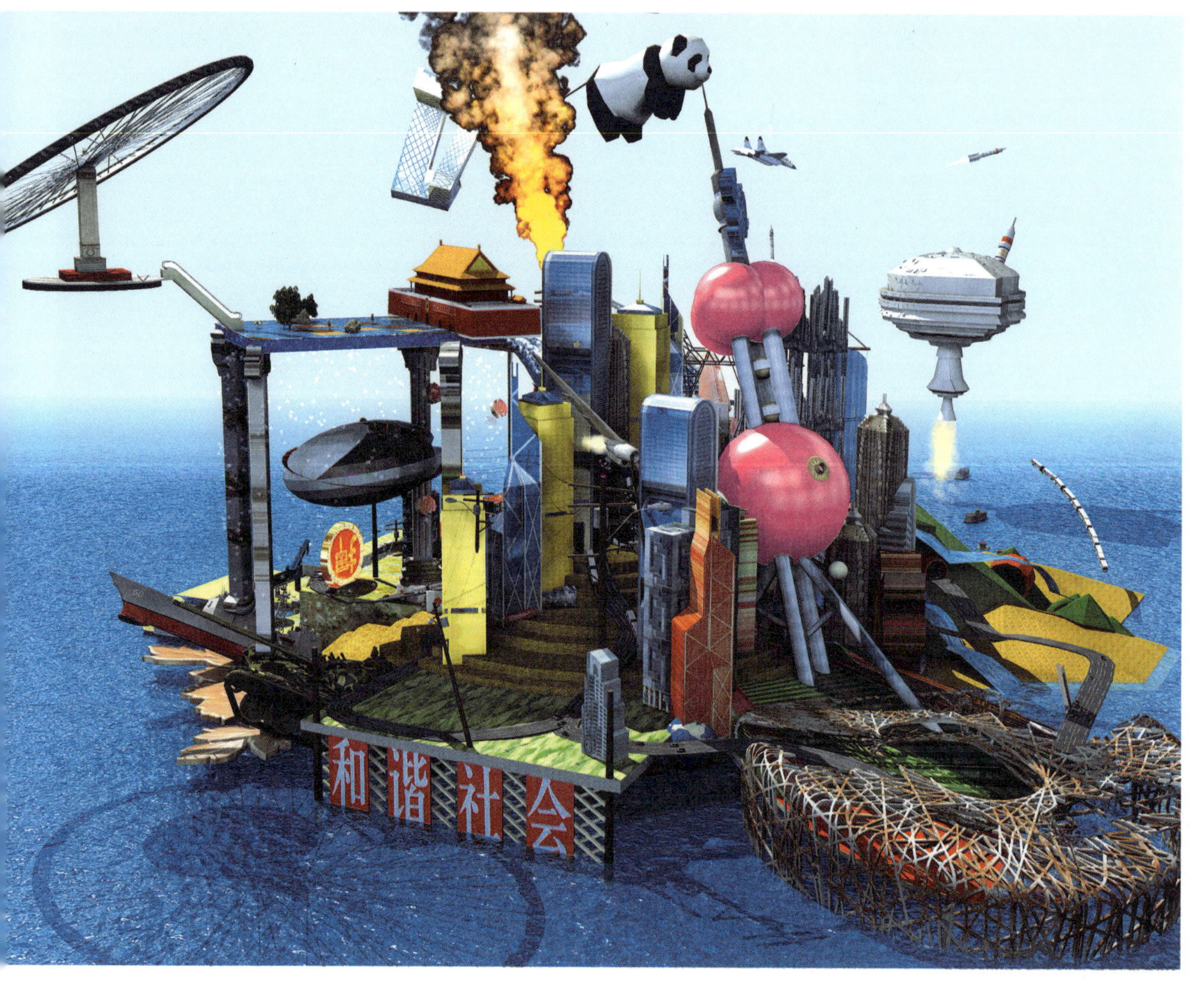

Preceding double page
Cao Fei
Installation view
of *Strangers: City*
2015
Video
4′18″

Cao Fei
*RMB City: A Second Life
City Planning*
2007
Digital print
120 × 160 cm

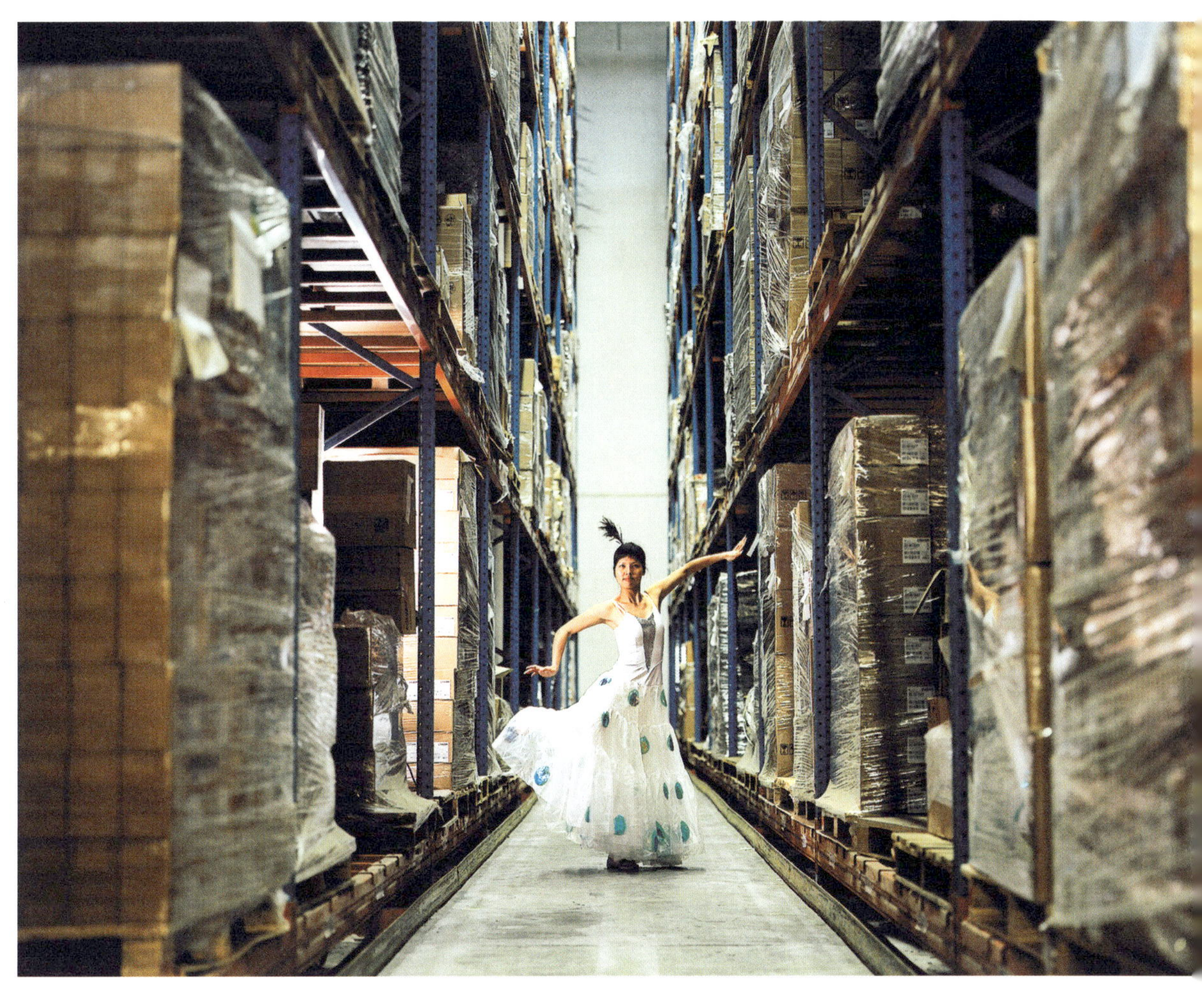

Cao Fei
*Whose Utopia:
My Future is Not a Dream*
2006
C-print
120×150 cm

HAO LIANG

Hao Liang
Yanshan Garden
2015
Photograph
12.4×18.8 cm

HAO
LIANG

CHINESE
PAINTING
AS
A
MEDIUM
FOR
CULTURAL
EXPLORATION

SUN DONGDONG

In reviewing the several major twentieth-century debates about Chinese painting, it becomes clear that nearly all of them revolved around the binary opposition between traditional (old) and modern (new) paradigms. The notion of "modernity" was widely discussed, either as the result of a gradual evolution or as a consequence of radical changes introduced by a particular ideology. These ideas about modernity, like the idea of "Chinese painting" itself, were influenced during this period by an emerging sense of national identity, but were also affected by concerns over the legacy of Chinese culture. Debates arose, for example, following the May Fourth Movement of 1919, with its emphasis on cultural enlightenment and national salvation, but also against the backdrop of the social transformations resulting from the Communist victory in 1949, and around the experimental ink painting movement that began after economic reforms in the 1980s. All of these debates about modernity had to confront the Western-centric and teleological view of history. Building on the ruins of the ancient Chinese empire, the historical context demanded the adoption of the Western cultural paradigm as synonymous with "truth". For Chinese painting, this Westernization ultimately led to a paradox. The constant pursuit of modernity bound it to the same destiny as Western painting. Rather than saying "Chinese painting had reached a dead end", it is better to say that the idea of historical narrative in art, both in China and the West, had come to an end. When historical purposes can no longer be ascribed to painting, it becomes a lifeless thing, taking its meaning from the past, with no hope for the future. In response to globalization, a growing number of Chinese painters have rediscovered "traditionalist" techniques, conforming to the Western understanding of Chinese painting: historical resonance and the legacy of cultural traditions. In contrast, Hao Liang, as an ink painter employing traditional techniques, brings a different and unique contemporary perspective to his work, which has attracted worldwide attention. He approaches Chinese painting as a means to explore Chinese traditional culture in its totality. Consequently, he does not focus on subtleties of style or the minutiae of technique.

Inspired by his teacher Xu Lei, Hao's method of studying traditional culture in its totality looks at ancient texts in parallel with classical paintings in order to extract new insights, pursuing what Foucault described as an "archaeology of knowledge". For example, by examining anecdotes in ancient Chinese texts, Hao sheds new light on the order of things. In his series "Searching the Wonders – Miscellanea on Leisurely Survival" (2013), he depicts the eight Chinese solar terms corresponding to seasonal changes, placing the paintings on facing pages. This is in contrast to the traditional presentation,

according to which only text appears on the left-hand
page and only painting on the right-hand page. The
relationship between these eight solar terms links
the pages of the album, giving visual representation
to the abstract concept of seasonality. Hao's scroll
paintings from the same period express the ethical
view of nature in Chinese traditional thought. The first
of these is *The Tale of Clouds* (2012–2013), with which
Hao tries to show the ways in which nihilism concerning
the world governed by the laws of nature is rooted
in Western systems of scientific knowledge, using
a distinctively East Asian art form. In a sense, *The Tale
of Clouds* is a critique of modernity, and this profound
and complex concept is a key inspiration for many of
the artist's creations. In a later scroll painting, *Fire
and Water* (2013), Hao exercises restraint, keeping the
composition rather simple. The scroll begins on the right
edge, gradually moving to a huge forest fire on the left,
trapping all the animals inside. How is one to interpret
the scene? Since the Han dynasty (206 BC–AD 220),
Confucianism has put forward the idea that interactions
between heaven and mankind serve as a system of
checks and balances on rulers. During the Song dynasty
(960–1279), people thus believed that natural disasters
were heaven's retribution. In *Fire and Water*, we can
assume that Hao is using this same metaphor, long
favoured by Chinese scholars, to project the anxiety
of a divided and conflicted world.

    Ci Jun (*The Virtuous Being*, 2013–2015) – the Chinese
title could be translated literally as "This Gentleman",
another name used for bamboo – is Hao's third scroll
painting. The title is another name for bamboo,
originating in a well-known anecdote from the Eastern
Jin dynasty (265–420). The famous calligrapher Wang
Huizhi (d. 388) had planted bamboo in the courtyard
of his new home even before furnishing its rooms.
When asked why, he replied that he could not let a day
pass without "this gentleman" for company. Bamboo
has often been used by Chinese scholars to express both
strength and integrity, a projection of the plant's lofty
image. For the most part, *Ci Jun* depicts landscapes.
However, the two gardens in the scroll, Wangchuan and
Yanshan, are each closely connected with a celebrated
ancient Chinese scholar, the first with Wang Wei and
the second with Wang Shizhen. Wangchuan Garden
disappeared without a trace long ago. However, Yanshan
Garden has survived for three hundred years and is now
a public park in the midst of the coastal city of Taicang.
At the end of the scroll, we see a giant Ferris wheel,
a replica of the one installed in Yanshan Garden today.
This painting seems to reflect the fate of these two
gardens throughout history. Before starting to paint
this scroll, Hao studied ancient paintings and collotypes
of Yanshan and Wangchuan, as well as recent satellite

images. Above and beyond the complicated history
of the gardens, the painting is more of a metaphor for
the relationship between mankind and nature. Stone
structures at the base of mountains, man-made marshes
and well-landscaped gardens all enjoyed common
currency among the Neo-Confucians, in line with
the idea that in order to extend knowledge, one must
investigate things. Although principle is given priority
over vitality, they cannot be separated. Both are said
to coexist between heaven and earth. These beliefs were
core concepts for ancient Chinese scholars, expressed
in their art and their lives. Thus, in this scroll, time
and the individual are interdependent. Dynasties and
generations are mere phenomena, part of the Chinese
rise-and-fall concept of history. As such, the scroll's
narrative is freed from the shackles of linear time,
engaging the conscious mind with the material world.
From this perspective, Hao asserts that immortality
exists beyond all dimensional boundaries. This assertion
reflects the metaphysical and historical influences still
lurking in contemporary Chinese aesthetics.

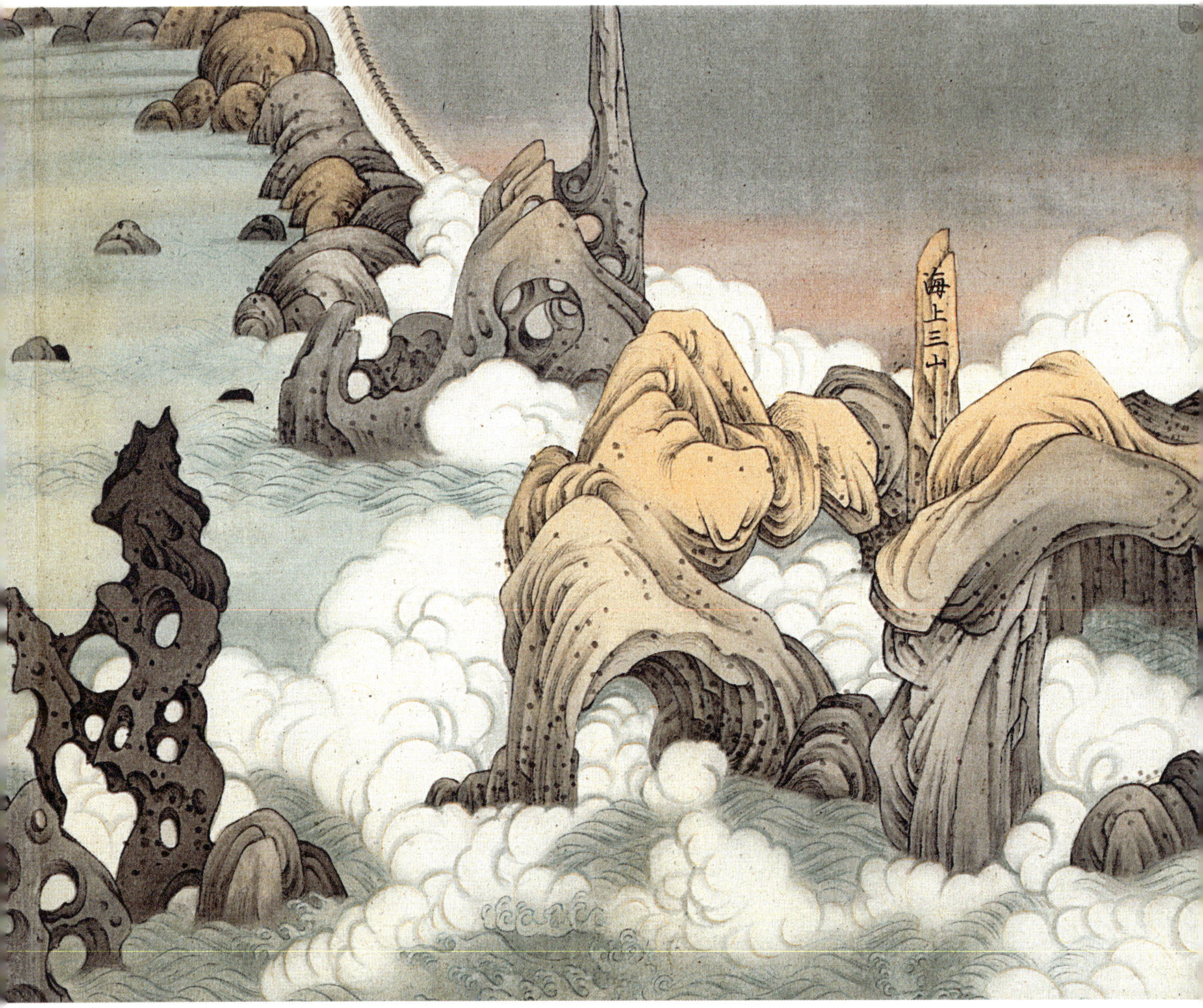

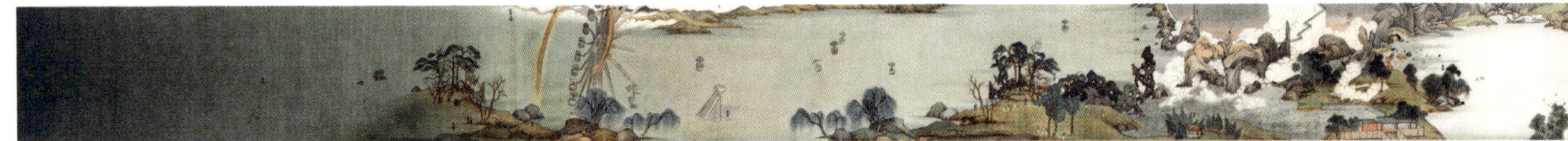

Hao Liang
The Virtuous Being
2015
Ink and colour on silk hand scroll
Hand scroll size: 40 × 1312 cm

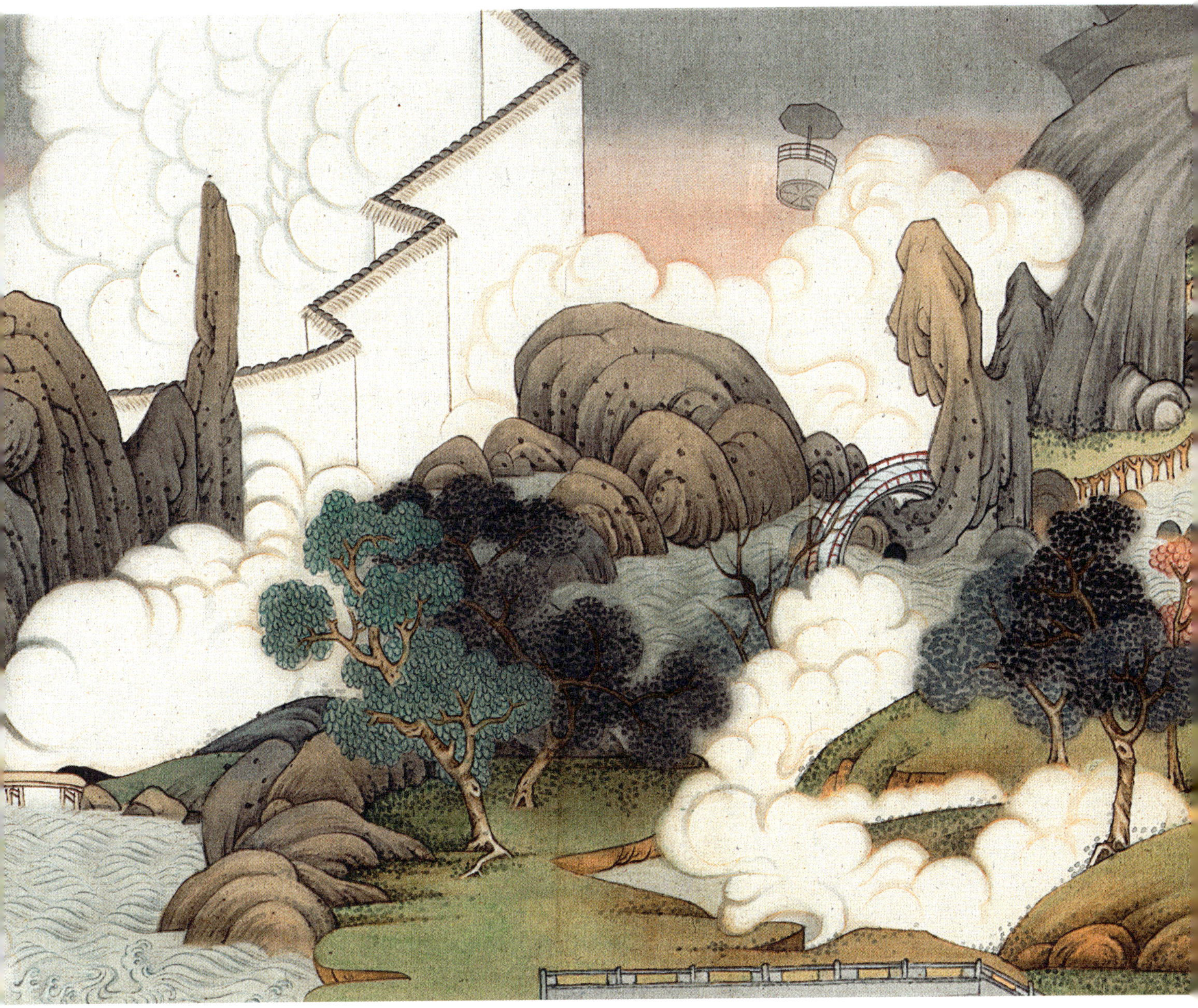

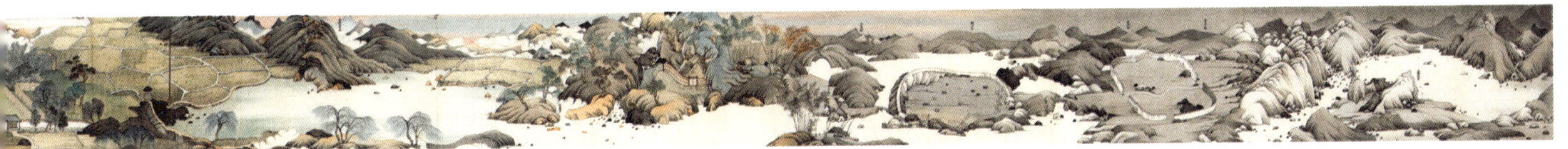

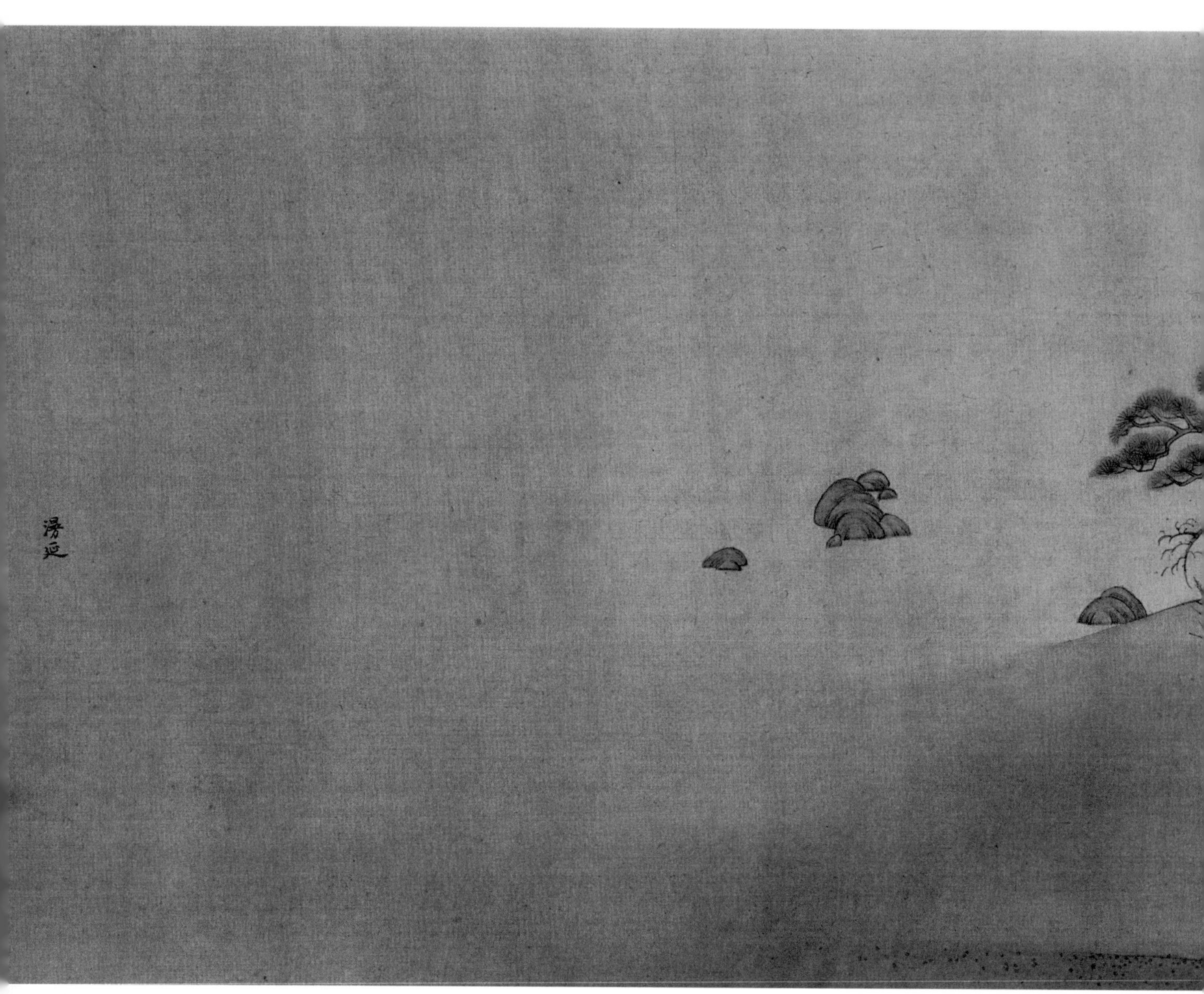

Hao Liang
The Virtuous Being (detail)
2015
Ink and colour on silk hand scroll

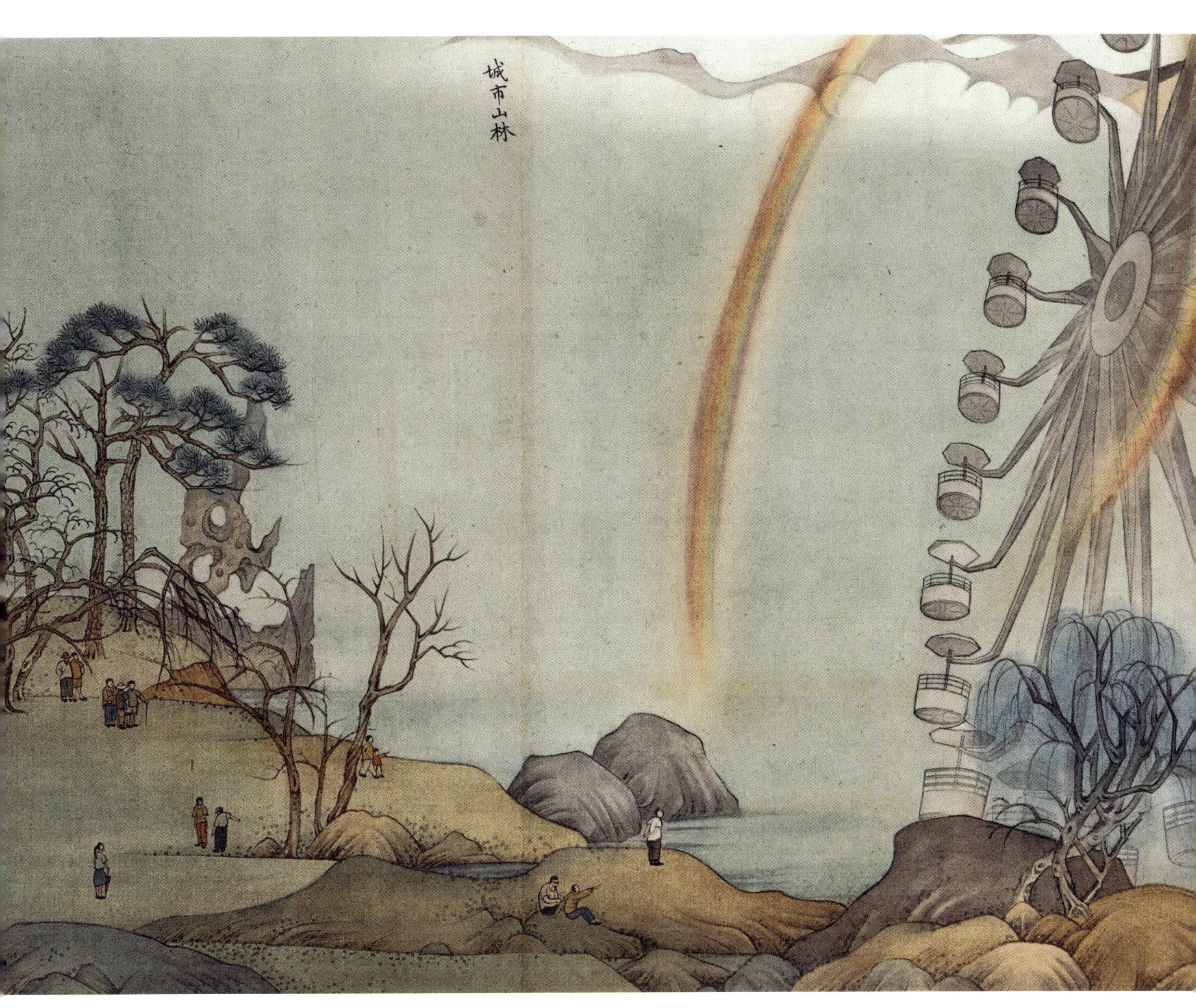
城市山林

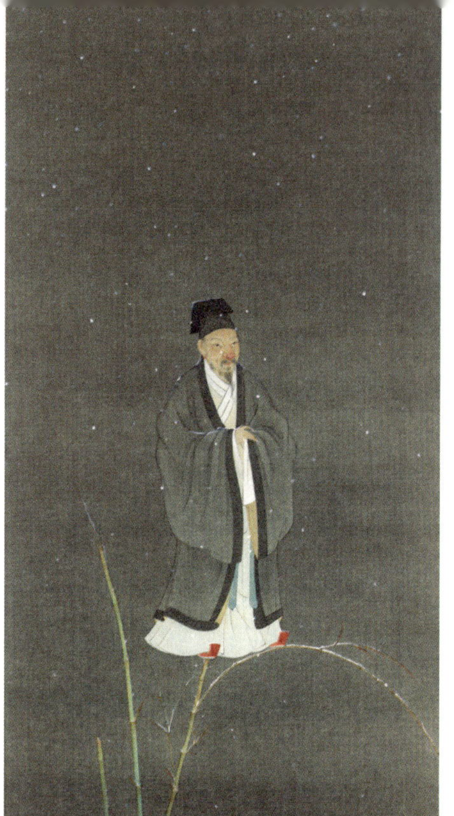

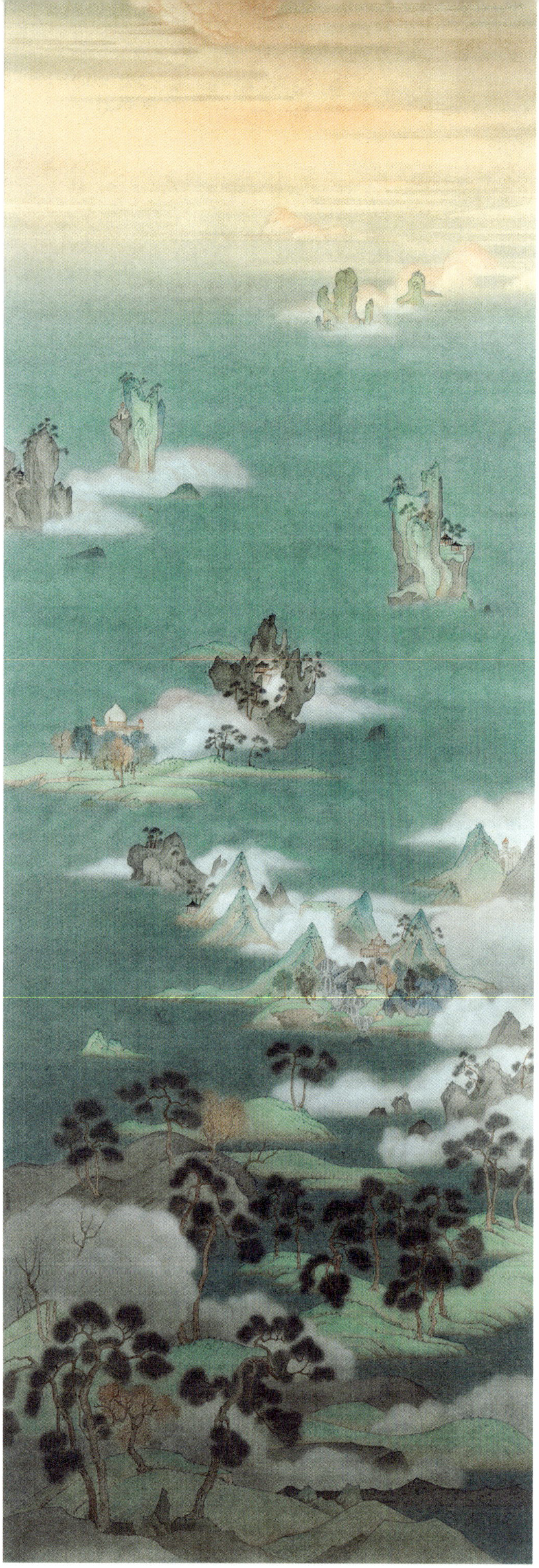

Hao Liang
Details of the installation
Passage from Xian to Ghost
2014

↑
Hao Liang
*Passage from Xian
to Ghost – Portrait
of Wang Shizen*
2014
Ink and colour on silk
hand scroll
37×75 cm

←
*Passage from Xian
to Ghost – The Legendary
Land Penglai*
2014
Ink and colour on silk
hand scroll
62×180 cm

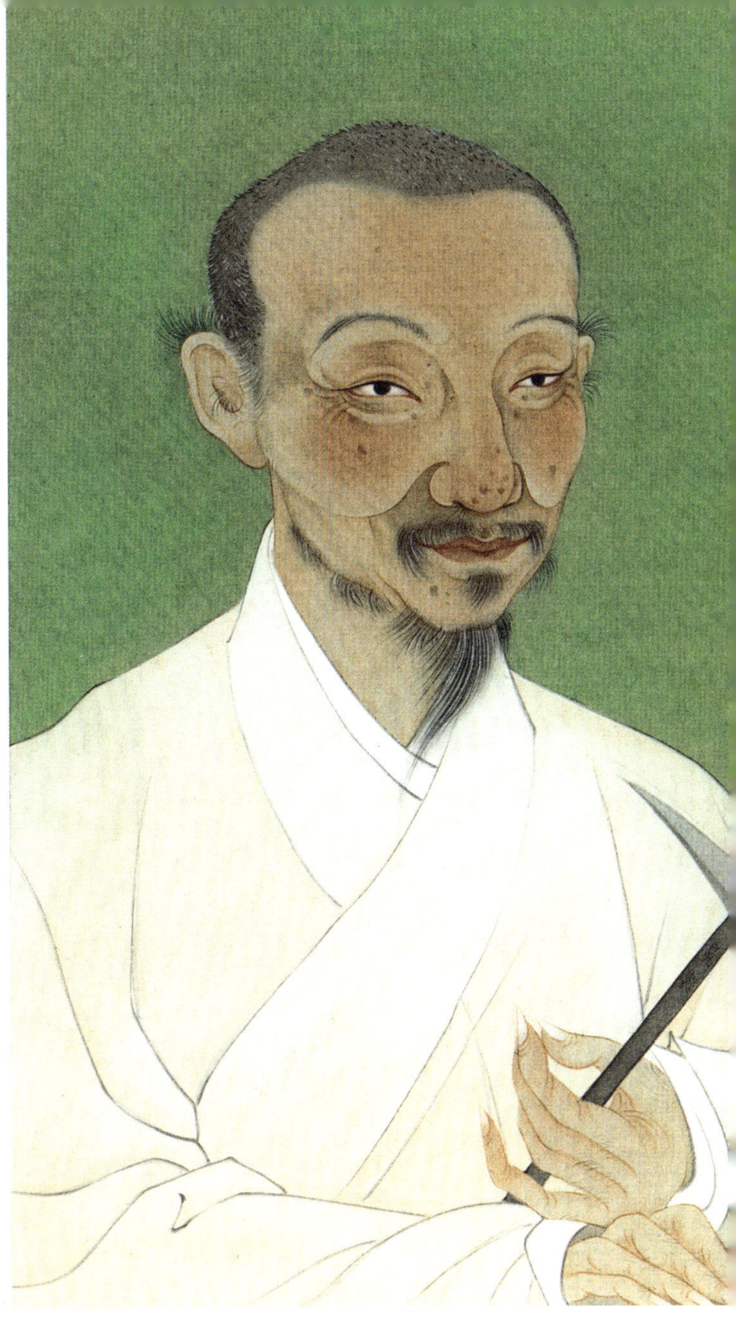

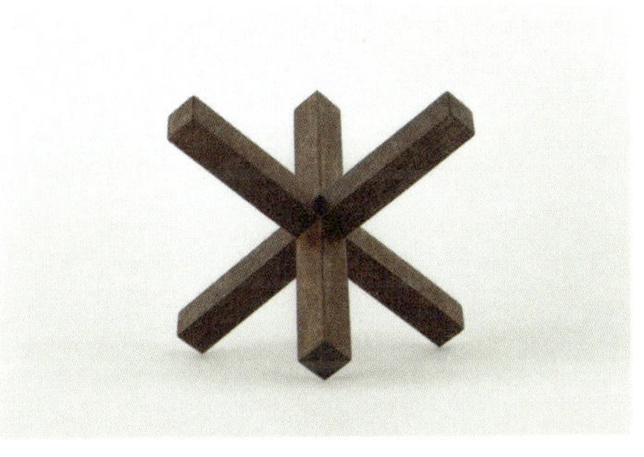

↗
*Passage from
Xian to Ghost – Portrait
of Virtuoso*
2014
Ink and colour on silk
hand scroll
28 × 47 cm

→
Two Sculptures
3 × 3 × 33 cm (× 3)

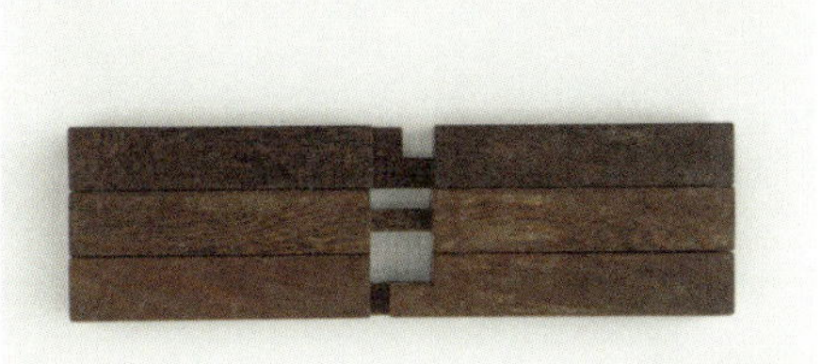

HU XIANGQIAN

Hu Xiangqian
Notes

ALL
THE
WORLD'S
A
STAGE[1]

CLAIRE STAEBLER

1.
William Shakespeare, *As You Like It*, act II, scene VII.

2.
Zhang Yulin, "La vigilance envers le regard" *LEAP magazine*, 2015 (French edition).

"I try to be a cultureless artist"
Hu Xiangqian

Founded uniquely on performance and its methodical recording on video, the work of Hu Xiangqian reflects his critical observation of his environment. Chameleon-like in his approach, the artist absorbs the spirit of the times, which he then scenarizes in various actions that alternate humour and derision. Inspired by popular and high culture (comics, literature, cinema, music, etc.) as well as by personal experiences, Hu produces work that is immaterial, driven by a permanent question: should the artist play a role, and if so, *what* role?

Born in 1983 in Leizhou, in the remote province of Guandong, Hu belongs to a generation that was exposed to globalisation and whose practice was changed as a result. When performance art began to develop in China in the 1980s and 1990s in parallel with the nascent institutional scene, this took a distinctive form, confirming its legitimacy in its ability to elude censorship. Circulating in the forms of photographs, videos and documents, it played a seminal role in the recent history of Chinese contemporary art and placed the figure of the artist at the centre — witness the cases of Song Dong (1966), Zhang Huan (1965) and Lin Yilin (1964), in whose work the presence of the body and the endurance forced upon it are so resonant. Indeed, although performance reflects a certain political climate prevailing at the end of the 20th century, Hu's practice emerged in a context of vigorous change which was both close to and remote from this history. Whereas the subjects addressed by the artist have gained a certain degree of lightness, his actions always stem from considerable mastery. Aware of the attention that he attracts, like his contemporaries, Hu pays great attention to the details.[2]

In one of his first works, *Blue Flags Everywhere* (2006), the artist engages in a spoof electrical campaign to be mayor of his hometown. In this utopian, left-field piece, Hu entered the art arena in the skin of a shady politician who hands out both leaflets and bribes. In 2014 Hu went back to Leizhou in his video *Speech at the Edge of the World* — first shown at the Gwangju Biennale, "Burning Down the House" — in which the artist states his motivations in front of a perplexed audience of college and school students. His postures and gestures remind us of the clichés of this kind of propaganda exercise. Confronted with this caricature, we hesitate between doubt and the desire to understand. These emblematic works consolidated his interest in appropriation and subversion, the here and the elsewhere.

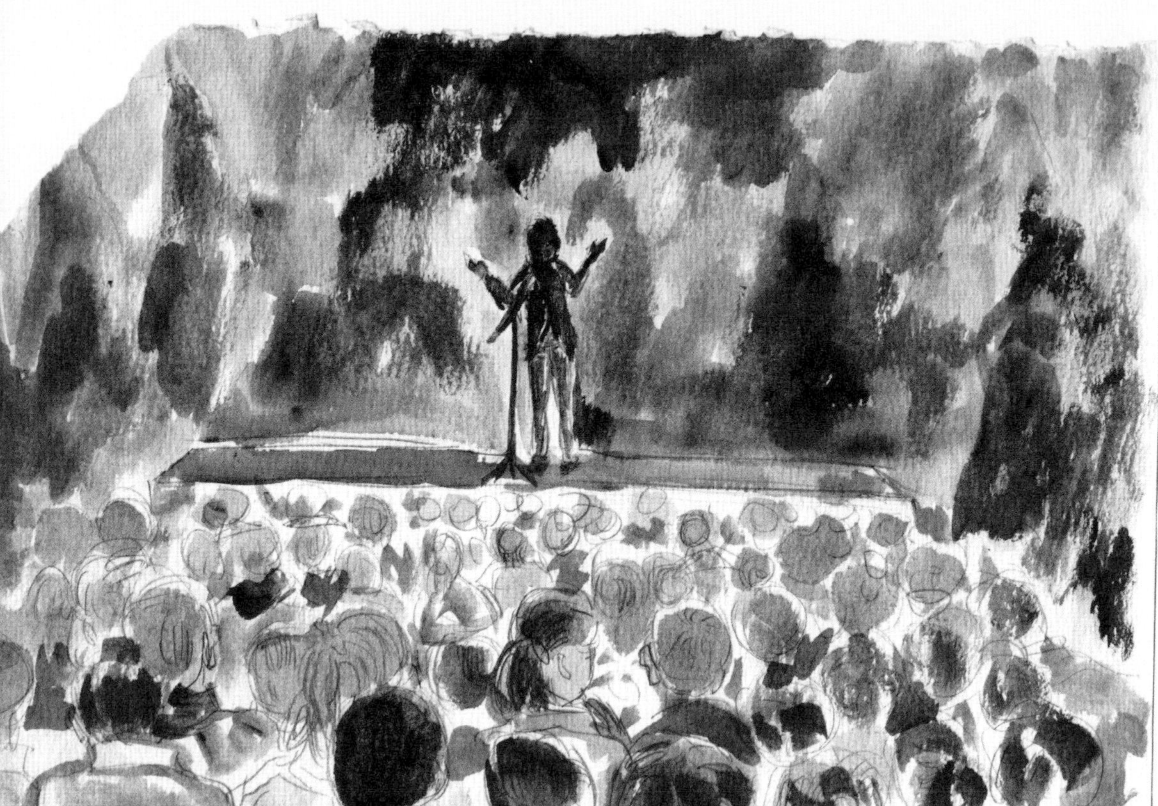

A narrator above all else, Hu has a compulsion
to tell stories. In the video *The Secret Mission* (2015),
he plays the lead role, that of an "Assassin of Chinese
Antiquity". Wearing a period costume inspired by the
fantasies of the Wuxia sabre and martial arts genres,
the artist performs a series of rather banal actions, far
from the chivalrous adventures usually associated with
this kind of story. He is more antihero than superhero.
This relation to the body and its occupation of space
is also present in *Reconstructing Michelangelo* (2015),
in which the artist creates a learning process for a
disciple – his assistant – inspired by a very romantic
vision of the Renaissance. Can the practice of
performance be taught in the same way as painting
or sculpture? Warming-up exercises, sports training,
discussion and practical exercises in public spaces
and in the Beijing gallery constitute the corpus of
these videos, which were shown in the exhibition
"A Performance a Day Keeps the Doctor Away".

The video *The Woman in front of the Camera*
(2015) features a woman dancing in a park in Beijing,
to a soundtrack of typically Chinese noises added
by the artist. This is the first piece in which Hu leaves
the performing role to another person. As walkers
enter the frame, pause briefly and then continue
on their way, the woman performs her choreography
with a scarf as her only prop, conveying a sense of
lightness and expressing a desire for simplicity. Rather
like Chris Marker, who, in *Un dimanche à Pékin* (1956),[3]
manages to show all the creative modernity of China
through the inactivity of its citizens, Hu tries to capture
the history of his country through the portrait of

Hu Xiangqian
Sketch for *Speech
at the Edge of the World*
2013
25 × 17 cm

3.
In 1955 Marker was invited
on a group tour organised
by the Franco-Chinese
friendship society. With
only modest equipment
and unable to film workers
in the factories, he made
a documentary showing
the people of Beijing on
their day of rest, Sunday.

a crowd and that of a woman, who seems to be making herself free of everything by affirming her individual liberty.

Hu is intrepid when it comes to taking on clichés. His work of the last ten years or so shows another, more human face of China, at the geographical, social and cultural limits of a country in perpetual motion, striving to endow local situations with a universal resonance.

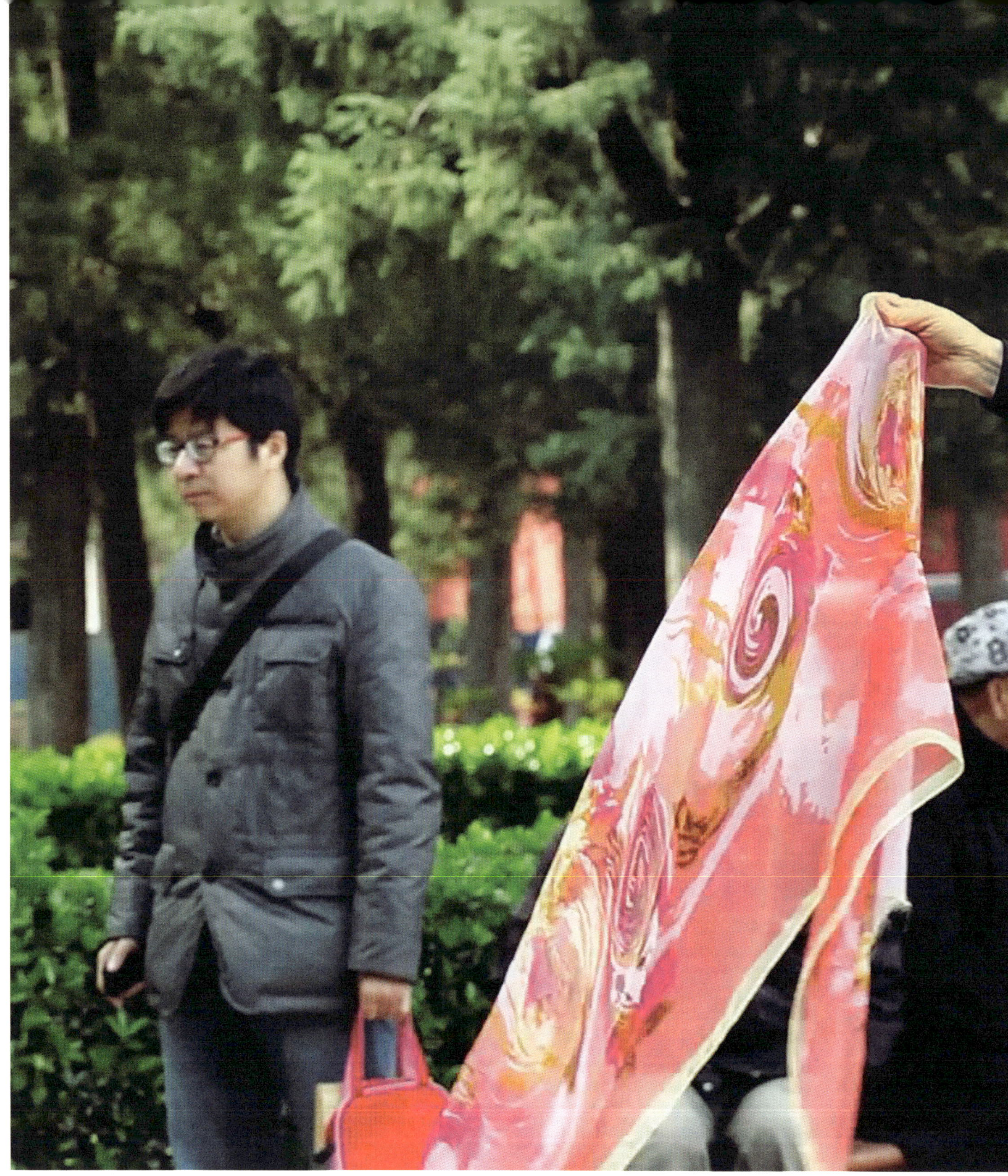

Hu Xiangqian
The Woman in Front of the Camera
2015
HD video
2'53''

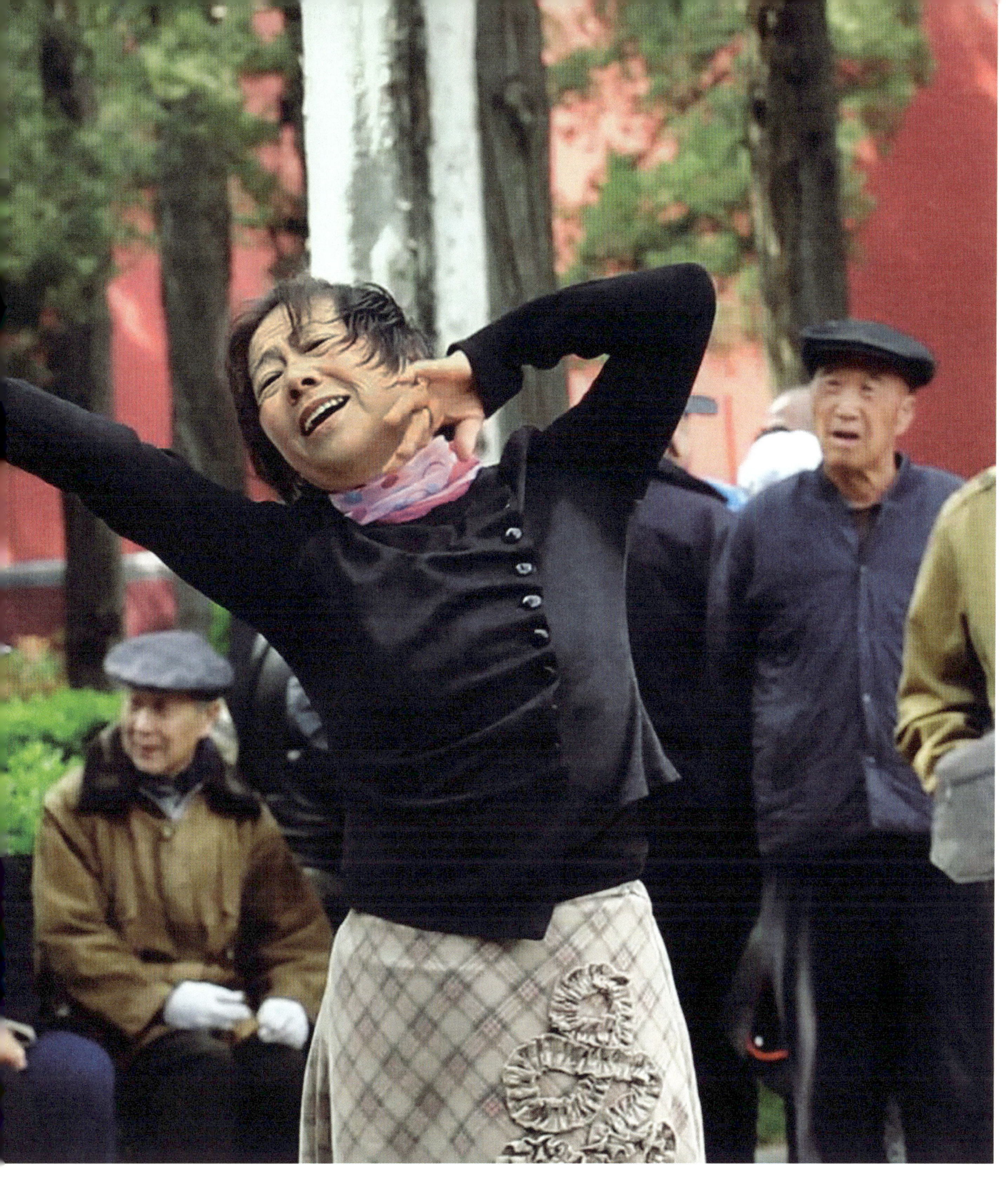

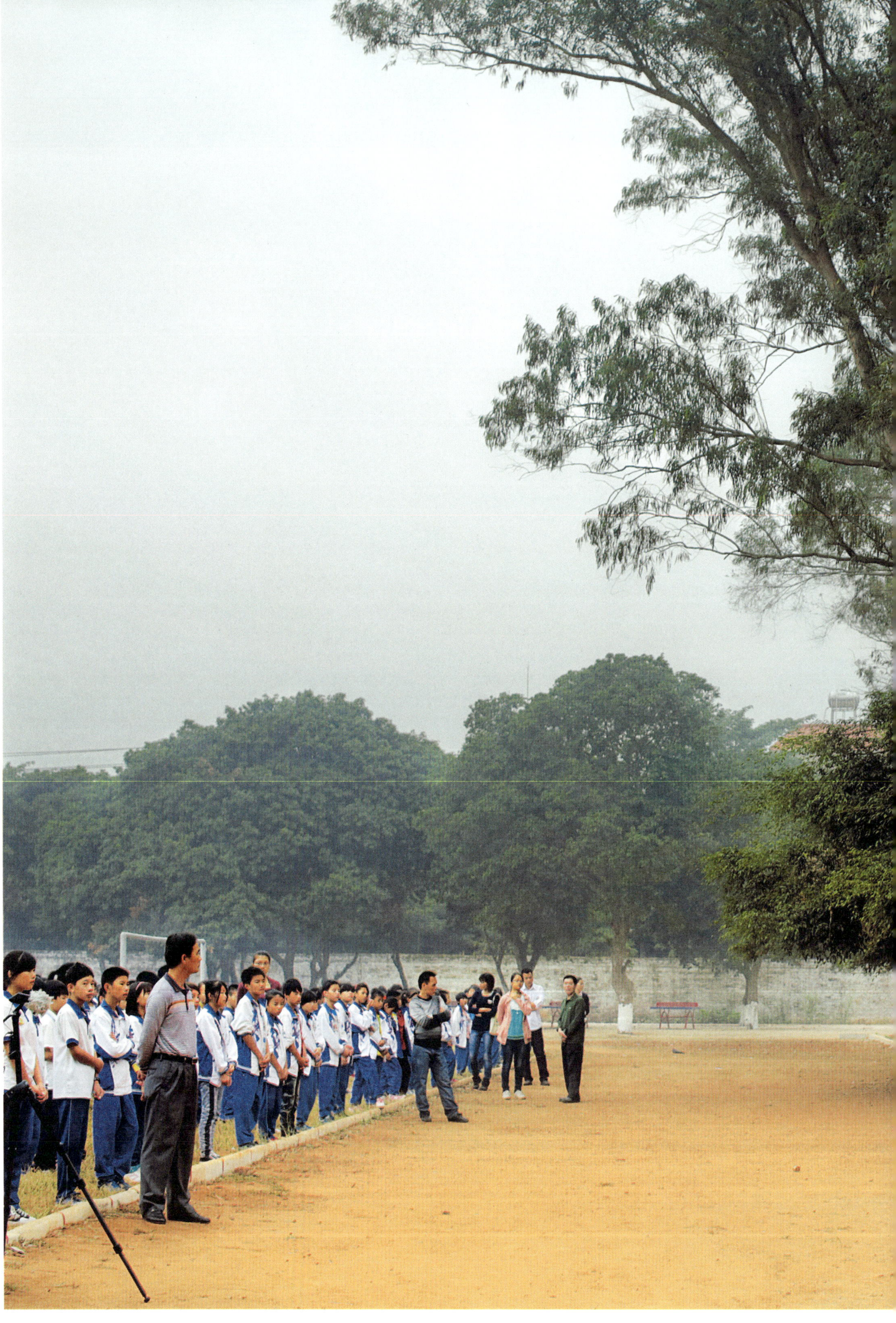

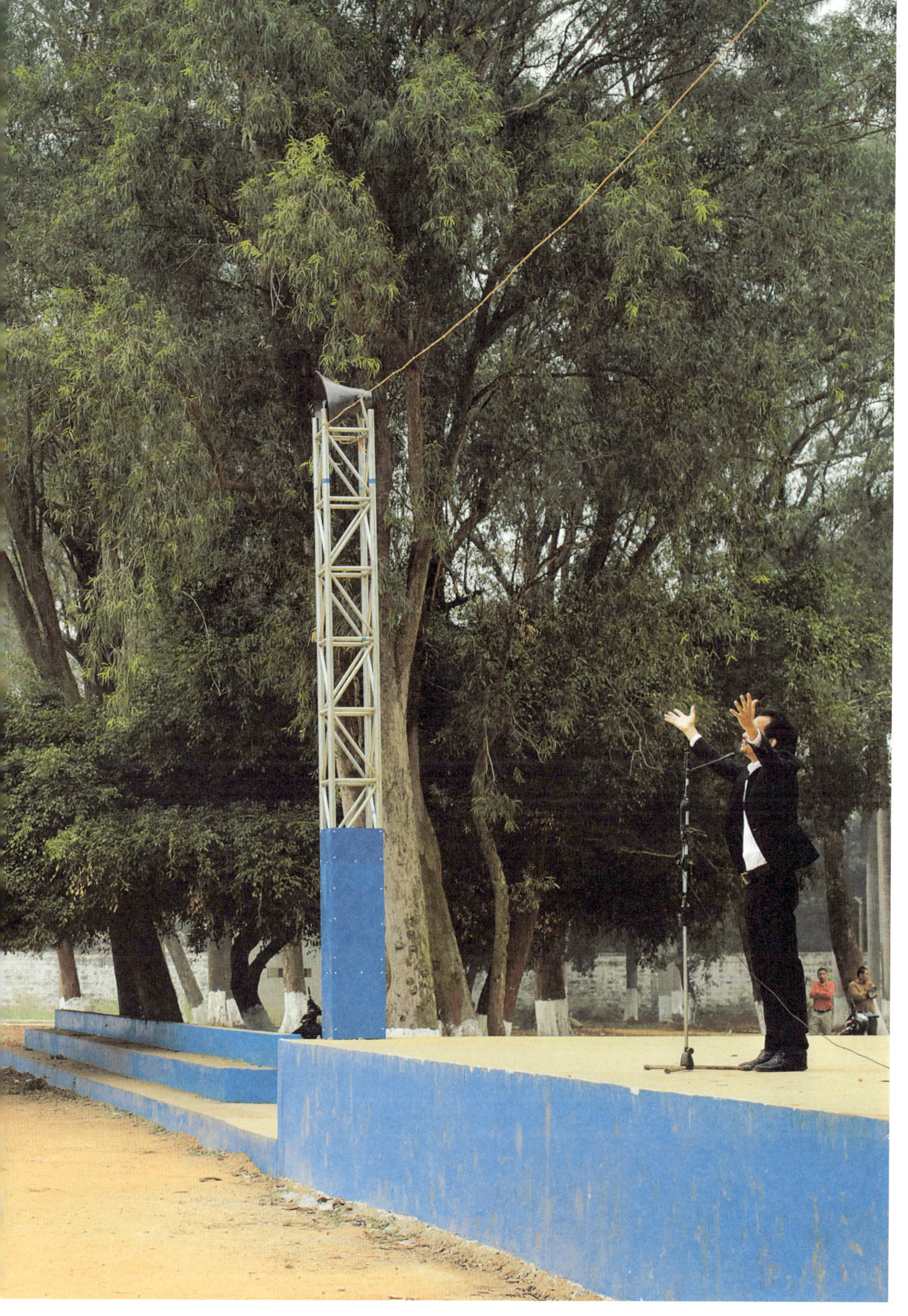

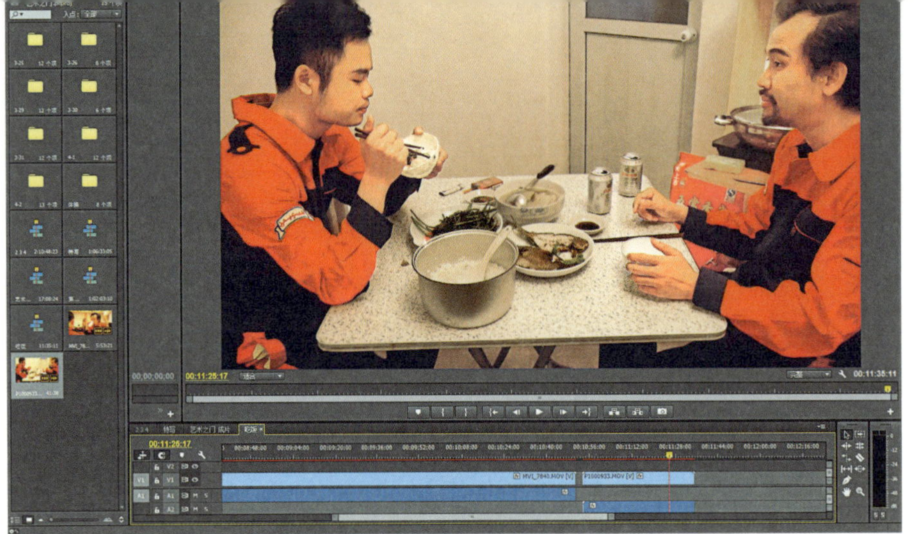

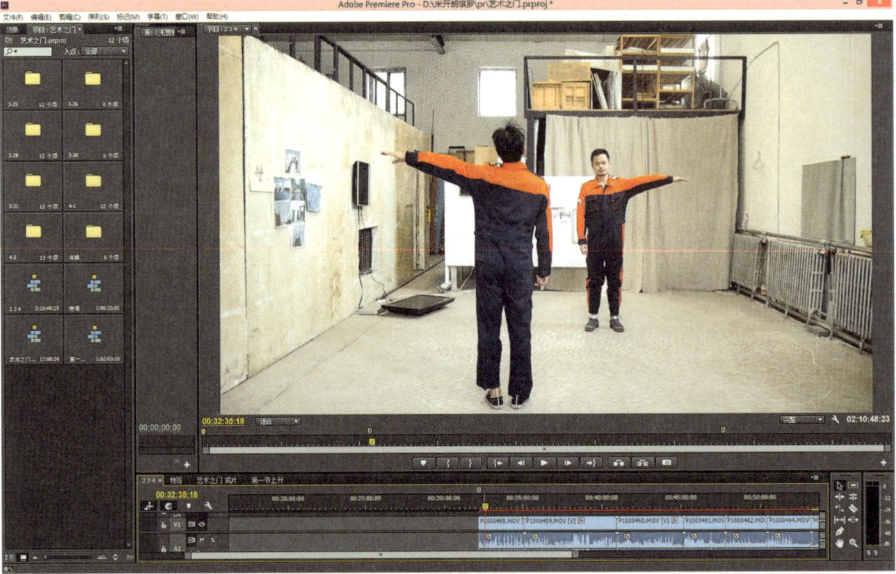

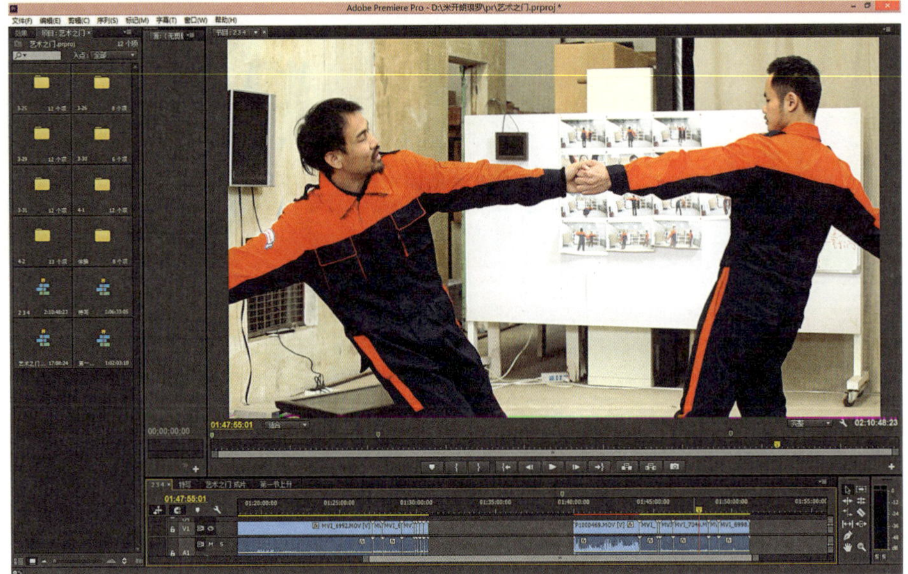

Preceding double page
Hu Xiangqian
*Speech at the Edge
of the World*
2013
Single channel HD video
12'23''

Hu Xiangqian
*Reconstructing
Michelangelo –
Sketch I & Reconstructing
Michelangelo – Threshold*
2015
HD video, wood
56'24'' and 11'19''

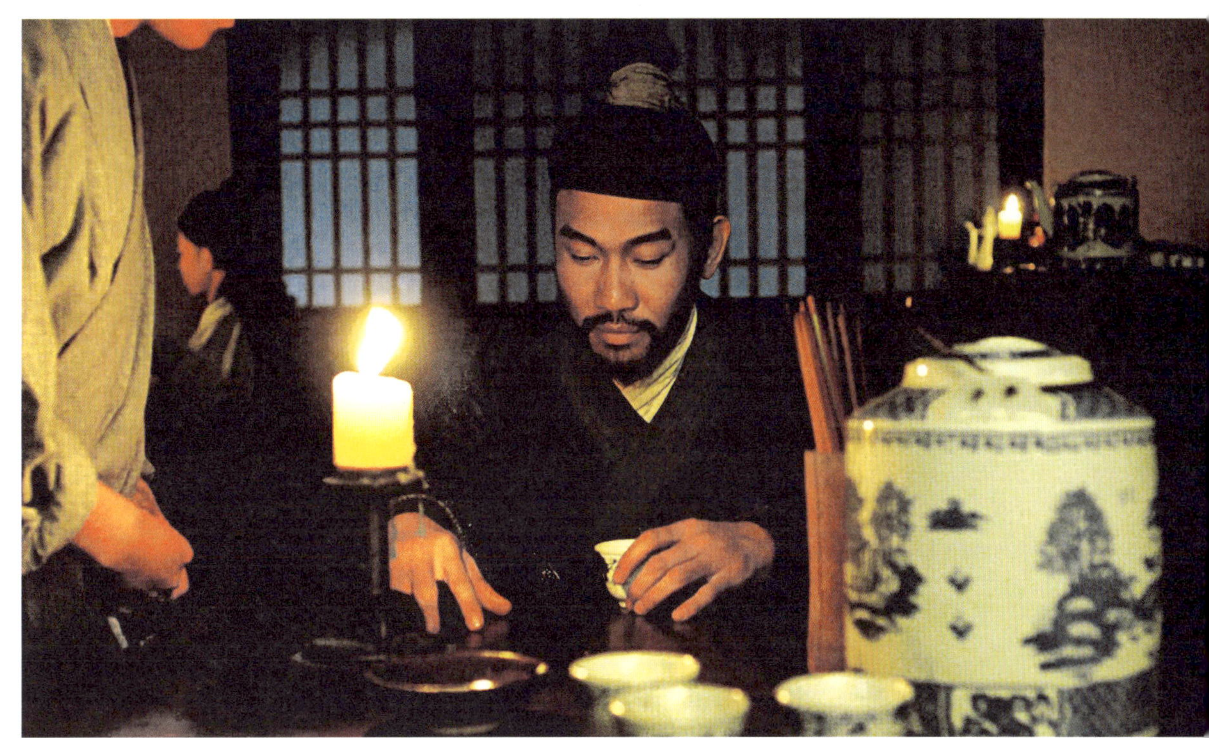

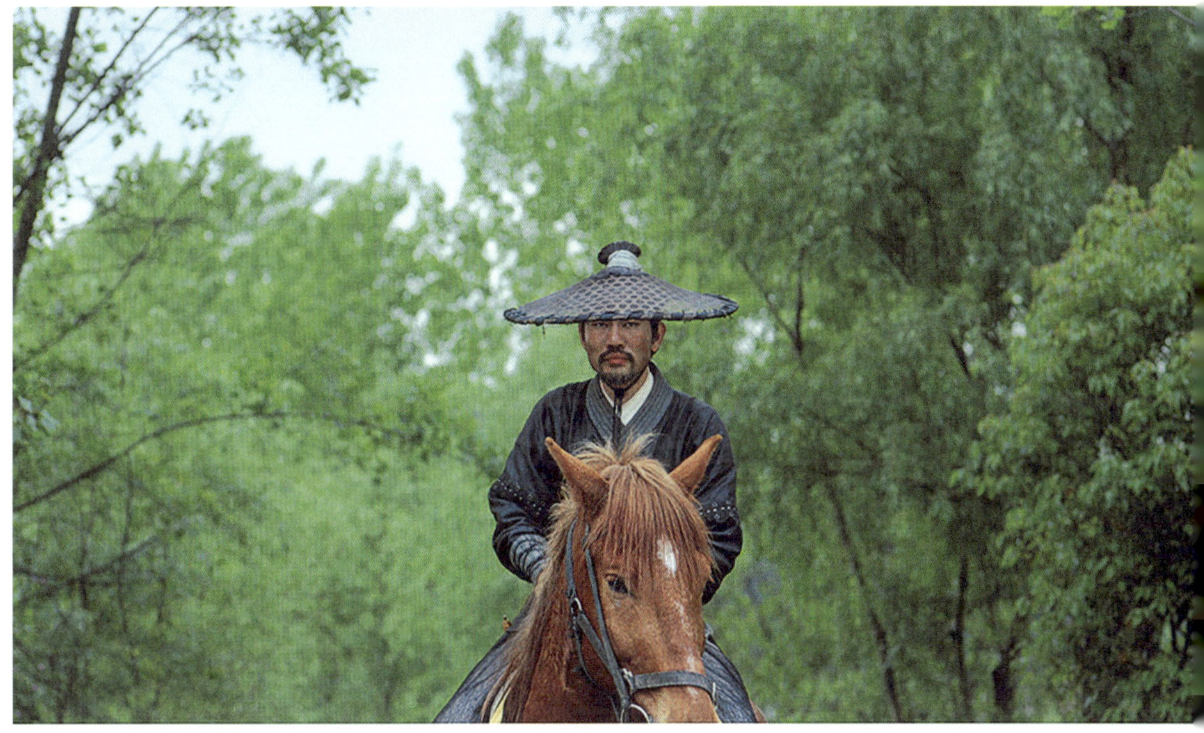

Hu Xiangqian
The Secret Mission
2015
HD video
38′06″

LIU CHUANG

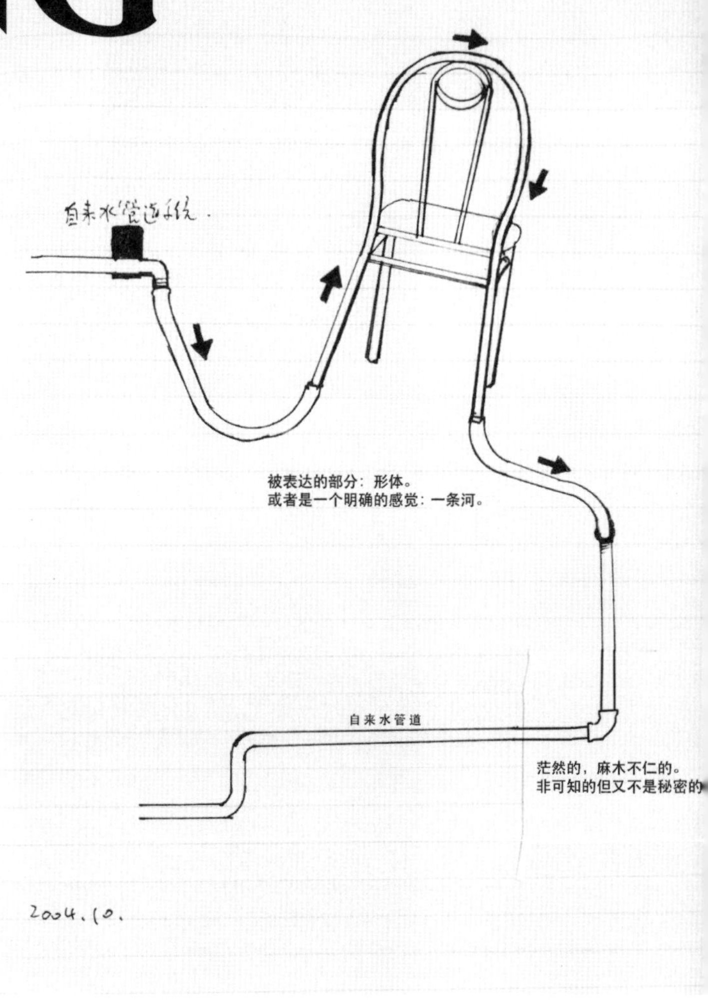

Liu Chuang
Untitled (Unknown River)
2014
Drawing on paper
19 × 20 cm

To explore the porous membrane between society and language, Liu Chuang exploits the diversity and flexibility of available media. His recent video *BBR1 (No. 1 of Blossom Bud Restrainer)* focuses on poplar trees, one of the main contributors to China's drive towards urban greening, and whose spread has kept pace with China's urbanization rate in the last century. Vigorous and resistant to cold, millions of these trees thrive in Beijing, but in spite of their contribution to the city's greening, they have created issues that are themselves emblematic of deficiencies in long-term urban planning. In the spring, the catkins of female poplars fill the air, irritating the skin and lungs like any allergen, and adding another burden to the public medical system. "The snow of poplar catkins" creates a semi-artificial spectacle, its density limiting visibility in the city, blocking traffic and clogging machines. The problem is almost impossible to resolve within the massive administrative body of the capital. One non-sustainable solution to this problem, the result of poor urban planning, has been the invention of the "Blossom Bud Restrainer", a plant hormone that acts as an annual plant contraceptive.

The poplar catkins disaster sounds a note of social disharmony, a noise and a short circuit in society's "normal" workings. To create the video *BBR1 (No. 1 of Blossom Bud Restrainer)*, Liu Chuang has used key words and concepts that link closely to this phenomenon, such as poplar, snow, nature and traditional Chinese medicine, to amass a substantial corpus of visual and audio materials from social media, soundtrack libraries and photo galleries. The visual language switches between documentary, advertising and music video, editing the cacophony caused by China's urban greening into a visual language that is less harsh to digest. "There is no real death in plants. They just grow without any purpose." Modern society attempts to control nature with sense and functionality. The word "anthropocene" describes a world in which the earth's surface is wrapped by the transformations of human activity, an "ecology without nature". The very topography of the earth reflects back the face of humanity – its activities, expectations and exploitation. Alphonso Lingis compares human faces to features on a blank wall – like smooth surfaces, faces are ready to be inscribed by systems (including those of symbols), their voids like black holes compressing matter and signals excluded from known systems, dissolving transparent and naturalized epistemological horizons through their density. *BBR1 (No. 1 of Blossom Bud Restrainer)* works much in this way: society and nature exist as each other's hyper-object, engaged in a mutual act of translation and blending.

For Liu Chuang, windows (the "Chuang" in Liu's name means "window" in Chinese) are spectral voids, bisecting gazes into inside and out. Security windows, commonly seen in South China, serve Liu Chuang well in his series *Segmented Landscape.* Deconstructed, they cast shadows on a white cloth like Rayographs. The intermediate space of the window not only lies between indoors and outdoors, but defines the histories of public and private housing in China. After the "Reform and Opening" of China, the importance and function of private living space gained prominence as apartments with independent kitchens and bathrooms started to appear. Half closed, barred windows can not only "frame" the commercial, political and domestic nexus, but the bars themselves are a source of visual production in the urban fabric. Among all the patterns that decorate these windows, Liu focuses most on "Fang Sheng" — two diamonds overlapping in the centre whose origins as an auspicious pattern date back to the Yuan dynasty. Though it has lost its original meaning over the years and become pure decoration, it has become a white noise standing still after rounds of explosions of images, revealing the structure of glossolalia in visual language. In a similar way, in Liu's *Unknown River* (2008) tubes are used to create desk and chair-like objects. Connected to the building's water supply system they reveal the daily directional flow of water in a poetic way, exposing its hidden complicated structure under the cement.

Untitled *(The Dancing Partner)* demonstrates the ebb and flow, short-circuits and ruptures of currents within a road network. Two identical white cars start from Caochangdi, a village agglomerating galleries and studios, and move at the legal minimum speed along the Fourth Ring Road. As they mirror each other's movements, the cars are continuously passed by impatient drivers, their shared tango acting as a tangible demonstration of the gap between law and ethics of road users.

After graduation, Liu Chuang managed a company named Picabia in Dongguan for over a year, providing decorative pictures to hotels and families in the Pearl River Delta region. Dongguan's prosperity is built on two industries, sex and manufacturing, but the predominantly female migrant workers suffer the loneliness of being far away from home. Pocket-size romance novels provide cheap recreation for millions of these workers. Passing from hand to hand, the margins of these stereotypical love stories bear witness to their readers' sorrows with tears and jottings: the first draft of a love poem, a work address, scribbles and doodlings. Thus *Love Story* intertwines the migrant workers' impulse and desire to write with the emotional restlessness of romantic fictions. Liu collects thousands of old novels, categorizes their marginalia and transplants the workers' writing to the white walls of the gallery. His works mobilize the echoes and cast-offs of pre-existing systems, offering fresh perspectives and a re-examination of a range of social systems and scenarios.

Liu Chuang
BBR1 (No. 1 of Blossom Bud Restrainer)
2015
Video
4′56′′

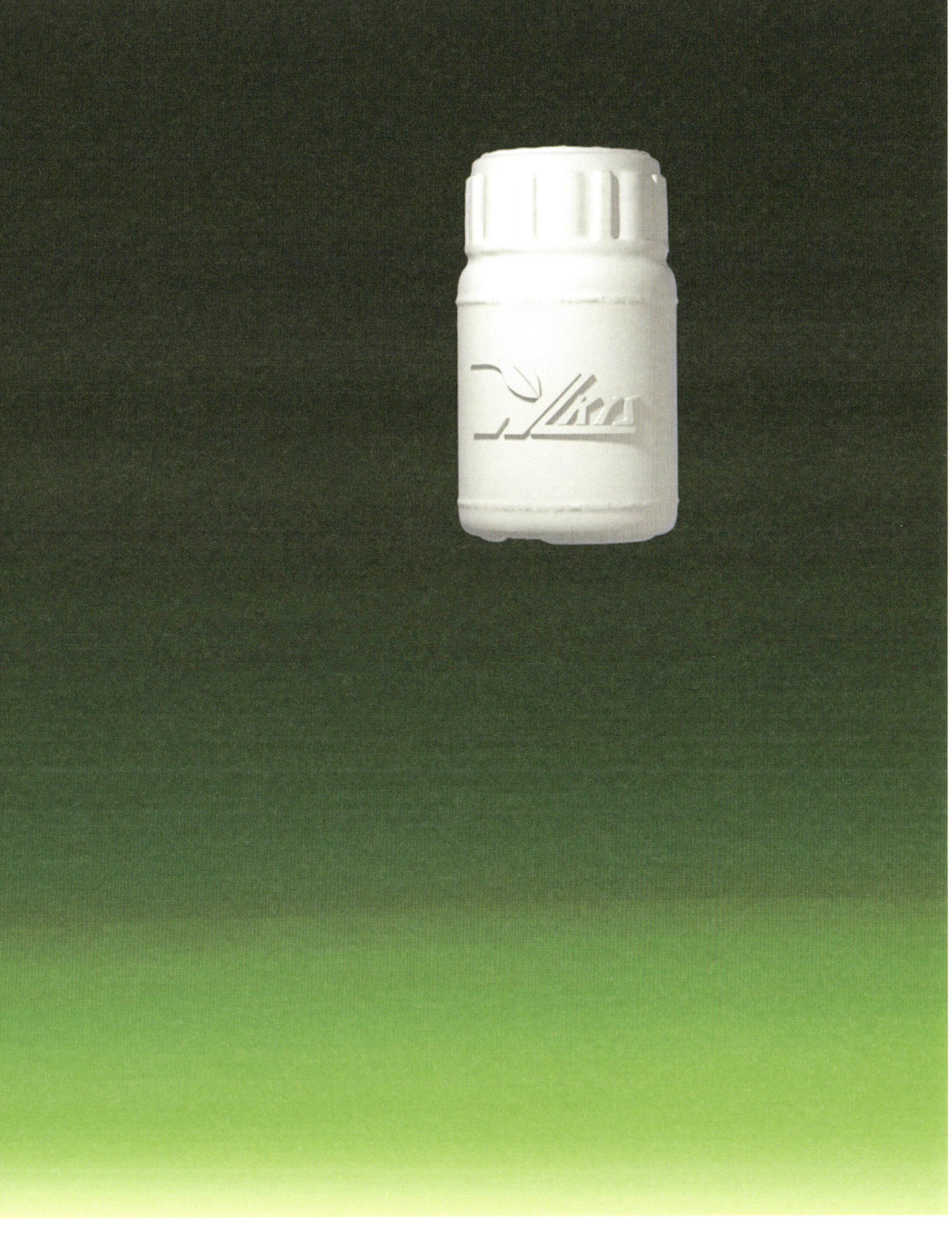

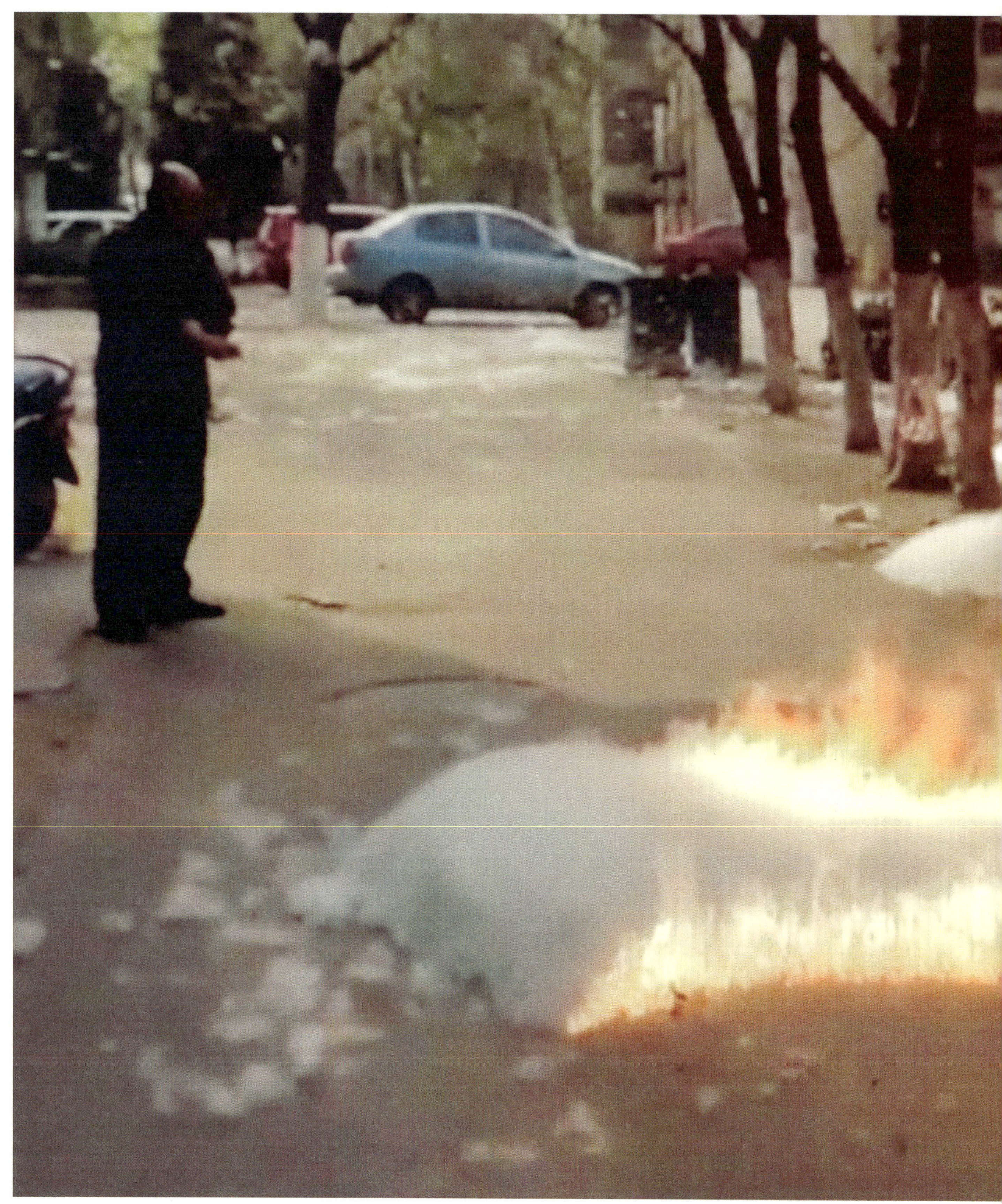

Liu Chuang
BBR1 (No. 1 of Blossom Bud Restrainer)
2015
Video
4′56″

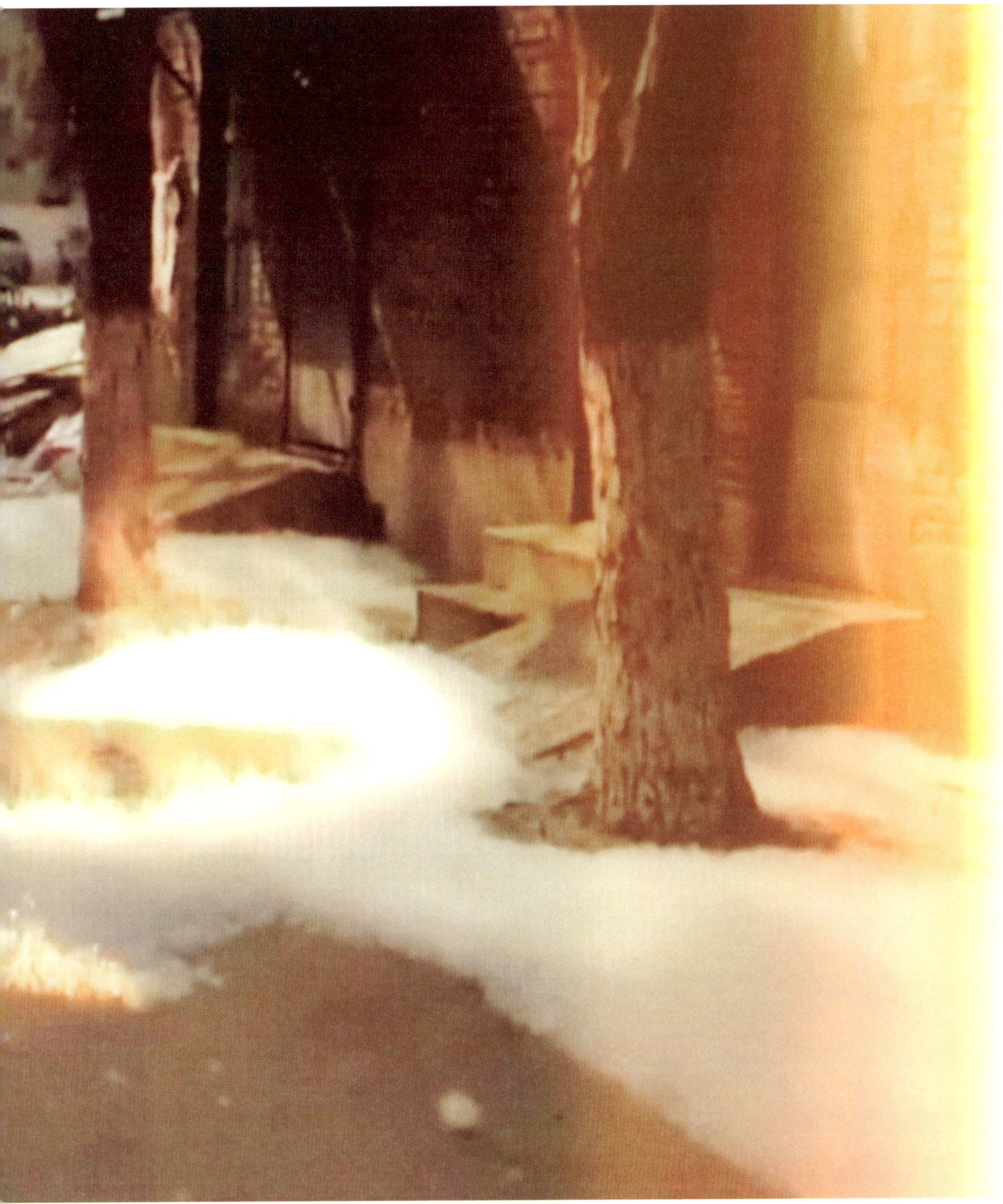

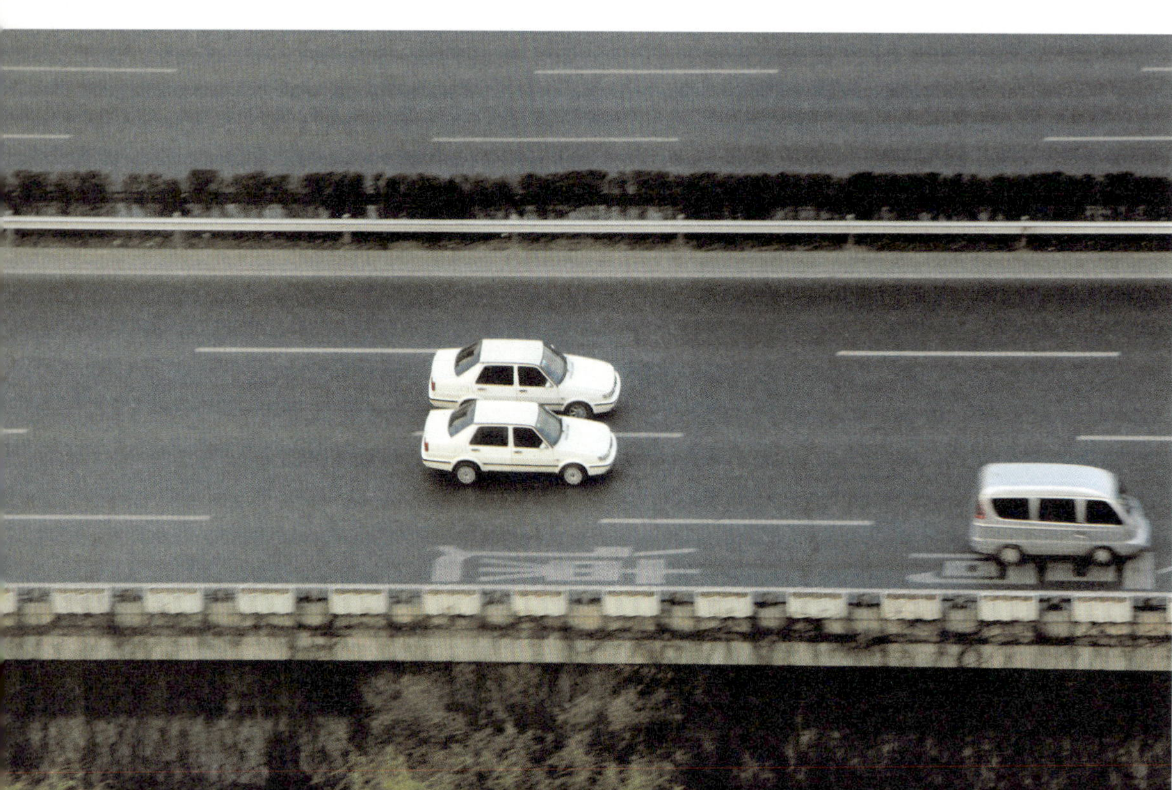

Liu Chuang
Untitled (The Dancing Partner)
2010
Video
5'15"

LIU
CHUANG

Liu Chuang
*Buying Everything on You
(Li Shuanghu)*
2006
Mixed media
120 × 240 × 20 cm

85

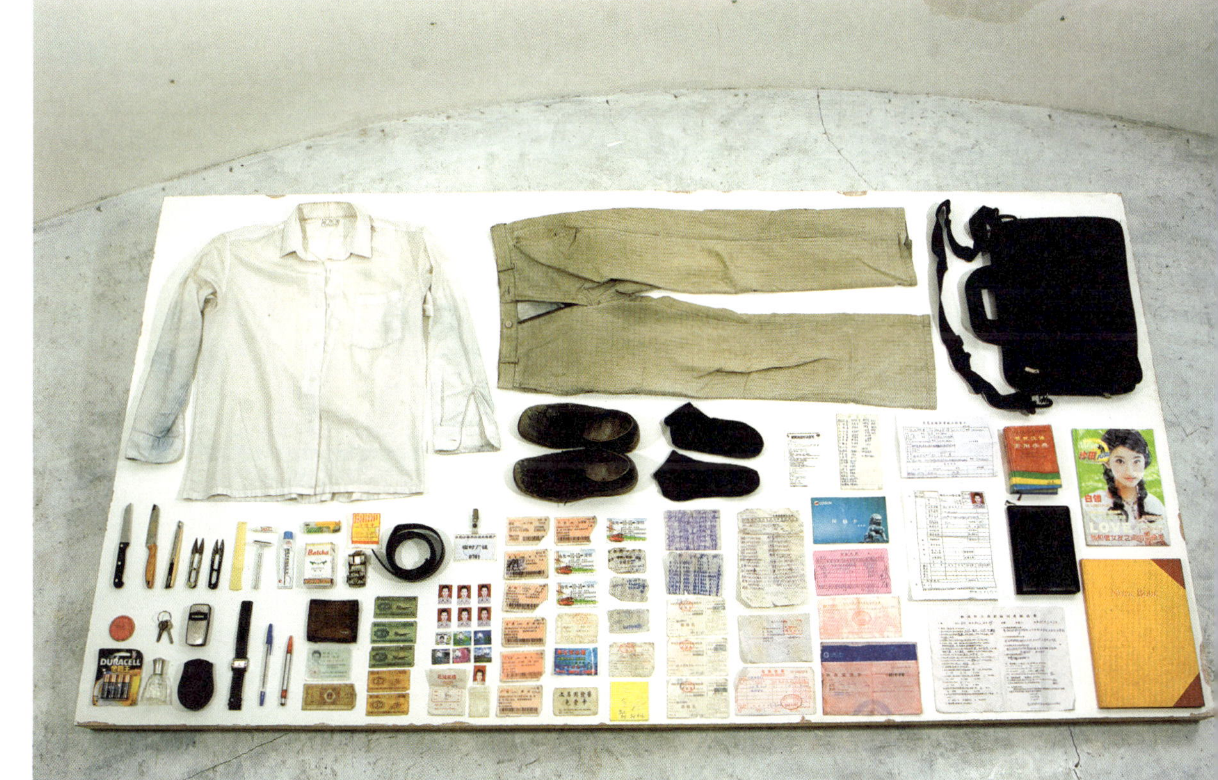

LIU SHIYUAN

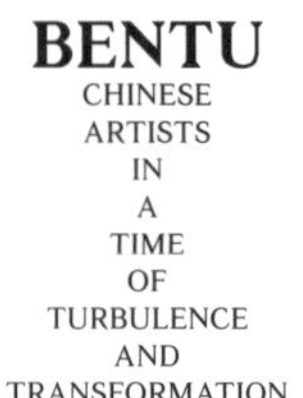

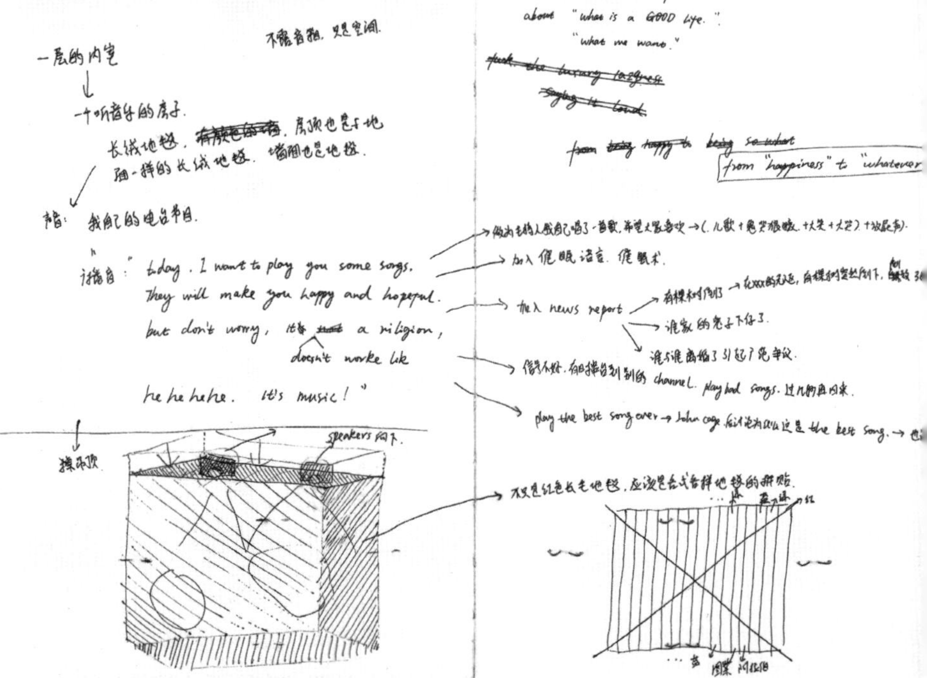

Liu Shiyuan
Sketch for "From
Happiness to Whatever"
2015
24×36cm

LIU
SHIYUAN

EVOKING
AND
CAPTURING
EMOTIONS

SASHA ZHAO

As you step into this temporary meditation room, you are bowled over by the tightly knit wool carpets in different patterns covering the entire surface from floor to ceiling. Before your eyes adjust to the environment, you may feel that the space is about to collapse in on you the very next second. And you are also struck by how sensitive your hearing has become, due to the absorption of sound by the carpets. A radio programme called *From Happiness to Whatever* (which also gives the installation piece its title) is playing, recorded by Liu Shiyuan and her husband Kristian Mondrup Nielsen, a jazz drummer and music producer. The sound installation seems to reproduce the everyday scene of a Danish family listening to the radio. This radio show, broadcast in a country consistently topping world happiness rankings, seems to advocate a positive culture or ideology. As these words of happiness float in the air, putting you into a meditative state, you are awakened by the artist's whispers, alerting you to the danger of being lulled into a false sense of security.

The radio show's scripts seem like a set of courses on positive psychology. The programme brings to mind those amateur broadcasters who attract people's attention by playing the same tunes as popular rock stations or imitating TV shopping channels. "Moon Letter", the first part of the sound installation, comes from a speech that was never given in public. It was drafted by White House spin doctors for Richard Nixon in the event that the Apollo 11 astronauts failed to return from the moon. This inspiring speech shows how a disaster can be turned into a triumph of will. Certainly, this is a very human mechanism, manipulating results to make a failure look like a victory.

The second part, entitled "Brain Spa", is designed to induce a state of relaxation through hypnosis, during which deeper realms of the mind become more accessible. By following the prompts, the exercise helps you to "free your mind from all limits, bringing you greater satisfaction and hinting at ways to fulfil your potential and become all that you can be". This self-actualisation approach obviously imposes its own values. The popularity of psychotherapy confirms the mainstream desire for happiness: you need to be happy. Only those able to adjust themselves can fit in, while those full of dread and remorse are considered morbid and to be shunned. Just then, a cut-in piece breaks the soothing meditative atmosphere, an advertisement in the form of a poem, read with a Chinese accent, sounding strange and ridiculous. For this, Liu Shiyuan collected advertising slogans for household items from Chinese TV commercials and translated them into English using Google Translate. The asymmetry between the information communicated in the two languages, devoid of the original context, helps us to better understand how advertisements use words to guide our behaviour as consumers.

Visitors may feel the most confused by the last part of the installation, entitled "Making It". Given the previous content, one would expect to hear specific advice on how to be successful (the topic itself is absurd), but what follows is a long, vague description. Kristian has taken excerpts from the Discovery Channel's *How It's Made* series showing how various items are mass-produced in factories. The underlying comparison may be only partly in jest, but these images of mass production hint at the growing mechanisation of art production today and the success of this trend, along with the huge sums involved.

Mass media pervade our lives without needing permission. As a traditional vector for information, broadcasting has functions other than advertising and entertainment. For example, people can acquire knowledge, follow the news and even learn about the latest government policies. But in China, a country lacking credibility for the information made available to the public, broadcasting is more about form than content. To a certain extent, the auditory experience for Chinese listeners is one in which the art of propaganda engenders political hegemony through the discourse itself. This piece by Liu Shiyuan engages your eyes and ears. The space is designed to break down barriers between the private and the public (an immersive environment can readily inspire thoughts of home and the maternal bond), thus showing that the public nature of the media and the privacy of meditation are not mutually exclusive. Media voices and images coexist effectively in this playful parody. Elements of propaganda and hypnosis are used in turns by the artist to stimulate the audience's comfort zones, invoking emotions and reflection. Ultimately, the artist's intention, like a Trojan horse, makes its way into each visitor's mind.

Finding connections among existing materials is a technique frequently employed by Liu Shiyuan in her work. For her installation piece *As Simple as Clay* (2013), she Googled images of clay and decorated an entire wall with these thousands of photos in order to underscore cultural diversity. And in *From Happiness to Whatever*, the tiles of carpets from countries around the world remind us that different cultures have varied notions of comfort, while the irregular composition suggests the frequent difficulty in bridging the gap between these cultures. The feeling of diaspora, frequently present in Liu's pieces, takes on an urgent dimension in this one. Appropriately, she points out that "happiness" as referred to in country rankings is only a mean value and cannot represent the real experience of any one individual. For her, although the Danish welfare system is often upheld as a socialist ideal, it cannot guarantee happiness for everyone.

On the contrary, a high "happiness" ranking becomes the face of the national ideology, building a way of life that conforms to the expected patterns of social development and economic principles.

It is worth noting that the different accents from Asia, North America, the Nordic countries and the United Kingdom in this installation piece, like the varying protagonists in Liu's *Lost in Export* (2014), demonstrate the artist's desire to remain language neutral. She refuses any kind of cultural hegemony. *From Happiness to Whatever* draws us into a space where emotions can circulate freely, hoping to inspire discussions on the individual's role in society.

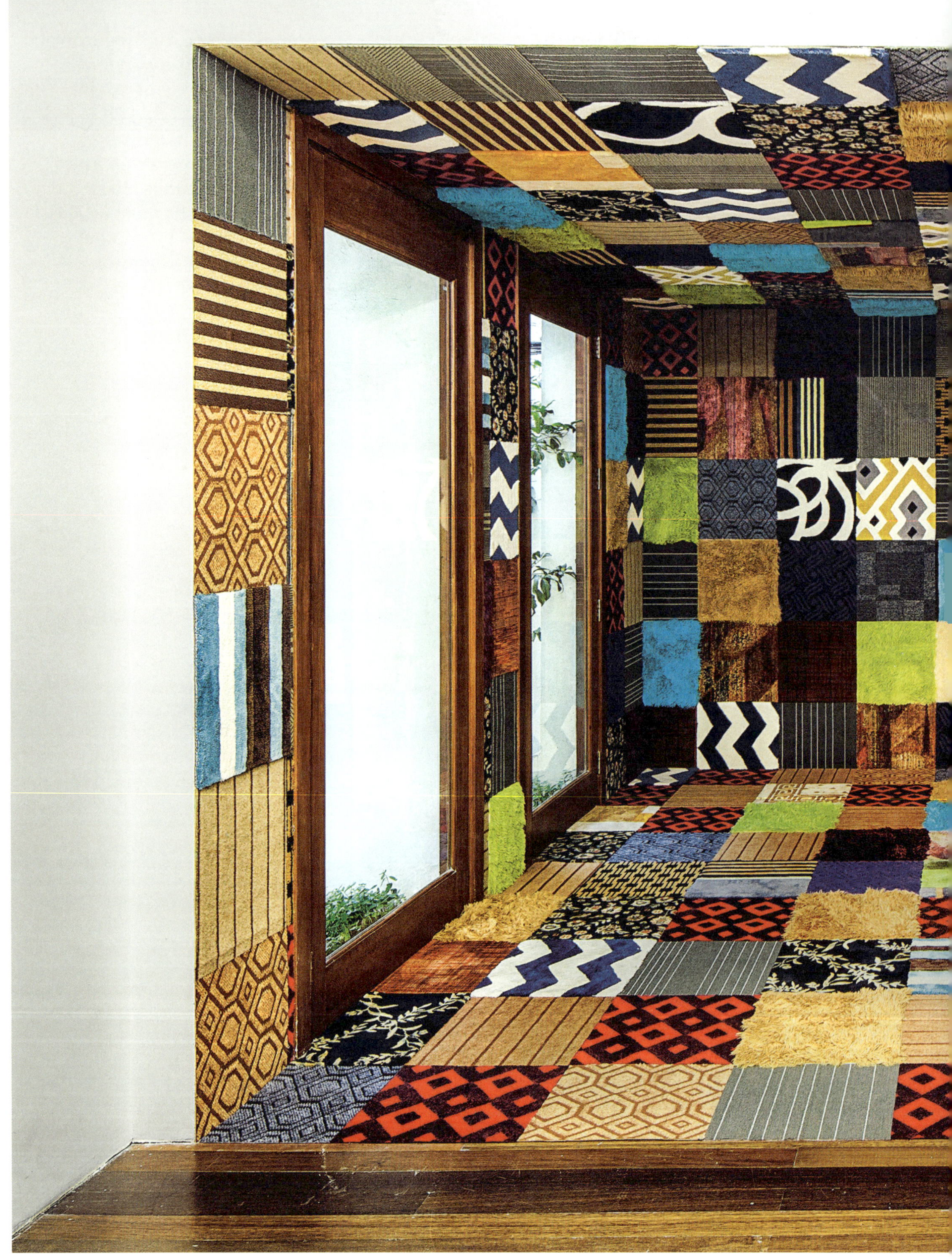

Liu Shiyuan
From Happiness to Whatever
2015
Carpets, speakers, iPod
Variable dimensions
Installation view at Leo Xu Projects gallery, Shanghai

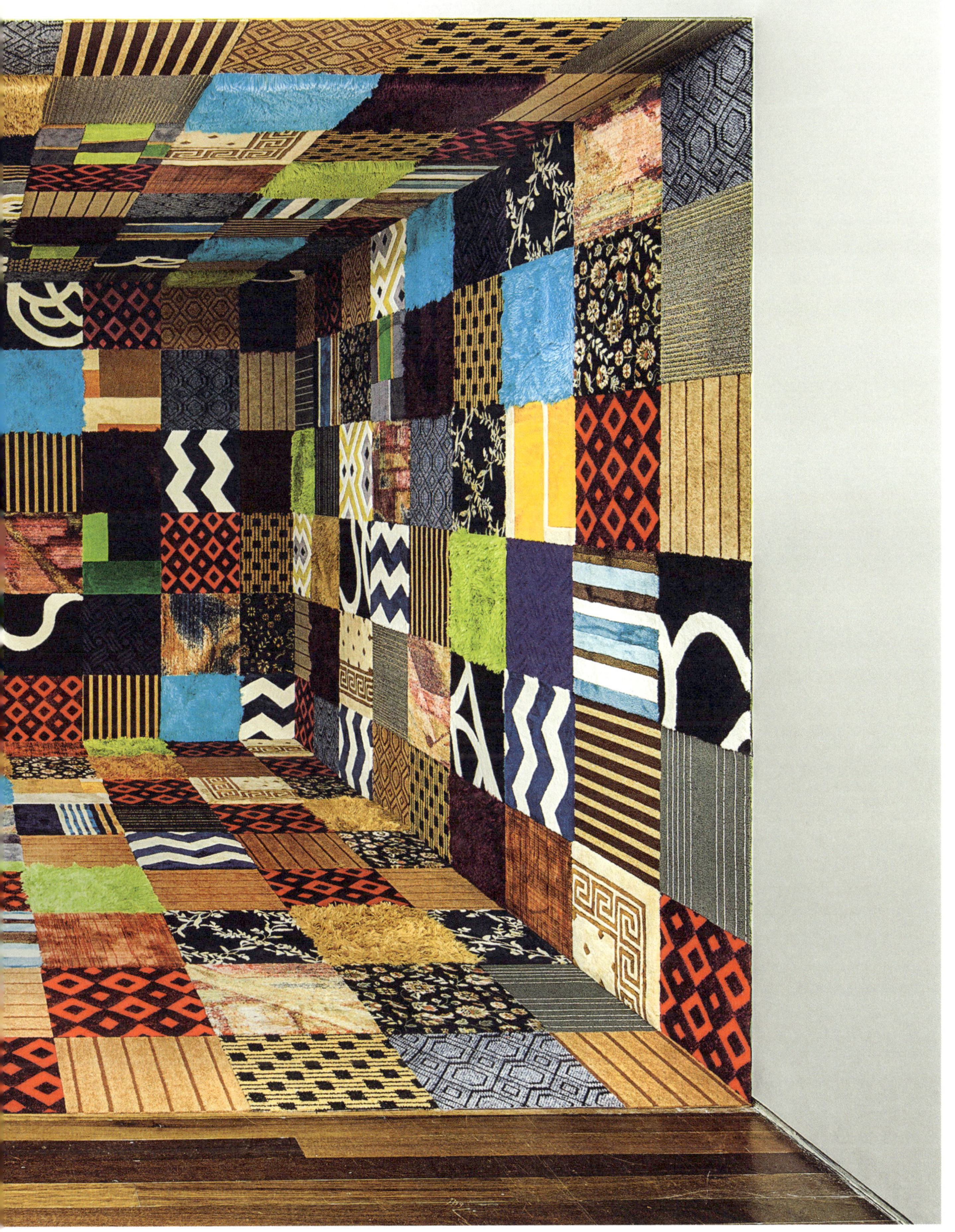

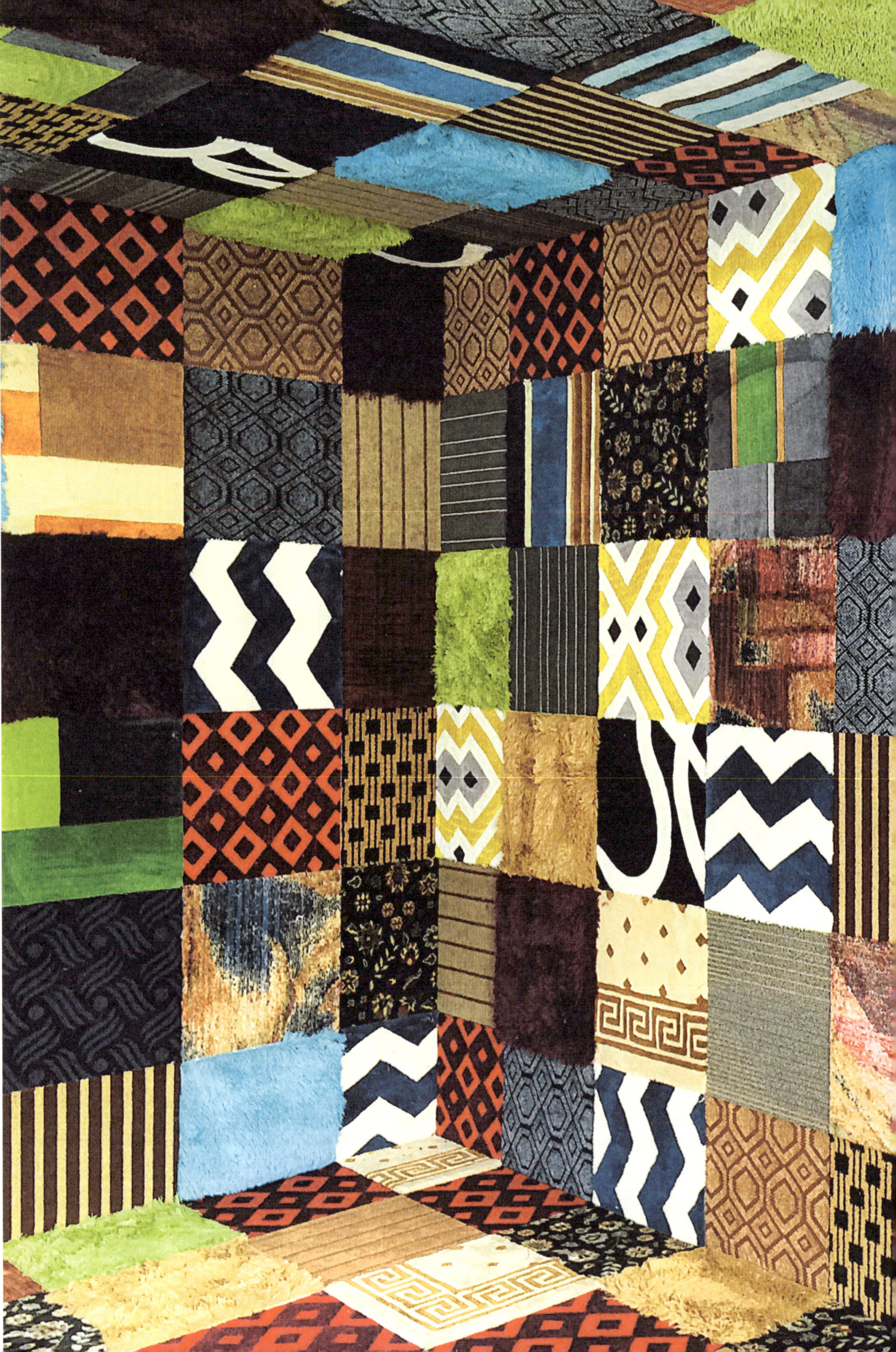

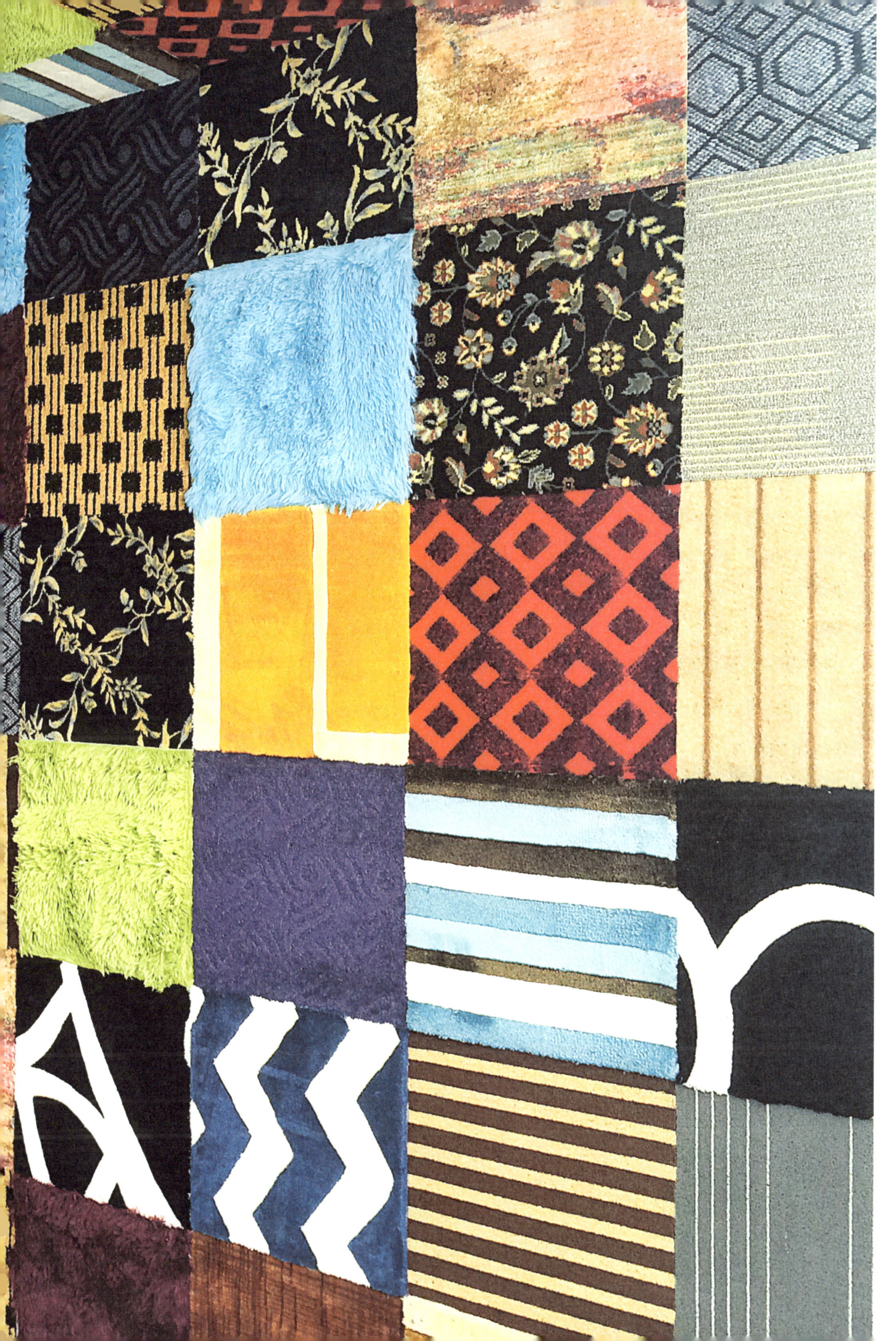

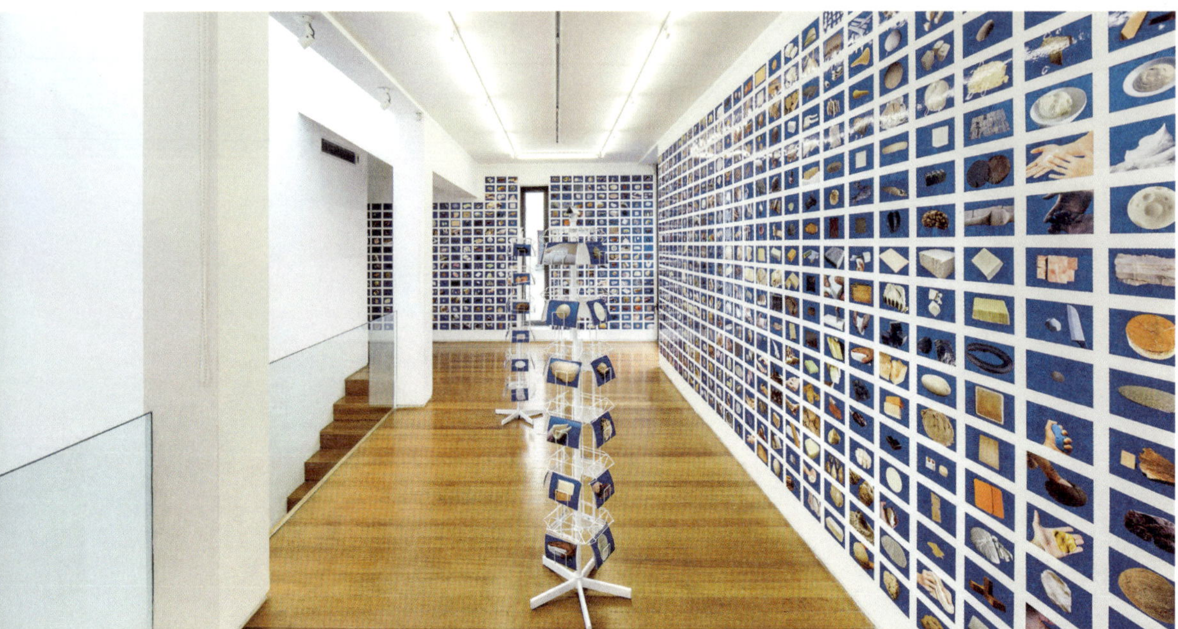

Preceding double page
Liu Shiyuan
*From Happiness
to Whatever* (detail)
2015

Liu Shiyuan
As Simple As Clay
2013
Installation view at
Leo Xu Projects gallery,
Shanghai, 2015
Variable dimensions
(each unit: 15.2 × 10.2 cm)

94

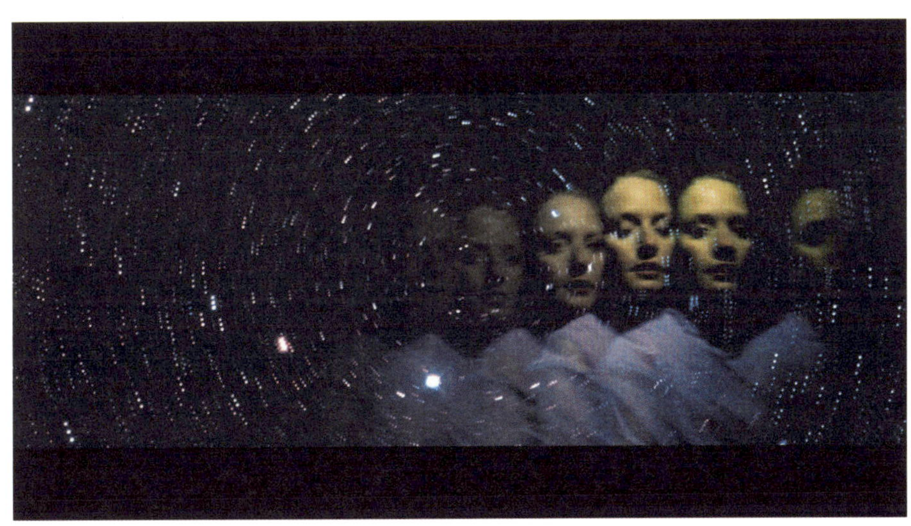

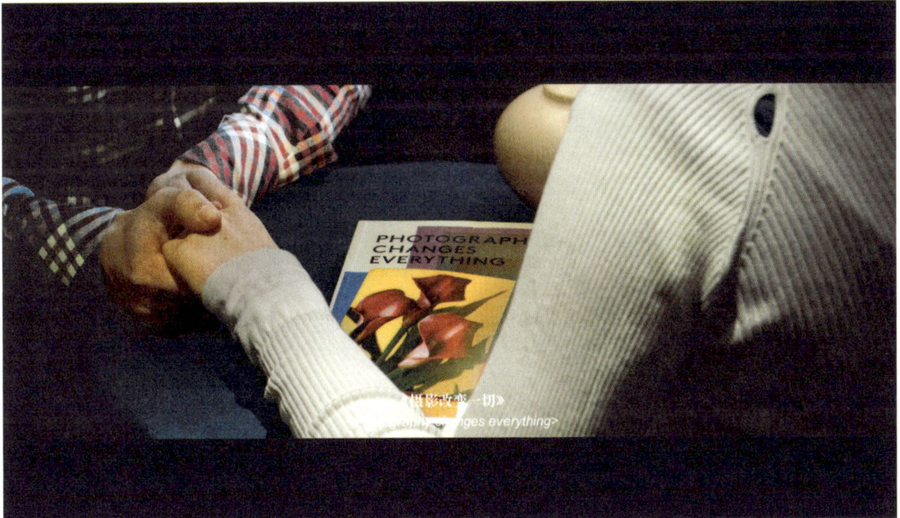

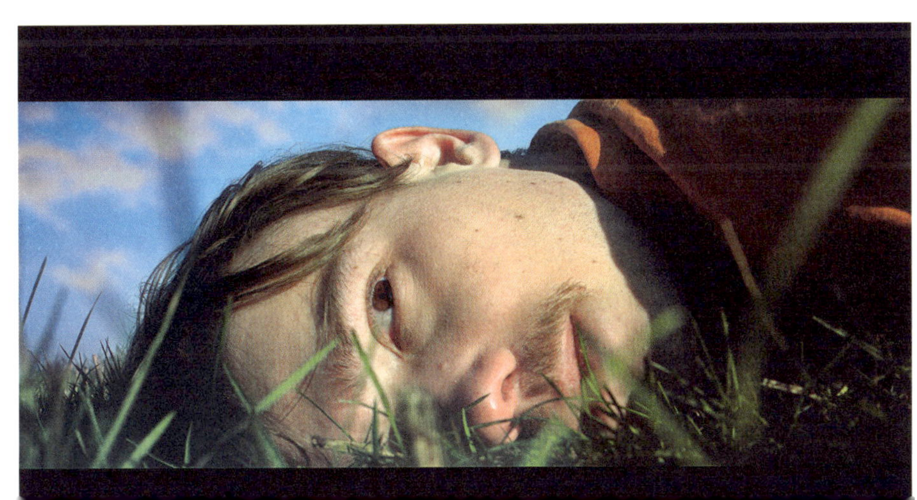

Liu Shiyuan
Video stills from
Lost in Export
2014
Video, stereo sound
33′34′′
Music composed by
Kristian Mondrup Nielsen

LIU WEI

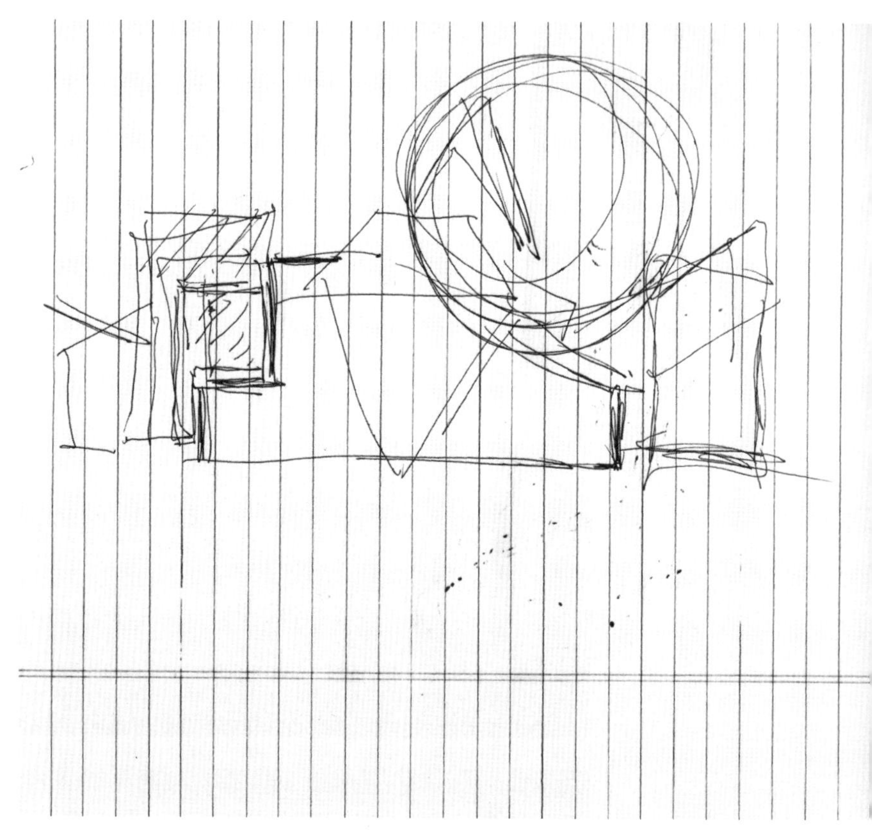

Project for the installation
at the Fondation
Louis Vuitton, Paris
2015
Sketch

LETTING THE WORLD LEAK IN

ROBIN PECKHAM

Liu Wei has spent the better part of a decade trimming the fat from his practice: gradually, he has tried to eliminate questions of representation, intervention and subjectivity from his practice, ending up with environments of sheer experience through which he intends to reflect the shared realities of his audience. Theoretically, he is what one might call a brute-force realist. Liu believes that social, political and phenomenological realities are reflected in artistic work not only through the intention of the artist but by logical necessity, making concrete references to the world beyond his work largely extraneous. He does concede to a crasser – which is to say, conscious – form of realism on one level, not by representing the world but by directly importing the materials of its structure. Most recently, Liu has been particularly interested in those standardized units of production interchangeable the world over: shipping containers, piping, tiling and other measures that speak of globalization in concrete, palpable terms: *Enigma* (2014), among other works, uses the measure of an ideal shape, the sphere, to measure and reconfigure standard plywood boards and shipping crates.

Up to and including his contribution to this exhibition and publication, Liu has been working in this vein for almost ten years now. The process has picked up within the last two years, as the artist has recognized that this way of working is beginning to reach an end. His practice is chiefly an art of negation. Liu knows when something must change, when something isn't working, when something has to go, and he has this feeling more often than not. His last major solo exhibition, at the Ullens Center for Contemporary Art in Beijing in early 2015, was a beautiful demonstration of this process: each one of the series he had worked on over the past years was summarized, presented as if it were the end of a sentence, and mashed into an uncompromising, ritualistic layout. *Puzzle* (2014), an expansive maze of mirrors cut and ground into various shapes, sat uneasily alongside "Jungle", an on-going series of dark canvas sheets stretched over steel frames. Both make for immersive environments meant to confuse, immerse and ultimately repel the viewer, and both work all too well.

With the recognition that the time had come to move on from the process of minimalizing his work, Liu is now working in two directions at once. The first involves simply taking the minimal components he has perfected and maximalizing them, combining them in ever more complex forms and permutations so that they confront and take over spaces and institutions. He adds colour, height, density; this strategy was evident in his last Hong Kong solo exhibition, "Silver", where the neon colour-field video *Shapeshifting* (2014) was reflected in dozens of faceted mirror works, and in his presentation in Paris, where massive spheres orbit one another like the visualization of a gravity field. A second direction turns its back on the minimal project more dramatically, albeit while retaining the successful construction models minimalism was able to produce. (It would be difficult to overestimate the success of this approach: from its inception, with the solo exhibition "Outcast", 2007, Liu's largely cubic installations of glass, wood and other construction materials have made for compelling spatial experiences.)

There is an undercurrent of roguish humour to Liu's work, and it is this strand that was largely elided when he began sanding everything down into right angles. Think of *Looks Like a Landscape* (2004), that infamous black-and-white photograph in which knees, elbows and derrieres form a preternaturally misty landscape in the classical tradition. Then there is "Indigestion", a series of tar mounds sculpted into piles of excrement and populated with toy soldiers. This kind of work doesn't show up much in the catalogues of the sorts of galleries that exhibit Liu Wei now, but an understanding of this sense of humour is integral to the meaning of the more alluring minimalism that he has recently been pursuing. Or take the series of dog toy sculptures, "Love It, Bite It", which began with maquettes of state and religious architecture recreated in oxhide before expanding to include the totality of the world's built environment writ large, effectively merging, in concept if not in form, with the "Library" series, which sees skyscrapers emerge from densely compressed stacks of books. Now the oxhide is back, and with a new approach: calling the new series "Big Dog", Liu makes massive toys for a giant canine, a figurative form that, though it remains visually absent, is a welcome return. As he insists, the dog was only ever interested in the flavour, not the form — the form is for us.

In another new work, what amounts to an oversized asphalt testicle — plus or minus details here and there for the sake of abstraction — dangles over a rather furry vaginal hole mounted in a plush, white leather structure recalling the architecture of the public fountain. Liu appreciates asphalt because it is a liquid substance that behaves like a solid, but retains its potential for motion on a glacial scale. Echoed in mirrors of vaguely Abrahamic ornament on the walls, the installation is not only a space but also an event. Liu Wei's realist commitments return here with a vengeance, and he appears increasingly interested in the idea of an accidental encounter, and the responsibility of making his work relevant not only to the north-eastern quadrant of Beijing where he lives and works, but also to the political and identitarian concerns of the publics and places in which he exhibits. Projects like this, which

quote the on-going refugee crisis and global violence
in crude yet obtuse ways, reflect reality in a way
that allows the concerns of their viewers to become
concrete. A collective psychological state becomes
tangible, something solid that intervenes again in the
fabric of the real. At a certain moment, the figurative
and representational pressures around him become
too much to bear, and Liu Wei steps aside to let the
world leak in.

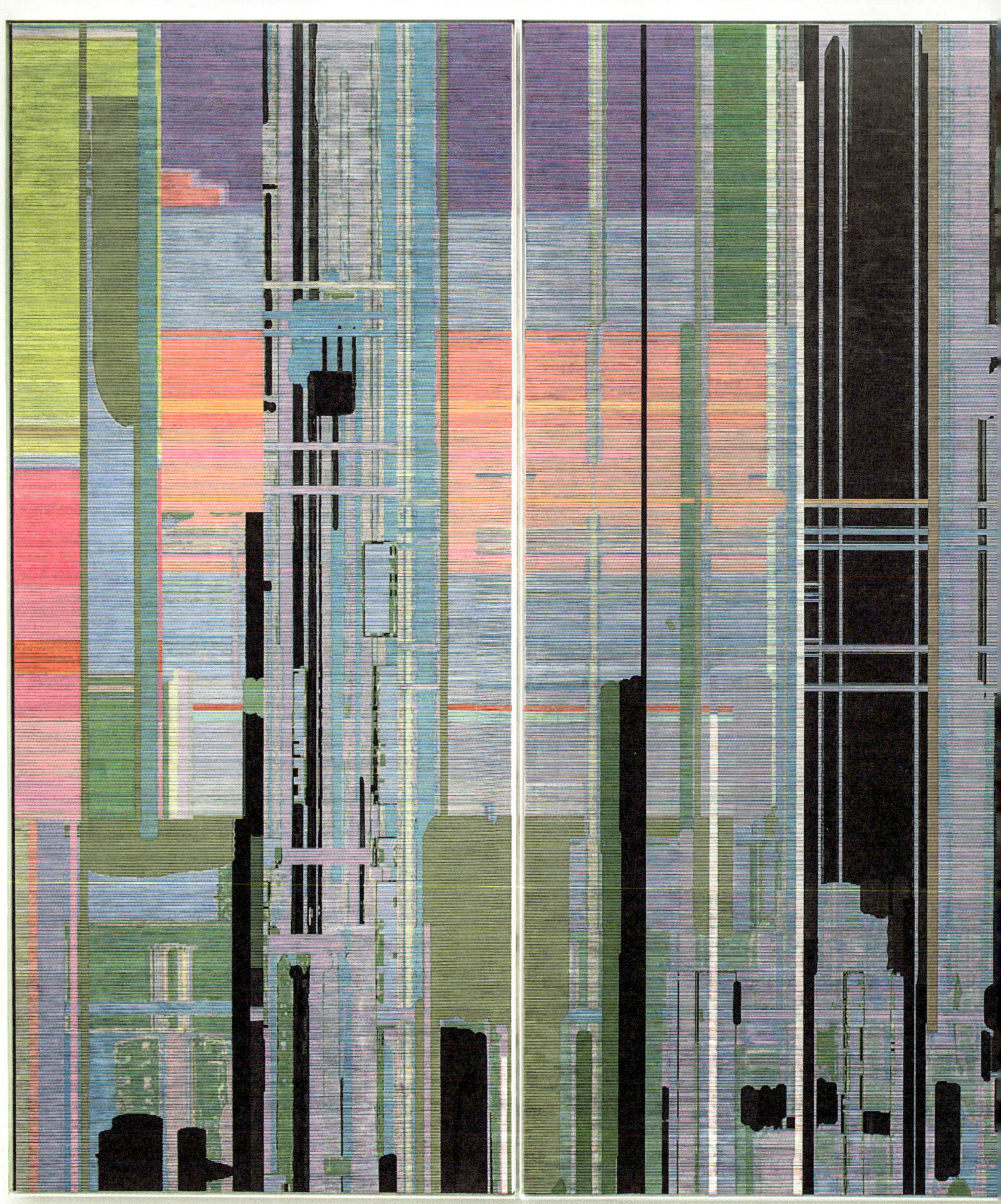

Liu Wei
Liberation No. 16
2014
Oil on canvas
400×720cm

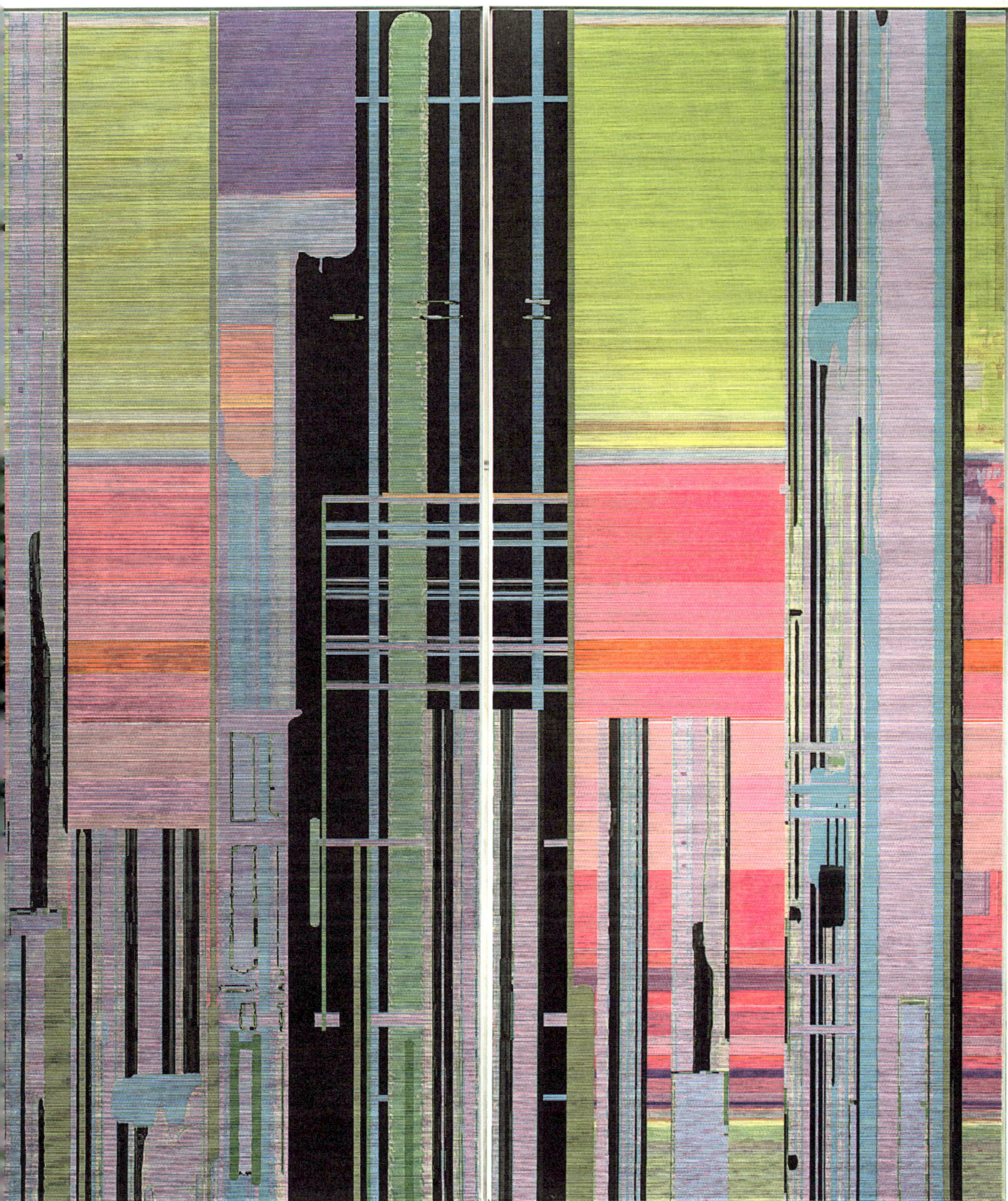

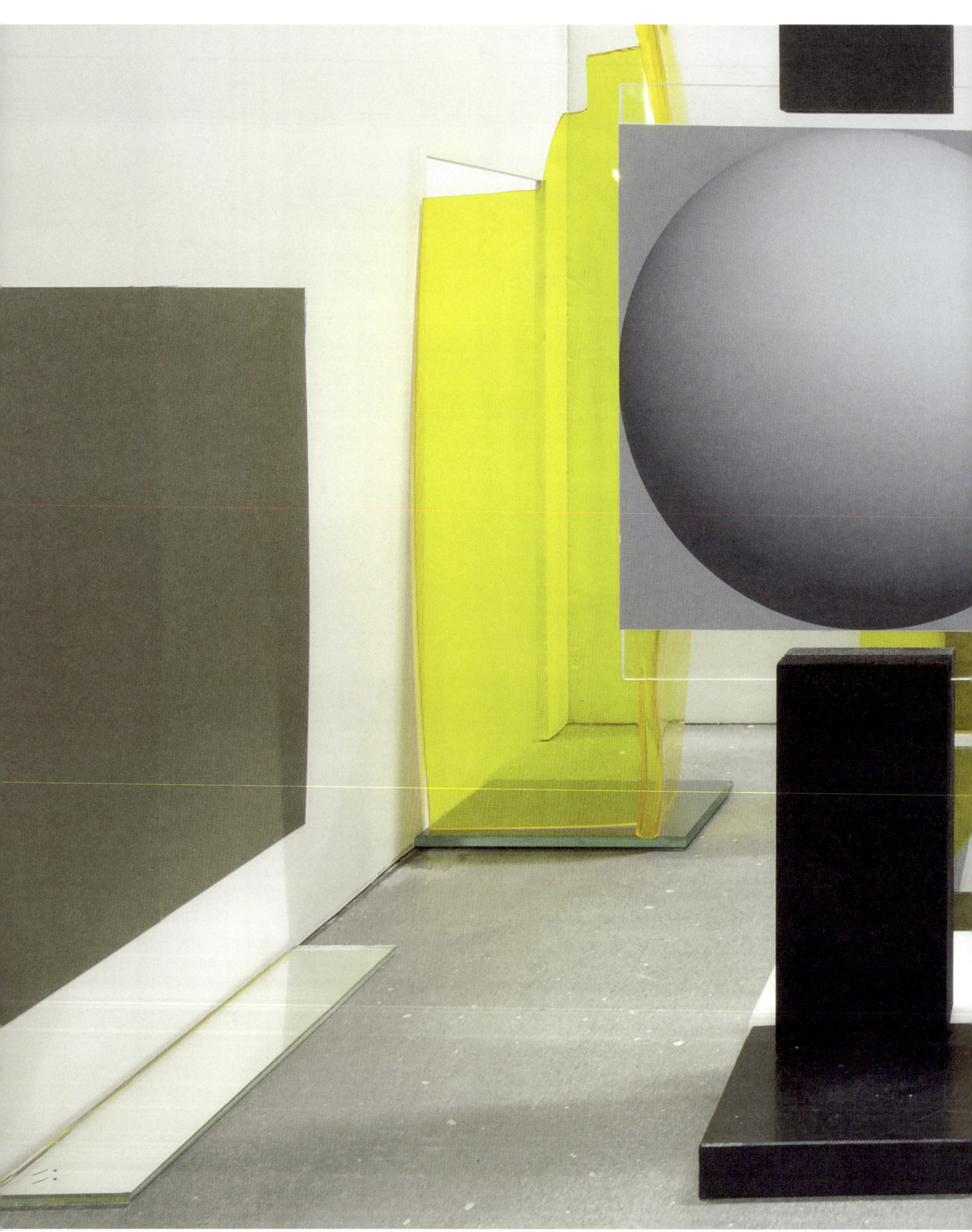

Liu Wei
Untitled (project for the
Fondation Louis Vuitton, Paris)
2015

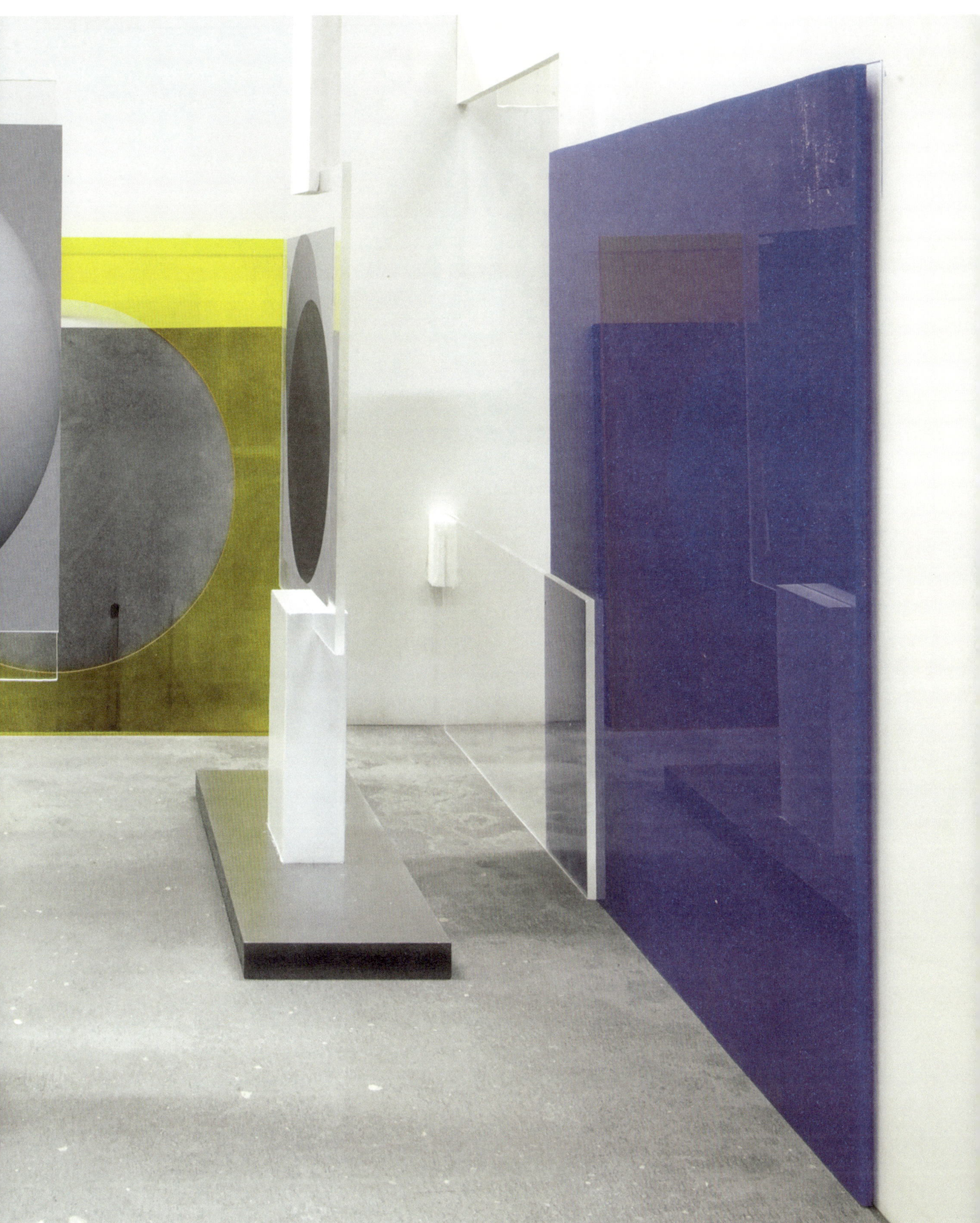

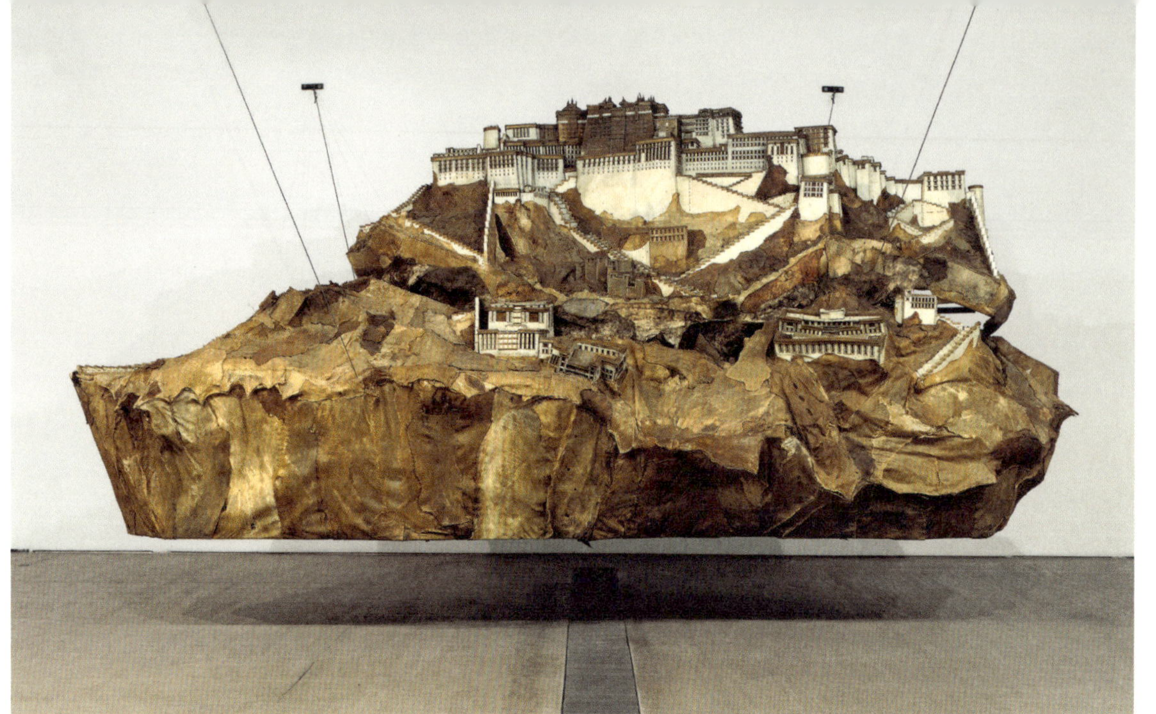

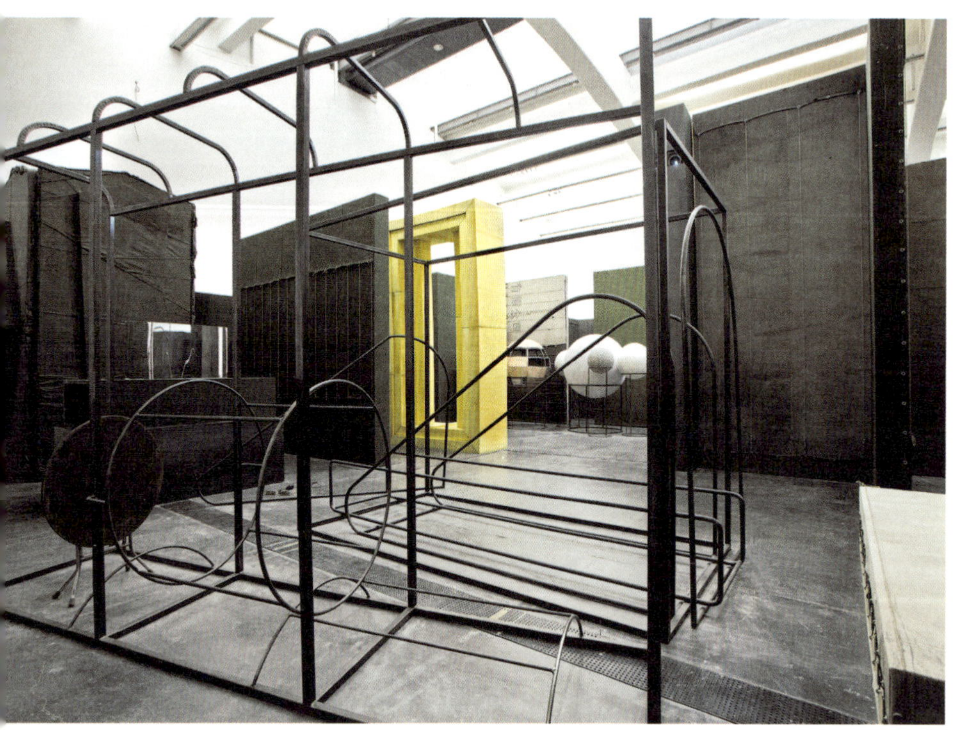

Liu Wei
Don't touch
2011
Oxhide, wood, steel
Variable dimensions

Liu Wei
Enigma
2014
Variable dimensions
Mixed media

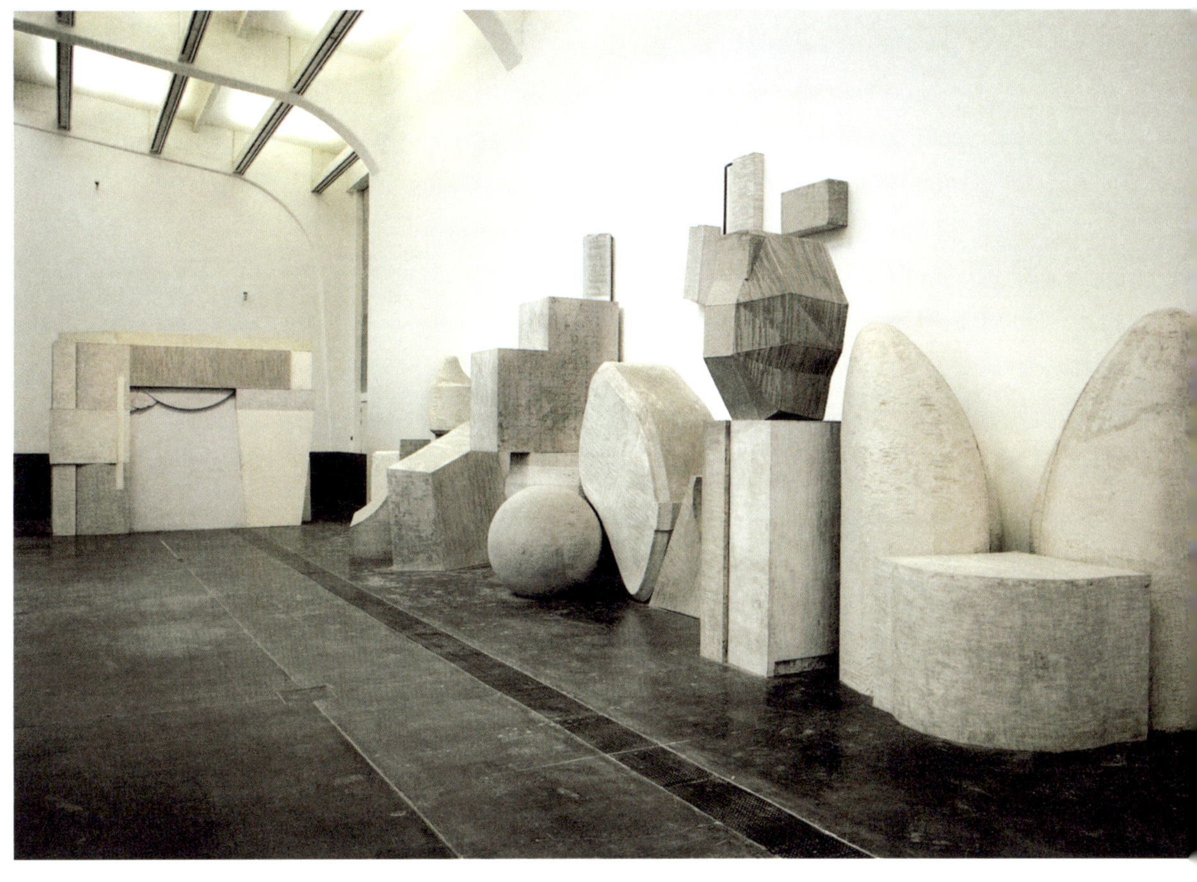

Liu Wei
Look! Book
2014
Variable dimensions
Books, wood, steel

LIU XIAODONG

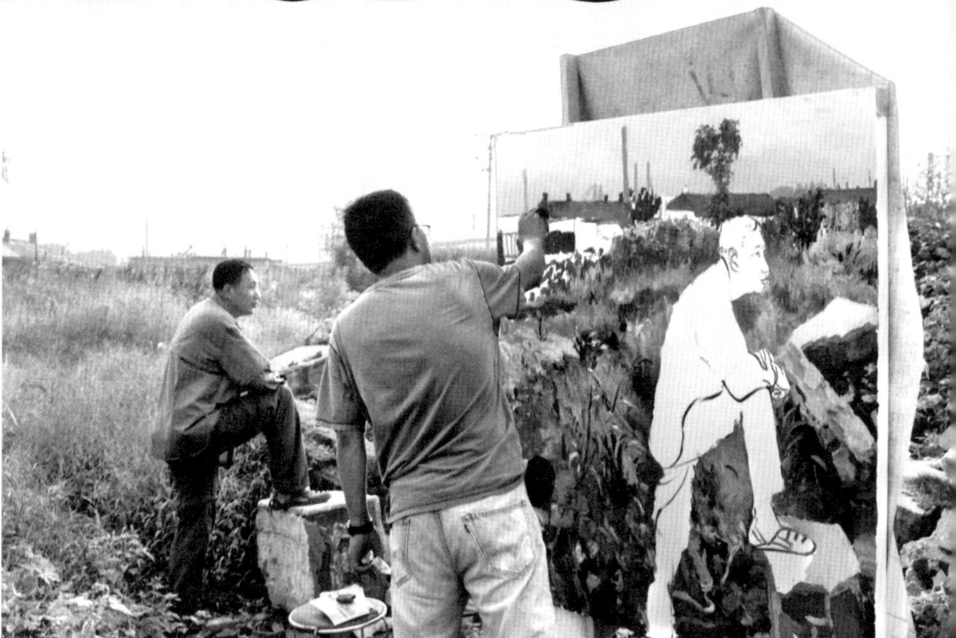

JOURNAL
OF
THE
CONTEMPORARY
WORLD

JÉRÔME SANS

Although Liu Xiaodong is seen as one of the leading figures in the "new generation" of contemporary Chinese realists, his practice differs considerably from that of his peers by virtue of the cross-disciplinary, conceptual approach that makes him one of the key figures on today's art scene, both in China and internationally.

For several decades now, Liu has been painting the everyday life and immediate surroundings of various communities. From his series showing jade miners in Hotan (*Hotan Project*) to his project on the Three Gorges Dam and his recent work in Ordos, Mongolia (*Diary of An Empty City*), Liu always cleaves to reality, while retaining a humanist approach and sense of historical awareness. His work draws on the great social, economic and environmental upheavals of contemporary life. In his large-format paintings, with their broad, spontaneous brush-strokes, the human dimension remains at the heart of these deep transformations. He depicts men and women in contemporary China, but also in turbulent territories such as Cuba, Israel and Palestine.

Who are these persons represented in their everyday world? While Liu's work was long considered a form of genre painting, showing ordinary moments, moments of life in families or among friends, his narratives also suggest a more paradoxical vision of reality, highlighting the contradictions of today's world and its race for development. The scene suddenly leads us behind the insouciance on its surface. Liu's incisive, complex vision brings out all the ambiguities of situations that few of us really care to look at: the existence of displaced, forgotten or abandoned communities (peasants, tribes, nomadic populations, migrant workers, victims of natural or ecological disasters, prostitutes, exiles, refugees, etc.). Liu is interested in all these communities and minorities living on the margins of the contemporary world and its movements, but also in inter-communal conflicts. In these, he refrains from offering a personal viewpoint. He questions or reverses mankind's shared dream or quest for a better life and a better world: is this "Chinese dream" promoted by the China's contemporary consumerism really a valid model?

In the age of globalization, this artist openly and repeatedly raises the question of the immaterial cultural heritage and its gradual disappearance. How can tradition and contemporaneity, rural and urban practices still manage to be meaningful? Liu offers neither apology nor critique, but openly explores a culture whose modes of expression are inclusive, similar and shared, even if these may be articulated in another language in the neighbouring city or at the other end of the world.

He reminds us that in the quest for an ideal world, no model is ultimately better than any other.

To make his "Hometown Boy" series in 2010, Liu went back to his hometown, the small industrial city of Jincheng which once had a flourishing paper mill, and which he left at the age of seventeen to study in Beijing and develop his art. Jincheng is the opposite of the glorious, progressive image of modern China that we usually see. There, Liu made a series of paintings showing his family home, which has remained unchanged since the old days, and his childhood friends, the very people he painted some thirty years ago now. In this series, he speaks to us of all the Chinese who have left their little rural towns to live in the megacities and find a form of development and a new setting. But he also shows the difficulties and misunderstandings between these different realities that are engendered by distance.

Liu is like an ethnologist in his exploration of this world and its communities. And, whatever the difficulties caused by the situations in which he sometimes finds himself, he always manages to find and capture the moments of grace. His approach is not that of the painter who goes to his studio every day and is prolifically productive. Liu's studio is the world itself. His output is infrequent and articulated in series, each one being generated by a particular societal issue. These ensembles are the result of long investigation, observation and reflection in the field. The artist constructs his path progressively in a log bringing together research, photographs, drawings, sketches, thoughts, testimony, sensations and information. This process, which has become a trademark, extends the perimeter of his work beyond the limits of the canvas.

It all begins with the exploration of a place, a city or a community that is symptomatic of deep changes. These sites exist on multiple scales: they reveal social, cultural and economic issues on a global scale and are platforms for debate. In these places Liu chooses sites that are conducive and eloquent, suitable locations for the nomadic studio – a simple tent – in which he can recreate everyday scenes by getting local inhabitants to pose for him. In his approach he is like a writer or filmmaker. The territory is the "set" and members of the community are his "actors", but also the protagonists of their own lives, as recounted by the artist. Every picture is made with a precise story and a context that Liu evokes not only in his paintings but also through the creative process, which is grounded in reality. Participation plays a crucial role in this search for truth.

Like the Italian Neorealist cinema that emerged during the Second World War, Liu's work represents real-life situations, showing the tribulations of modest individuals. The actors are non-professionals, so they

are familiar with the life that they are acting out.
Like the filmmakers of that movement, the artist believes
in the absolute necessity of emphasizing the reality
and personal nature of the everyday life he depicts.

For Liu, making the paintings is a kind of
performance, a live event that captures the very
essence of the scene and its protagonists, in the heat
of the moment. The narrative consequently has
a special vibrancy and immediacy, as it responds
directly to the terrain and its history.

On each of his projects, Liu collaborates with
filmmakers with whom he co-constructs and records
its different phases, giving a voice to the process of
painting. These documentary films enrich the considerable
preparatory work and accompany the artist's progress.
It is in developing this multidisciplinary approach around
the culture of the image that Liu Xiaodong's series
are creating a veritable fresco of contemporary life in
all its complexity.

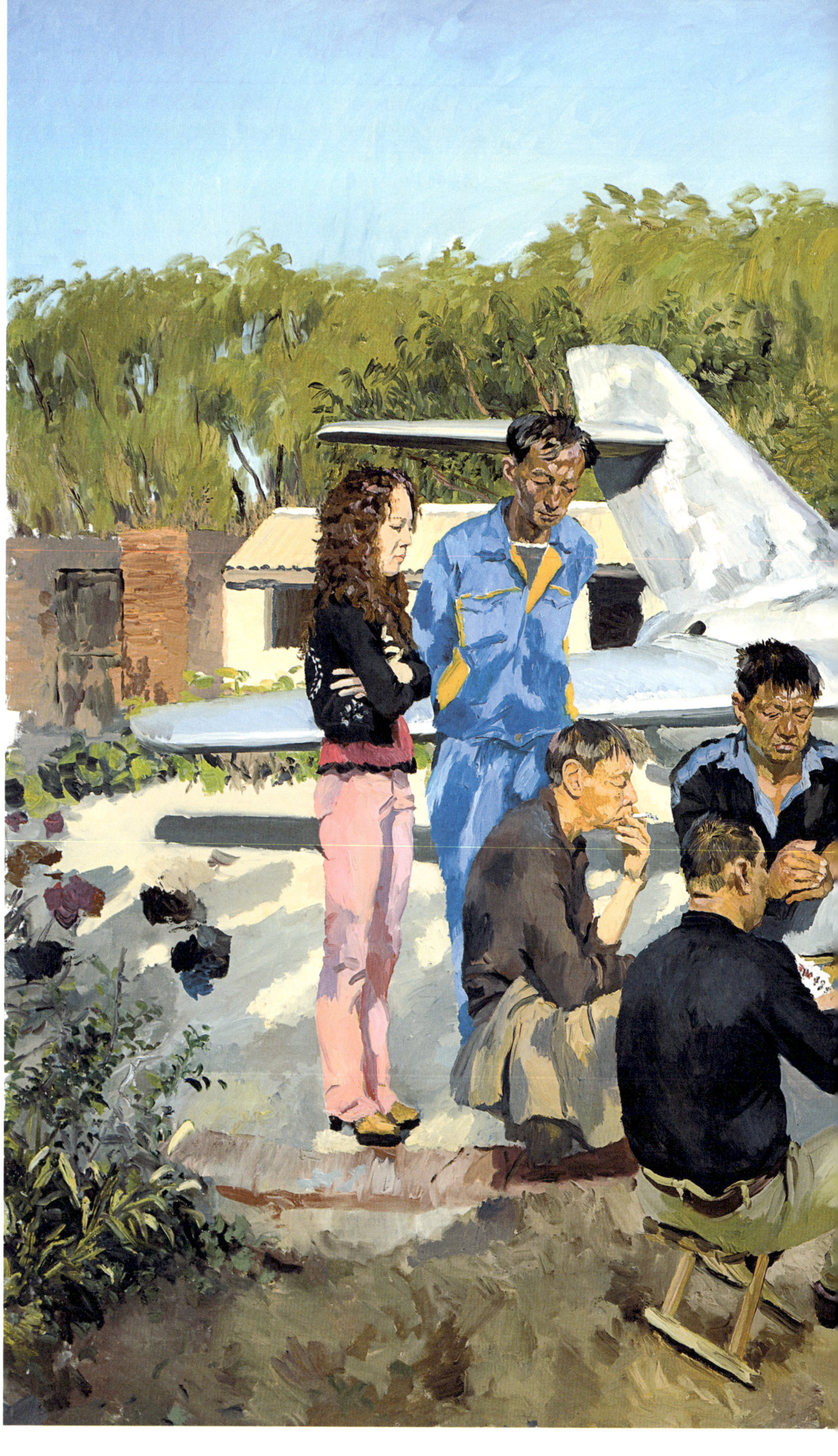

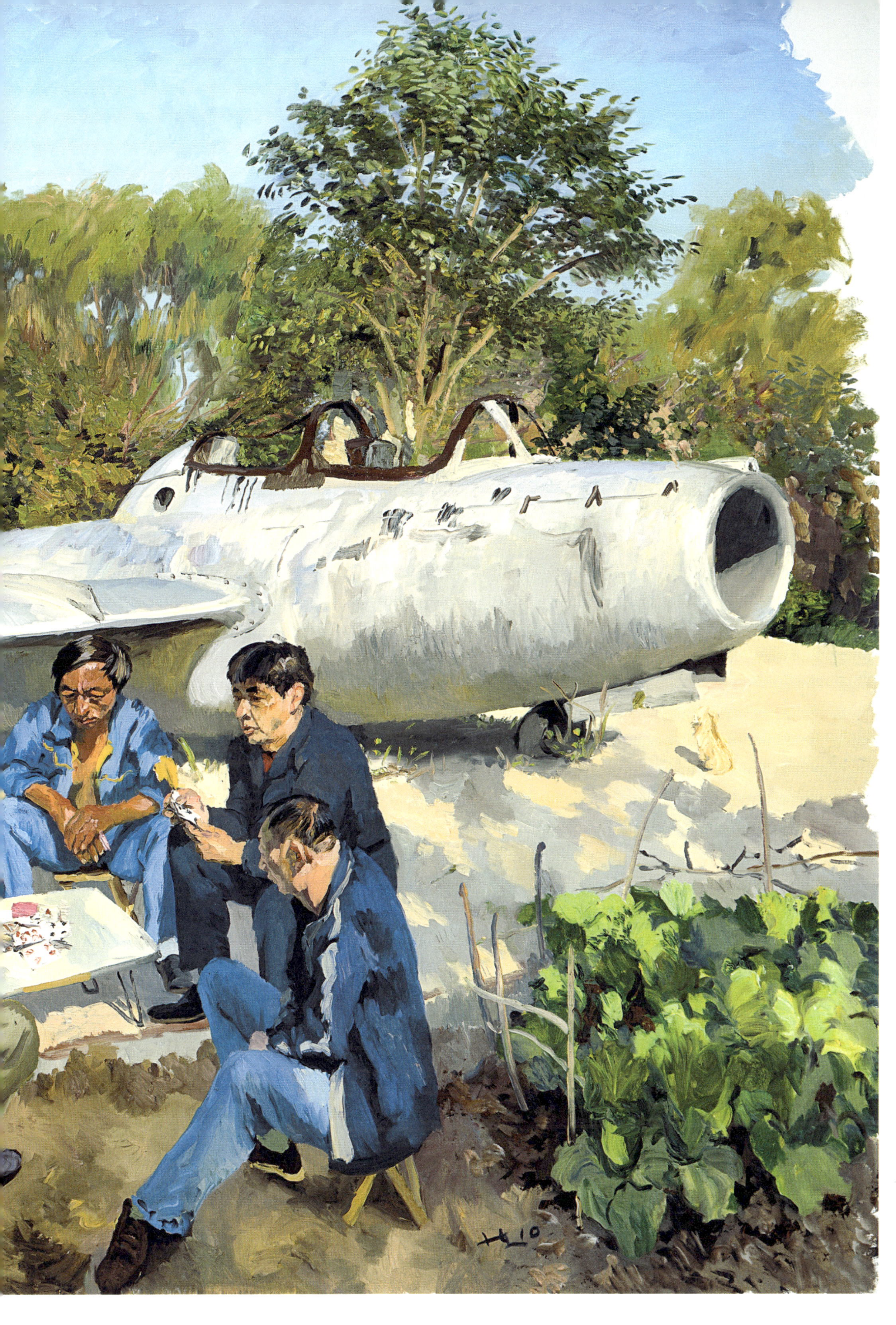

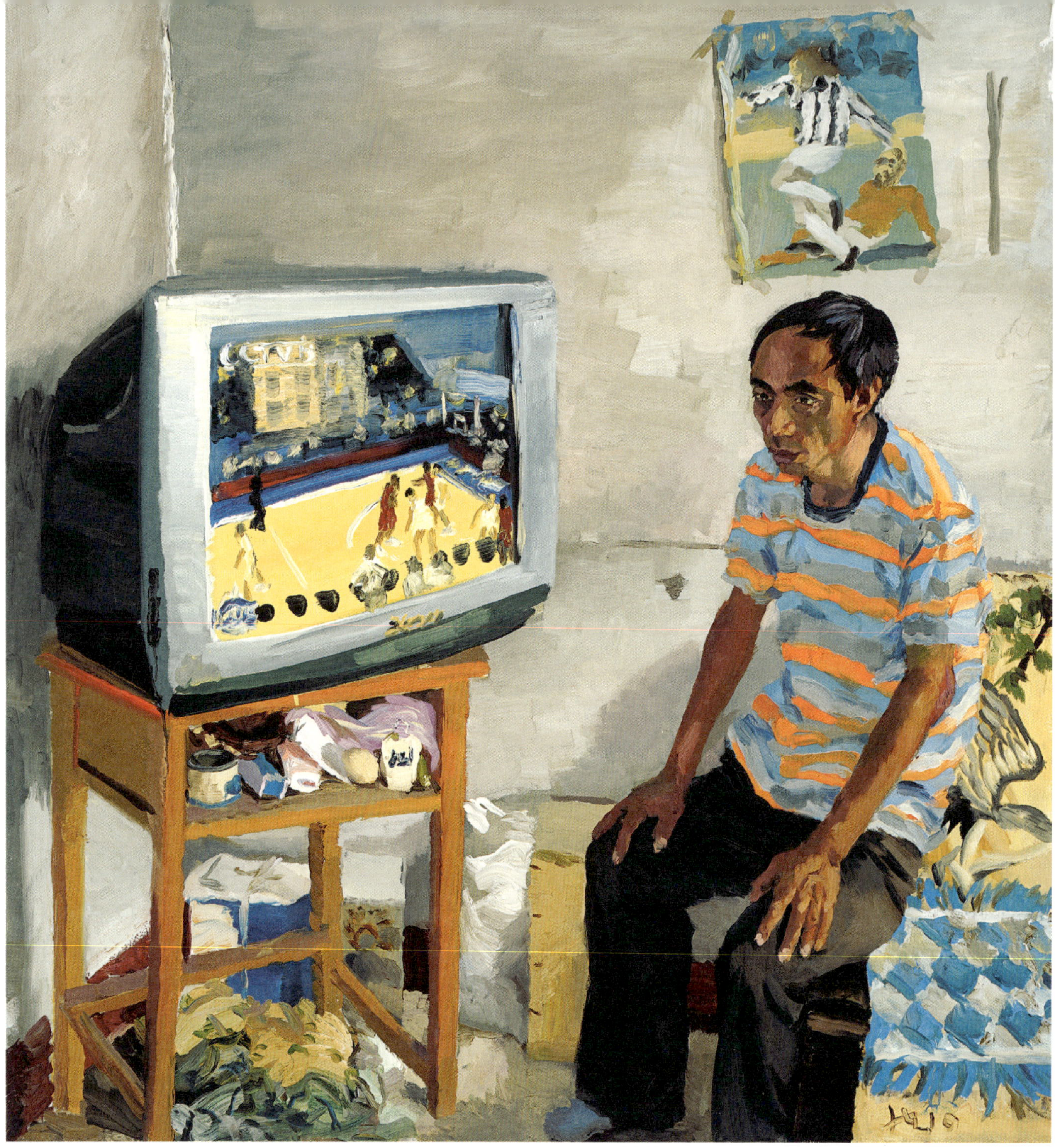

Preceding double page
Liu Xiaodong
Jincheng Airport
2010
Oil on canvas
300 × 400 cm

Liu Xiaodong
Li Wu works the nightshift and still cannot sleep by day
2010
Oil on canvas
150 × 140 cm

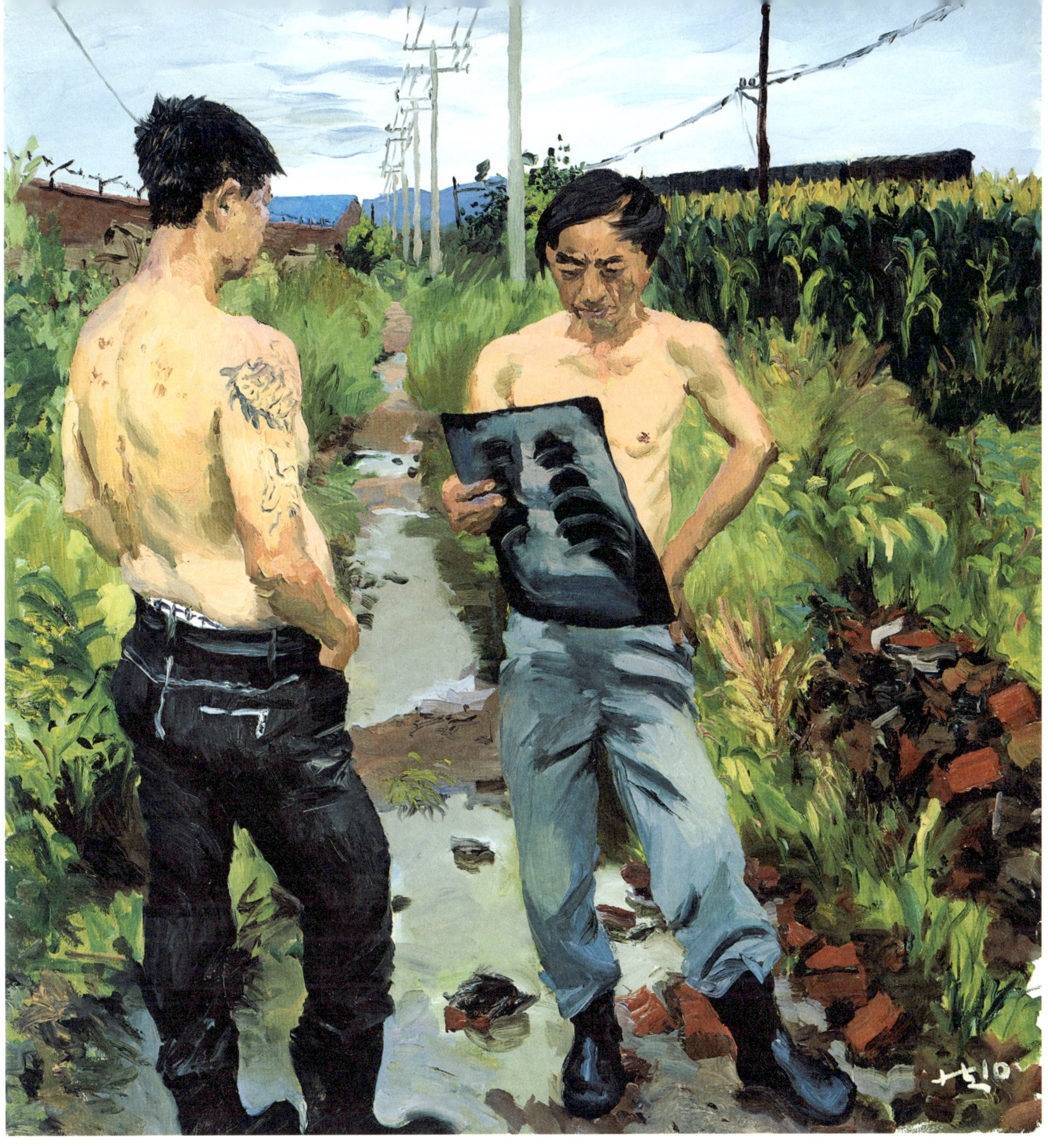

Liu Xiaodong
Bent Rib
2010
Oil on canvas
150 × 140 cm

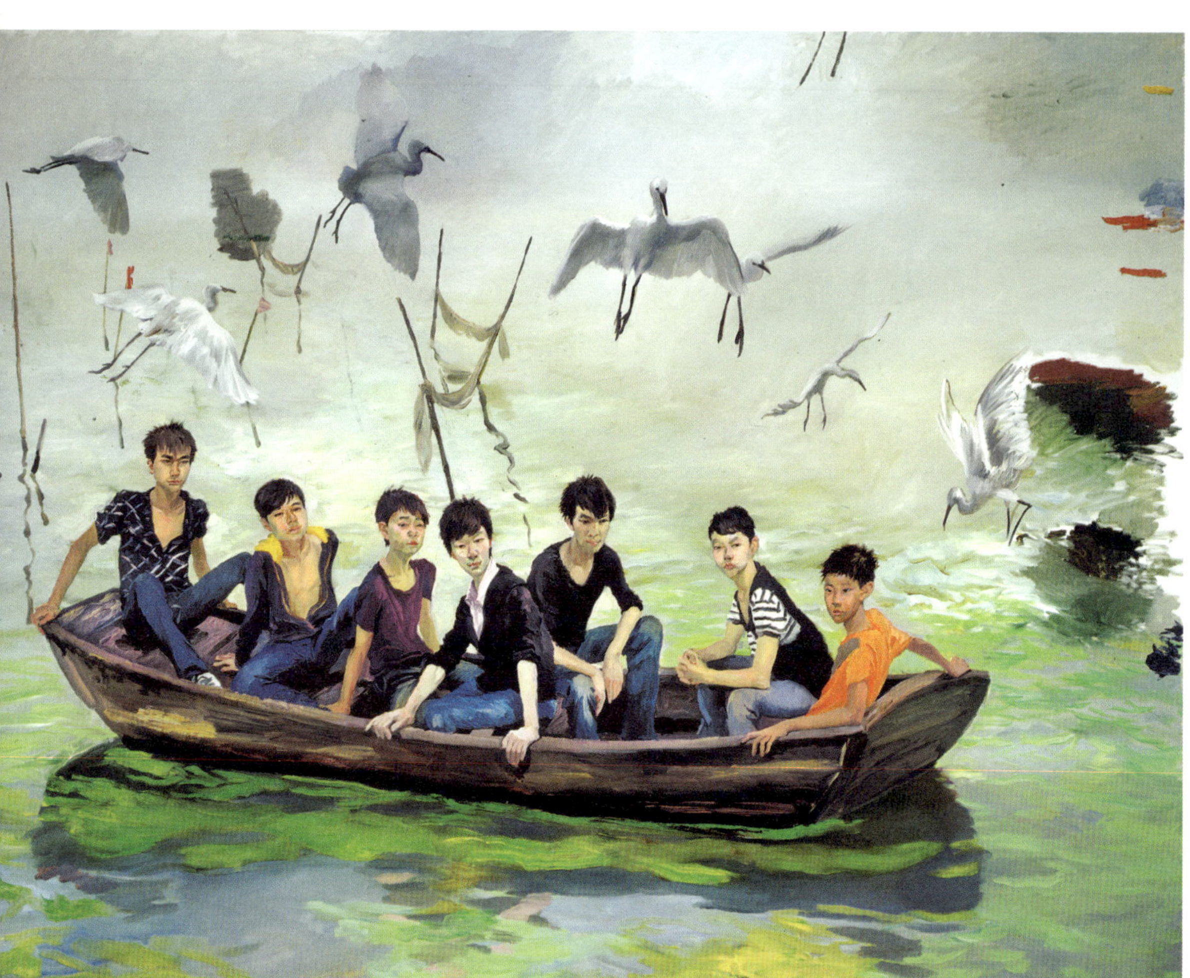

Liu Xiaodong
Into Taihu
2010
Oil on canvas
300 × 400 cm

LIU
XIAODONG

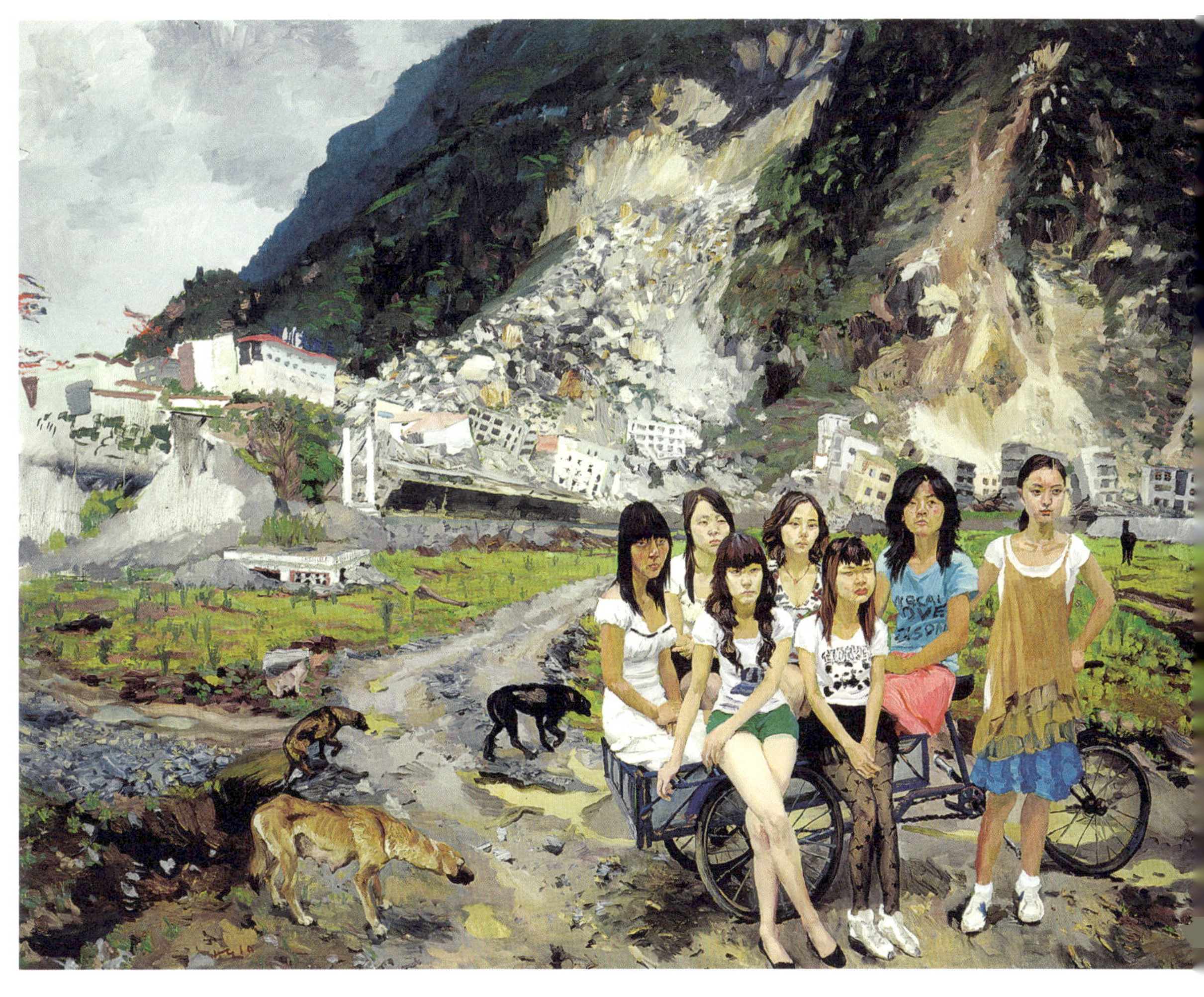

Liu Xiaodong
Out of Beichuan
2010
Oil on canvas
300 × 400 cm

QIU ZHIJIE

MAP BEYOND BOUNDARIES: QIU ZHIJIE AND *MAPPING THE WORLD* PROJECT

LIU TIAN

1.
Liu Xie, *The Literary Mind and the Carving of Dragons*, chapter 1, "On Tao, the Source", c. AD 500.

The beauty of mountains and hills mantled by the rich textures of the earth, this is the way that nature writes its own verses of Tao. Liu Xie[1]

Qiu Zhijie graduated from the Zhejiang Academy of Fine Arts (now the China Academy of Art) in 1992, where he studied printmaking. At his graduation show, he presented *About a New Life*, a maze-like installation of sixteen glass panels of differing sizes, covered with intertwined and overlapping silk prints and ink drawings of images and texts. The panels were arranged so that viewers could walk among them. A noteworthy but rarely mentioned fact is that Qiu washed all of the glass panels clean after the exhibition and sold them to a construction company. At the time, he was an ardent follower of the Fluxus movement. Another of the artist's well-known works from this same period, *Writing the "Orchid Pavilion Preface" One Thousand Times* conveys a similar message: the loss of history entailed by the obliteration of a revered text in an attempt to perpetuate its memory, as the layered words dissolve into a thick solidified mass of ink. The invisible calligraphy underneath the layers of dried ink reflects the philosophical ideas of this treatise penned by Wang Xizhi, China's most famous calligrapher (303–361), with its oft-quoted fatalistic doctrines, such as "What we used to be fond of will become the past instantaneously," "We can't help but to cheer ourselves by recollection" and "Life, long or short, always comes to an end." By wiping clean the glass panels of *About a New Life*, Qiu also makes an implicit reference to *Dream of the Red Chamber*, one of China's Four Great Classical Novels, which includes actions designed to "remove layers to return to the genuine" and "white out the earth to reveal its true beauty".

Even in these works from Qiu's student days, his predilection for the joining of elements inspired by contemporary art and local art forms, as well as Chinese traditional and folk arts, is clear. It later became his own creative approach across different art forms, media and materials, and even identities, which finally combined into a creation-education idea he calls "total art". Just as the lines of demarcation drawn on maps are made by humans and do not really exist on earth. A map is the totality of all particulars.

In general, maps are images of a civilization and the navigation of nature. However, in ancient Chinese philosophy, as expressed in *The Literary Mind and the Carving of Dragons*, Map comes from Text. The original Text (文) is the texture (纹) of earth and the pattern of creature. Then the complexity of topologies and the richness of life turn into the text of human beings and the text of words. Painting and writing/calligraphy are derived from the same original Text to depict the wonders of nature, so a map is a prototype of painting-writing practice.

The *Mapping the World* project is first of all about epistemology and methodology, as the Chinese character *tu (图)* can mean "map", "mapping" and "planning". Maps are a way to understand the world, to deal with the complicated relationships between events and objects, human concepts and perceptions, and ultimately the painter himself. In line with this philosophy, Qiu has initiated three separate series under this project: *All of the Objects Series (万物)*, *All Living Things Series (众生)* and *Autobiography Series*. Qiu extracts a theme from groups of objects, inspired by Ludwig Wittgenstein's "family resemblance"[2] principle, whereby things thought to be connected by a single essential feature common to all are in fact connected by a series of overlapping similarities. The objects in each theme are thus located on the map based on different relationships.

Historically, maps have often enabled military conquest, or been redrawn as a result of such an event. Qiu's maps are also about conquest, but instead in the areas of learning, thinking and cognition, in this case redrawn like evolving mind maps and defining the conquered territories. It is worth noting that when the maps are completely unfolded they are presented as a special power, as if representing the territories of state or the theatres of war. When fully opened, military maps show how authorities govern something known. But on Qiu's maps, objects appear in conglomerations based on merged knowledge. The paintings and texts emerge from his creative mindset and/or his interpretations of common knowledge, decisively positioned against the mainstream. The maps are in keeping with one of the artist's key principles, namely that creativity transcends the boundaries of human knowledge. Qiu's maps are actually "pictures", reflecting the ancient Chinese belief that "tracing the confusion wrought by the past presages the future not sprout yet".

During the winter of 2007, the artist and I flew to Lhasa from Beijing, and we were both awed by the sight of vast glaciers over the Tibetan plateau. This might have been the impetus for his future "Bird's-Eye View" series (2013). In 2010, Hans Ulrich Obrist, the moderator for the Digital-Life-Design (DLD) conference in Munich, asked Qiu to draw a "twenty-first-century map". This was the first time Qiu had used his maps to present his views on futurology and eschatology. For this, he mostly used pencil sketches and line drawings. But once he began the "Bird's-Eye View" series, he replaced the lines with brush strokes and ink painting, creating a new genre departing from traditional Chinese *shanshui* ("mountains and water") landscape painting. Breaking with the usual Chinese emphasis on horizontality, Qiu favours verticality and views from above. The significance of Qiu's maps lies both in their cohesive focus on a subject and the introduction of non-traditional painting techniques.

2.
Ludwig Wittgenstein, *Philosophical Investigations*, translation by G. E. M. Anscombe [first published 1953], Blackwell Publishing, Oxford, 2001. Wittgenstein refers to the concept of language games. He rejects the idea that language corresponds to reality and argues that concepts do not need to be clearly defined to be meaningful. He uses the concept of "family resemblance" "to bring into prominence the fact that speaking of language is part of an activity, or a form of life which gives language its meaning".

The *Mapping the World* project is a particularly powerful metaphor, touching on various realms, from the emotional and religious to adventure, utopia, revolution, social relations and even games. All are depicted as imaginary "landscape" aspects, as rivers and lakes, mountains and plains, valleys and ravines. Their placement, altitude and orientation on the maps reflect certain essential characteristics, groupings or ideas. From this perspective, Qiu's maps come close to recreating the classical Chinese gardens (a focus already evident with *About a New Life*). The creation of a map, like the organization of a garden or any work of art, passes through a succession of phases: selecting the location, arranging the terrain and constructing the edifices, in line with the notions of elegance, taxonomy and vantage points presented in Wen Zhenheng's seventeenth-century *Treatise on Superfluous Things*.

"On Exactitude in Science", the one-paragraph short story by Jorge Luis Borges,[3] deals with the relationship between maps and territories and is written as a quotation attributed to a fictional author, who imagines an empire where the art of cartography becomes so precise that only a map coinciding point for point with the empire itself could suffice. This is the limit of the map as a replica of the real world, infinitely close to the real. The Chinese art of studying nature's method does not mean replication or mimesis. Rather, it means following the principles of nature in order to create a reality beyond the bounds of nature. There are two types of maps in common use throughout history: the data (or thematic, mathematic) map and the narrative (or literary, imaginative) map. The first shows one or several variables (or themes) arranged spatially and is thus based on objective measurement, while the second tells a story plotted through space and thus serves to provide a visual counterpart to a conceptual proposition. Before the advent of modern geological survey maps, ancient cartographers based their work on drawings, pictures, writings and books, same as the *Mapping the World* project. Heaven and earth have great beauty outside languages, and we are fortunate to have had the opportunity to explore these on Text (maps). The breathtaking scope is given by nature transcending known boundaries, illustrating achievements of timeless Text beyond our capacity to write.

3.
Jorge Luis Borges, *On Exactitude in Science*, translated by Norman Thomas de Giovanni, Penguin Books, London, 1975. See also Jorge Luis Borges, *Collected Fictions*, translated by Andrew Hurley, Penguin Classics, New York, 1998, and *The Aleph and Other Stories* [first published 1945], Penguin Classics, London, 2004.

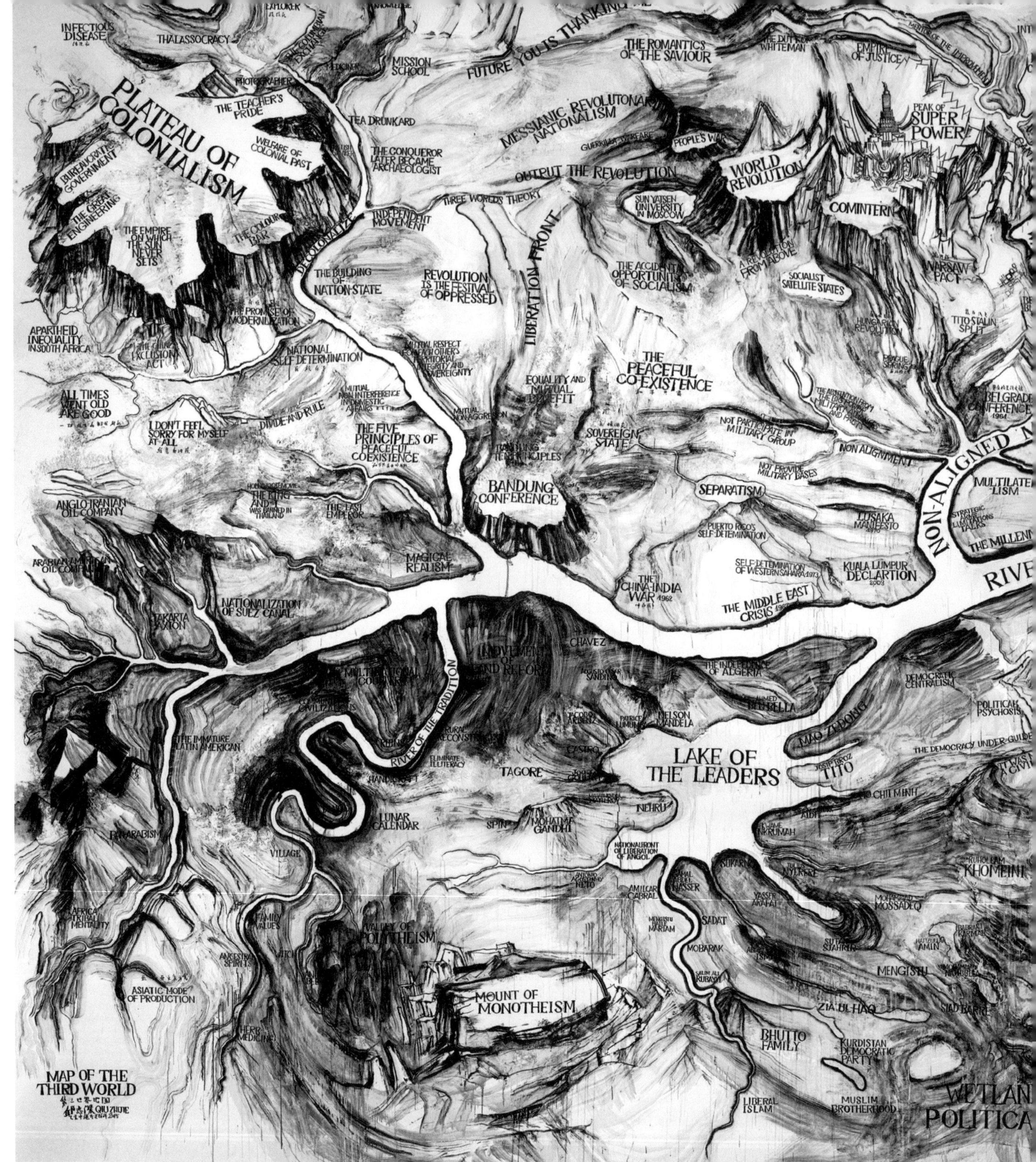

Qiu Zhijie
Map of the Third World
2015
Ink mural (for the 6th Moscow Biennial)
70×1400 cm

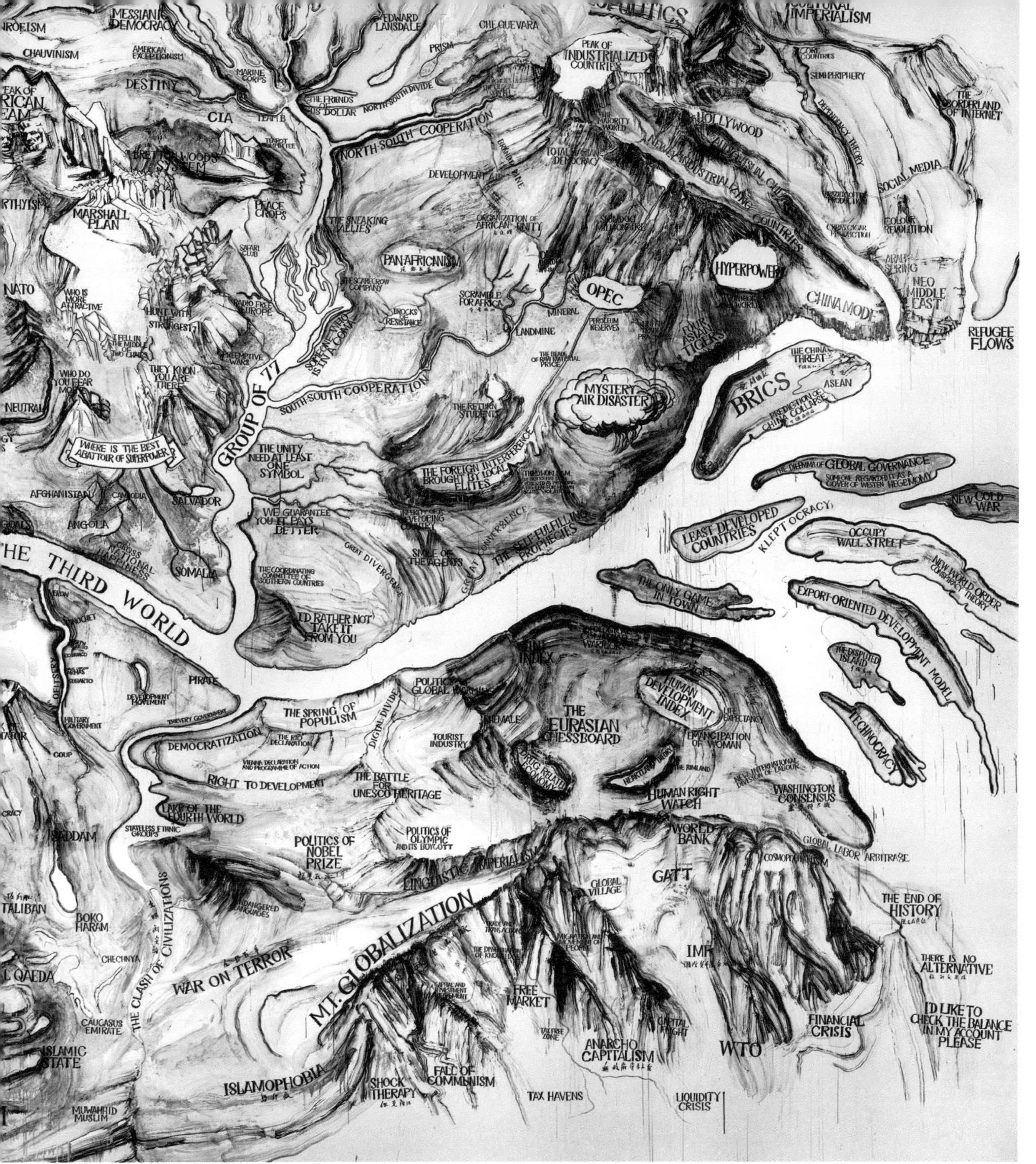

MESSIANIC DEMOCRACY
CHAUVINISM
AMERICAN EXCEPTIONALISM
DESTINY
PEAK OF AFRICAN DREAM
CIA
MARINE CORPS
TEAM B
EDWARD LANSDALE
CHE GUEVARA
PRISM
THE FRIENDS OF US DOLLAR
NORTH-SOUTH DIVIDE
POLITICS
PEAK OF INDUSTRIALIZED COUNTRIES
CULTURAL IMPERIALISM
CORE COUNTRIES
SEMI-PERIPHERY
THE BORDERLAND OF INTERNET
DEMOCRACY THEORY
BRETTON WOODS SYSTEM
NORTH-SOUTH COOPERATION
DEVELOPMENT
HOLLYWOOD
NEW INDUSTRIAL CULTURE
SOCIAL MEDIA
MARSHALL PLAN
PEACE CORPS
SAFARI CLUB
THE SNEAKING VALLEYS
ORGANIZATION OF AFRICAN UNITY
TOTALITARIAN DEMOCRACY
NEW INDUSTRIALIZING COUNTRIES
COLOUR REVOLUTION
NATO
WHO IS MORE ATTRACTIVE
HUNT WITH STRONGEST
RADIO FREE EUROPE
PAN-AFRICANISM
THE SCARECROW COMPANY
SCRAMBLE FOR AFRICA
MINERAL
OPEC
HYPERPOWER
FOUR ASIAN TIGERS
CHINA MODE
ARAB SPRING
NEO MIDDLE EAST
I FELL IN THE MIDDLE TWO CHAIRS
ROCKS OF RESISTANCE
LANDMINE
PETROLEUM RESERVES
THE CHINA THREAT
REFUGEE FLOWS
WHO DO YOU FEAR
THEY KNOW YOU ARE THERE
PREEMPTIVE WARS
THE RETURN STUDENT
A MYSTERY AIR DISASTER
BRICS
ASEAN
PREDICTION OF CHINA COLLAPSE
NEUTRAL
WHERE IS THE BEST ABATTOIR OF SUPERPOWER
GROUP OF 77
SOUTH-SOUTH COOPERATION
THE UNITY NEED AT LEAST ONE SYMBOL
THE FOREIGN INTERFERENCE BROUGHT BY LOCAL ELITES
THE DILEMMA OF GLOBAL GOVERNANCE
SOMEONE REGARDED IT AS A COVER OF WESTERN HEGEMONY
NEW COLD WAR
AFGHANISTAN
CAMBODIA
SALVADOR
WE GUARANTEE YOU IT PAYS BETTER
LEAST DEVELOPED COUNTRIES
KLEPTOCRACY
OCCUPY WALL STREET
NEW WORLD ORDER
ANGOLA
GROSS NATIONAL HAPPINESS
SOMALIA
THE COORDINATING COMMITTEE OF SOUTHERN COUNTRIES
GREAT DIVERGENCE
SMILE OF THE AGENTS
THE SELF-FULFILLING PROPHECIES
THE ONLY GAME IN TOWN
EXPORT-ORIENTED DEVELOPMENT MODEL
THE DISPUTED ISLAND
THE THIRD WORLD
PINOCHET
PIRATE
DEVELOPMENT MOVEMENT
THIEVERY GOVERNMENT
I'D RATHER NOT TAKE IT FROM YOU
THE SPRING OF POPULISM
POLITICAL GLOBAL WARMING
SHEMALE
HUMAN DEVELOPMENT INDEX
LIFE EXPECTANCY
EMANCIPATION OF WOMAN
TECHNOCRACY
MILITARY GOVERNMENT
COUP
DEMOCRATIZATION
THE RIO DECLARATION
VIENNA DECLARATION AND PROGRAMME OF ACTION
THE EURASIAN CHESSBOARD
TOURIST INDUSTRY
THE RIMLAND
HUMAN RIGHT WATCH
INTERNATIONAL DIVISION OF LABOUR
WASHINGTON CONSENSUS
SADDAM
STATELESS ETHNIC GROUPS
RIGHT TO DEVELOPMENT
THE BATTLE FOR UNESCO HERITAGE
DIGITAL DIVIDE
DRUG RELATED KINGDOM
WORLD BANK
GLOBAL LABOR ARBITRAGE
LAKE OF THE FOURTH WORLD
POLITICS OF NOBEL PRIZE
POLITICS OF OLYMPIC AND ITS BOYCOTT
COSMOPOLITANISM
TALIBAN
BOKO HARAM
CHECHNYA
ENDANGERED LANGUAGES
LINGUISTIC IMPERIALISM
GLOBAL VILLAGE
GATT
THE END OF HISTORY
AL QAEDA
THE CLASH OF CIVILIZATIONS
WAR ON TERROR
MT. GLOBALIZATION
TRADE AND INVESTMENT AGREEMENT
THE DIVISION OF KNOWLEDGE
IMF
THERE IS NO ALTERNATIVE
CAUCASUS EMIRATE
FREE MARKET
CAPITAL FLIGHT
FINANCIAL CRISIS
I'D LIKE TO CHECK THE BALANCE IN MY ACCOUNT PLEASE
ISLAMIC STATE
TARIFF-FREE ZONE
ANARCHO CAPITALISM
WTO
ISLAMOPHOBIA
SHOCK THERAPY
FALL OF COMMUNISM
TAX HAVENS
LIQUIDITY CRISIS
MUWAHHID MUSLIM

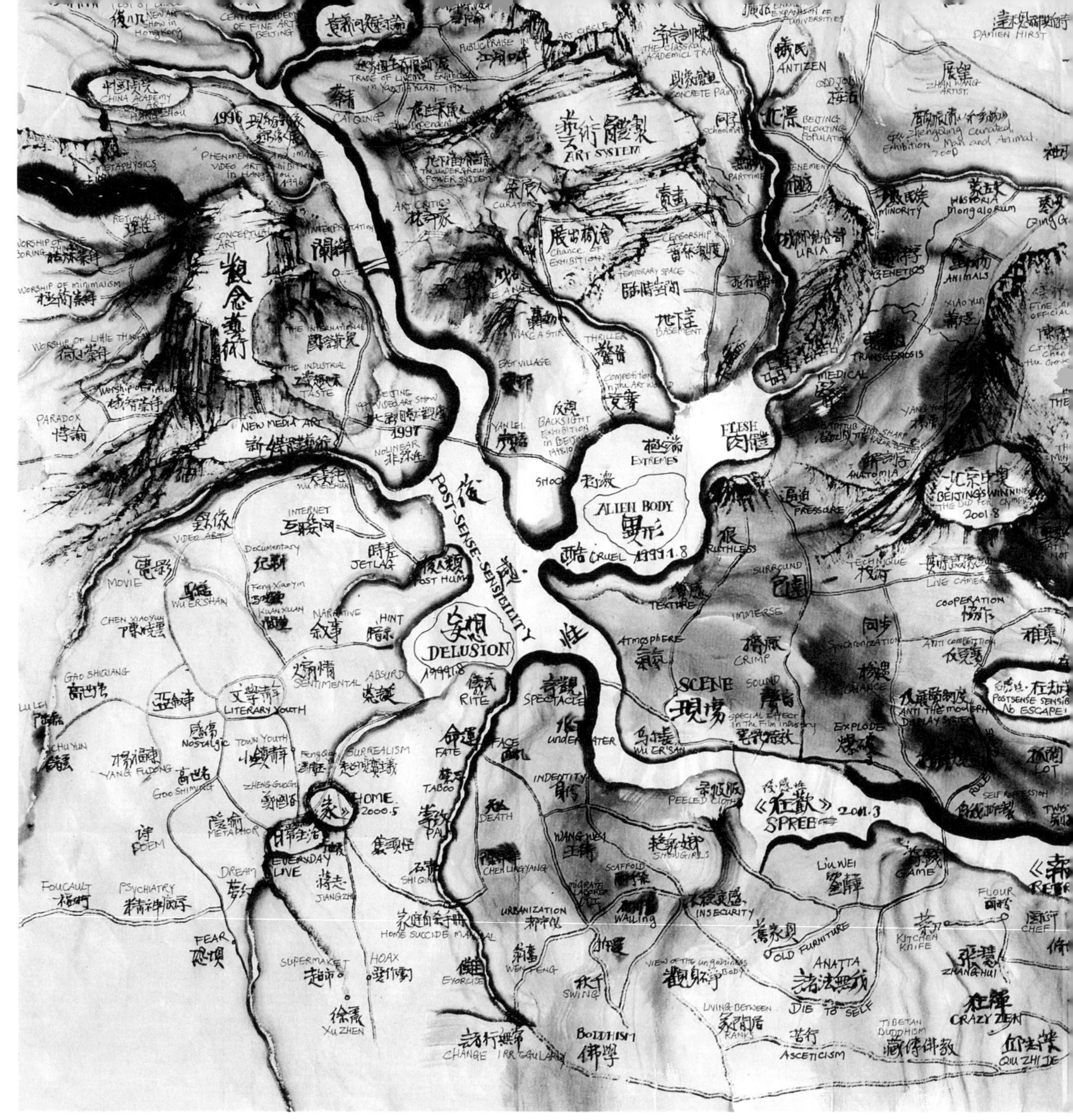

Qiu Zhijie
Memory about the Post-Sense Sensibility
2014
Ink on paper
70×140 cm

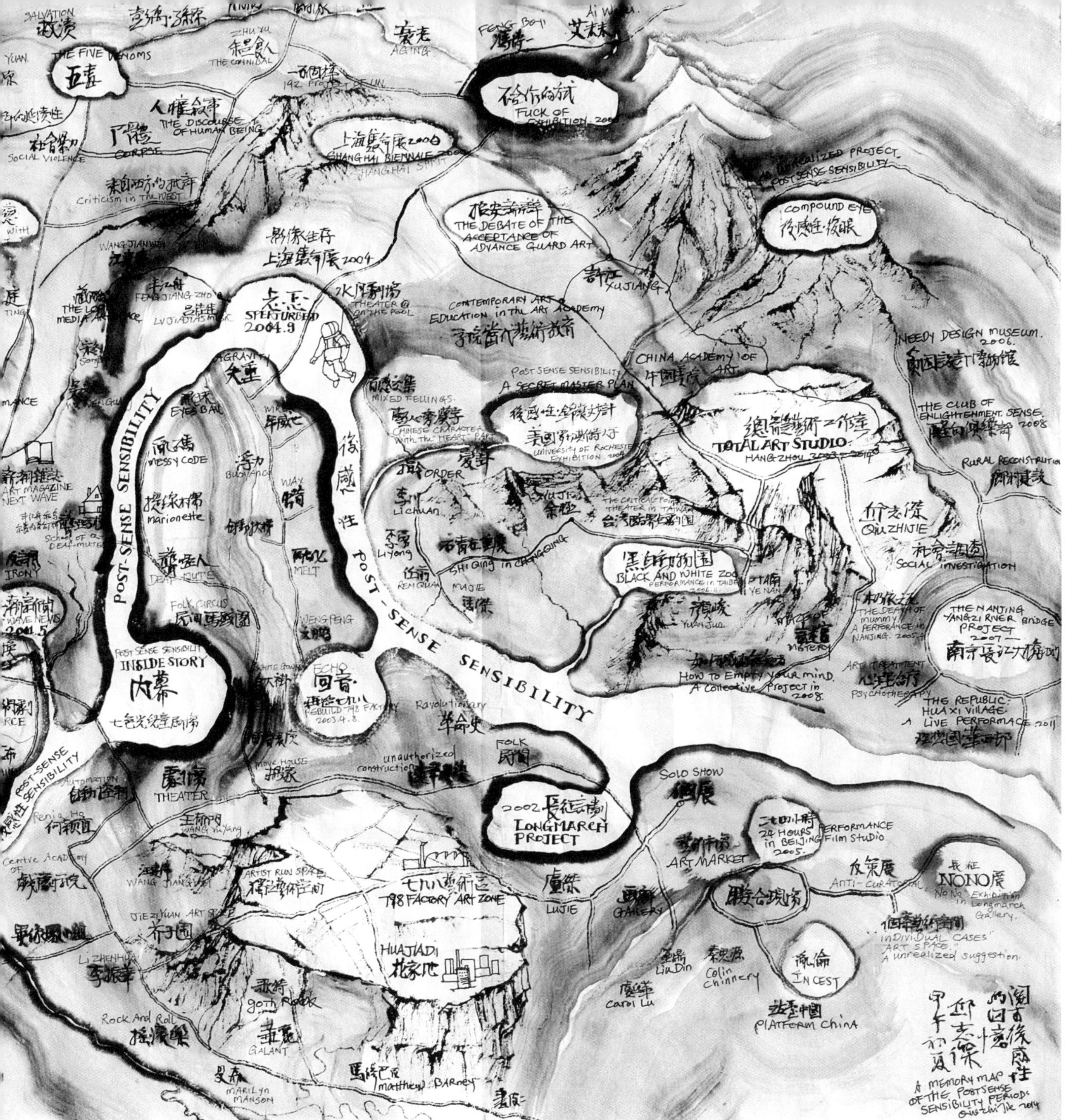
SALVATION
THE FIVE VENOMS
五毒
YUAN
THE DISCOURSE OF HUMAN BEING
人權公害
CORPSE
屍體
SOCIAL VIOLENCE
社會暴力
Criticism in the West
WANG JIANWEI
FENG BOYI
AI WEIWEI
艾未未
AQING
FUCK OF EXHIBITION 2000
不合作的方式
SHANGHAI BIENNALE 2000
上海雙年展 2000
THE DEBATE OF THE ACCEPTANCE OF ADVANCE GUARD ART
前衛論爭
REALIZED PROJECT
POST SENSE SENSIBILITY
COMPOUND EYE
後感性·複眼
YUJIANG
上海雙年展 2004
FENG JIANG ZHO
LVJIADTA
THEATER @ ON THE POOL
水月劇場
Contemporary Art Education in the Art Academy
學院當代藝術教育
CHINA ACADEMY OF ART
中國美院
NEEDY DESIGN MUSEUM 2006
THE LOCAL MEDIA ART SPACE
Post sense sensibility A Secret Master Plan
THE CLUB OF ENLIGHTENMENT SENSE 2008
啟蒙俱樂部
STED TURBED 2004.9
忐忑
GRAVITY
失重
EYES BALL
眼球
MESSY CODE
亂碼
BUOYANCY
浮力
MARIONETTE
提線木偶
MIXED FEELINGS
雜感共集
CHINESE CHARACTER WITH THE HEART PART
藝術慢蒙亭
後感性
Post Sense Sensibility
University of Rochester Exhibition 2006
後感性·秘密總體設計 美國羅徹斯特大學
ORDER
次序
LICHUAN
李川
LIYONG
李勇
TOTAL ART STUDIO
HANGZHOU 2003 - 2010
總體藝術工作室
QIU ZHIJIE
RURAL RECONSTRUCTION
社會調查
SOCIAL INVESTIGATION
POST-SENSE SENSIBILITY
THE CRITICAL POINT THEATER IN TAIWAN
台灣臨界點劇團
WAX MELT
網化
ART MAGAZINE NEXT WAVE
School of DEAF-MUTES
DEAF-MUTES
聾啞人
FOLK CIRCUS
民間馬戲團
IRONY
反諷
WAVE NEWS 2001.5
WENG PENG
文鵬
SHI QING IN CHONGQING
石青在重慶
REN QUAN
任前
MAJIE
馬傑
BLACK AND WHITE ZOO
PERFORMANCE IN TAIBEI 2006.11
黑白動物園
YE NAN
YUAN JIAO
袁嶠
MISTERY
秘境
THE DEATH OF mummy A PERFORMANCE IN NANJING 2005.7
木乃伊之死
THE NANJING YANGZI RIVER BRIDGE PROJECT 2007 —
南京長江大橋
How to Empty your mind. A Collective Project in 2008.
ART TREATMENT
心理治療
PSYCHOTHERAPY
THE REPUBLIC: HUA XI VILLAGE A LIVE PERFORMACE 2011
華西國華西村
INSIDE STORY
Post Sense Sensibility
內幕
七色光兒童劇場
ECHO
回音
REBUILD 798 FACTORY
2003.4.8
Revolutionary
革命史
POST SENSE SENSIBILITY
AUTOMATION
自動控制
Renjia Ho
何頑頁
THEATER
幻象劇場
WANG YUYANG
王郁洋
FOLK
民間
unauthorized construction
違章建築
SOLO SHOW
個展
ART MARKET
藝術市場
24 HOURS IN BEIJING PERFORMANCE 2005.
二十四小時 北京電影製片廠 Film Studio
Anti-curatorial
反策展
NONO展
NO No. Exhibition in Longmarch Gallery
長征 NONO 展
2002 LONGMARCH PROJECT
長征藝劇
Centre Academy of
戲劇學院
WANG JIANWEI
汪建偉
JIE ZI YUAN ART SPACE
芥子園藝術空間
藝術家工作間
ARTIST RUN SPACE
LUJIE
盧杰
GALLERY
畫廊
LIU DIN
劉鼎
Colin Chinnery
秦思源
CAROL LU
盧迎華
'individual CASES' 'ART SPACE' A unrealized suggestion
個案藝術空間
Li Zhenhua
李振華
798 FACTORY ART ZONE
七九八藝術區
HUAJIADI
花家地
GOTH ROCK
歌特
ROCK AND ROLL
搖滾樂
GALANT
畫麗
MARILYN MANSON
瑪麗蓮曼森
(Matthew) BARNEY
馬修巴尼
畫廊
UNITED DISPLAY
聯合現實
INCEST
亂倫
PLATFORM CHINA
站臺中國
A MEMORY MAP OF THE POSTSENSE SENSIBILITY PERIODS Qiu Zhijie 2014
關於後感性的回憶地圖 邱志傑 2014

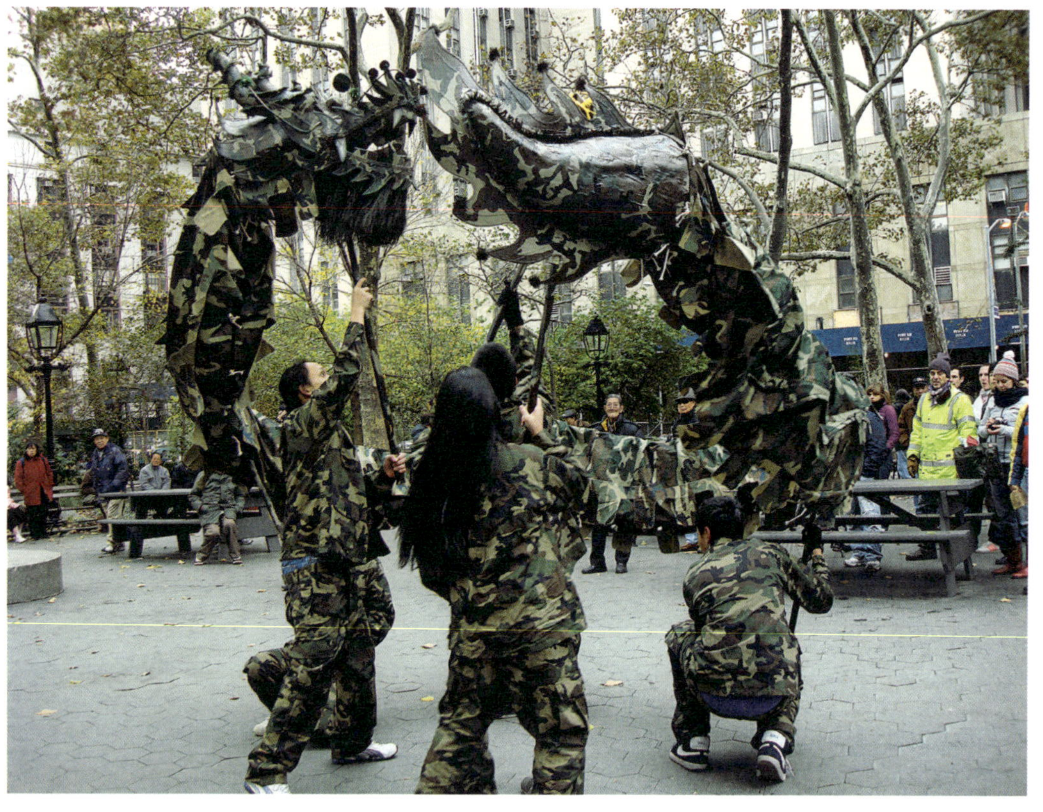

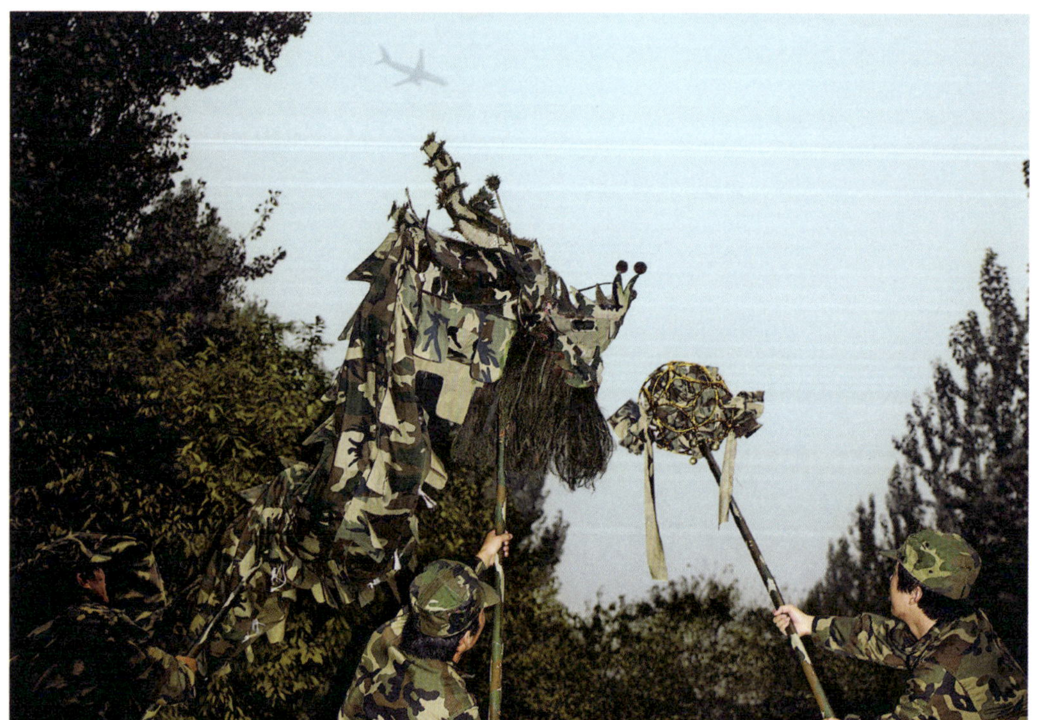

Qiu Zhijie
The Storm is coming
2007
Performance at PERFORMA
2007

124

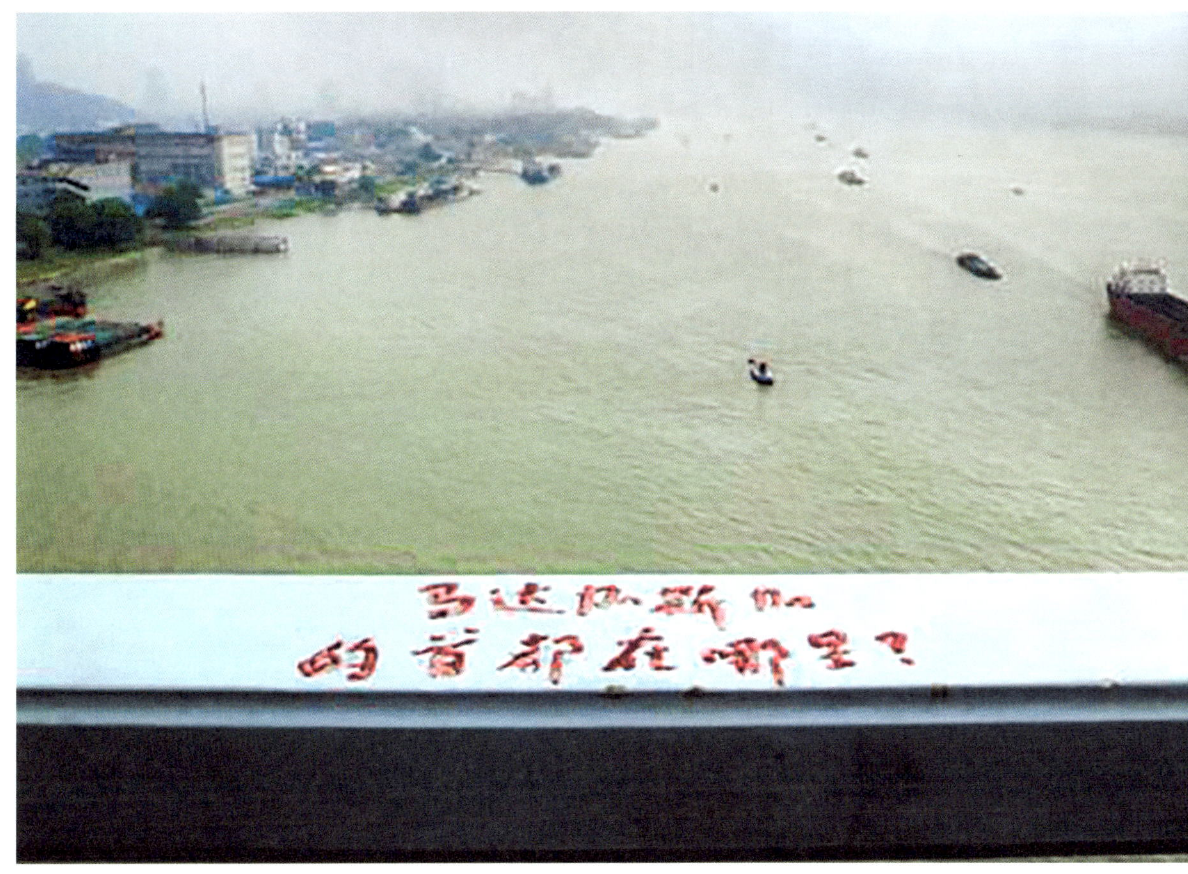

Qiu Zhijie
*When love is dead –
where is the capital
of Madagascar?*
2008
Photograph
11×17 cm
(Work from *A Suicidology
of the Nanjing Yangtze
River Bridge Project*)

125

TAO HUI

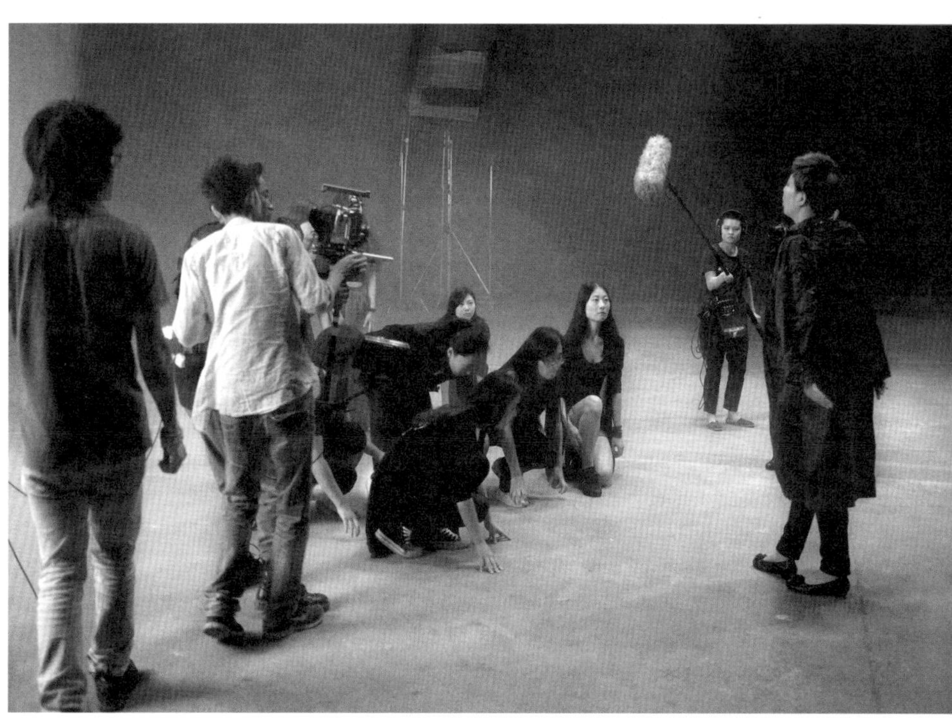

Photo shoot, *The Acting Tutorial*
2014

BEYOND
THE
FORM,
THE
STORY
BEGINS

YANG ZI

When he was a child, Tao Hui lived in a village at the summit of a mountain shrouded in mist, blocking the view of the Yangtze River below. The local people were forthright and simple folk, little acquainted with scientific and rational discourse. As a young lad, Tao loved chatting with his neighbours, who were fascinating storytellers, with a repertoire ranging from gossip to ghouls and goblins. By turns funny and mysterious, they were as likely to give their listeners goosebumps as to bring them to tears or peals of laughter. Illusions, fantasies, personal memories, folklore and facts were all intermingled, nourishing one another and imprinting themselves vividly on Tao's mind. Thus was formed his desire to represent them.

Later, television would tell its own stories, and Tao realized that illusions, fantasies and the rest could be seen as well as heard. This realization made a lasting impression on him. "Television was my first exposure to the world outside my village," says Tao. "When I was little, since my parents had to go to work, I always stayed at home alone. At that time, only one channel was available in the village, and a lot of the content was repetitive. Even so, for me television was a window into a completely different way of life." Tao quickly saw that TV soap operas and costume dramas, like the stories told by his neighbours, could distract people from their tedious and monotonous lives, cracking ever so slightly the cold edifice of reality to let in some light.

When, many years later, Tao Hui started to work as a video artist, he did not tell stories with his camera in the usual way. Tao says that when he was at university, he was "into making experimental films". So he purposefully juxtaposed the fantasies produced by the television industry with reality. Characters in his works *Miss Green, Remember to Forget!* (2008) and *Mongolism* (2010) come from two popular Chinese TV costume dramas of the 1990s: *The New Legend of Madame White Snake* and *My Fair Princess*. He had his classmates perform the scenes, often set in the Huangjiaoping area of Chongqing, where his alma mater, the Sichuan Fine Arts Institute, is located. Tao often plays with perceptions of time and space in these two video pieces. For example, in *Miss Green, Remember to Forget!* the actors are dressed in bright red and green outfits sewn by Tao Hui himself, using a mix of ancient and modern styles. Miss Green (a green snake in the Chinese fairy tale, servant of Madame White Snake) gulps down a goldfish after cooking it in an electric rice cooker. In *Mongolism*, a group of middle-aged women in red jackets, beating drums and clanging gongs, march in single file up to a Mongolian princess. In some ways, these works can be interpreted as remnants of a visual memory: leaving home after watching these kinds of dramas on TV and stepping out into a street like the one in the videos, we may find that the joys and sorrows experienced by the characters are insinuating themselves into our own lives. The jumpy camera work reinforces this same feeling. Tao's plots are often improvised on the set, depending upon the circumstances and the crew's decisions, rather than using thoroughly worked out scripts. His cinematographic techniques (anachronisms, parallelisms, juxtapositions, spatial disruptions) push the boundaries between the virtual reality of TV drama and real-world experience. In addition, frequent scene changes inspire a fragmented perception of time and space.

Since his graduation in 2011, Tao Hui has spent most of his time in Beijing, although he has returned to his home village on a number of occasions. He initially worked as an artist's assistant and art editor for a journal while developing his own voice as an artist. His 2011 installation piece *Emotional Manufacturing* consists of a set of three remodelled routers not connected to the Internet. Each of the routers broadcasts its wi-fi network name to all devices within range as a terrifying message: "-you might have cancers-", "-your baby was raped-" and "-your mom is dead-". This piece seems to be testing the threshold of tolerance for fantasy, but is perhaps also attempting to provide a justification for the interruption of drama into the real world. At this transitional phase in his career, Tao employs techniques very close to "contemporary" ones, providing limited hints for viewers and refusing them the comfort of familiar narrative conventions.

This was a necessary passage. Tao's increasing familiarity with the creative process has made him wary of these excessively conceptual works, and he has begun adding more narrative clues in an effort to tell a complete story. At the same time, he no longer deliberately eschews clear narrative progression, as he had done in *Mongolism*, but uses various methods to neutralize the explicit ideas or information, as in *Emotional Manufacturing*. For *The Dusk of Teheran* (2014), which was filmed during an artist residency in Iran, Tao invites an Iranian actress to narrate, in Persian translation, the heartfelt reflections shared by Hong Kong pop singer Anita Mui with her fans, at her farewell concert a month before her death. Thus, Mui's comments on societal expectations, the want and need for love and to be loved, become a metaphor for the limited rights granted to women in many Middle Eastern countries, including Iran, where female singers are not allowed to perform in public and women are under extreme pressure to marry, often at a very young age. Owing to this cultural displacement, Tao's work makes the message and the story all the more vivid and poignant. Far from the blind pursuit of "subtraction" by a number of Chinese contemporary artists, Tao clearly embraces an interest in "addition". Ever since high school, Tao has taken to jotting down his whimsical ideas in notebooks, often sketching them as scenes. For *1 Character and 7 Materials* (2015), he picks seven of these scenes and makes them into videos, each just a few minutes long. The seven surreal scenes depicted include a group of girls in folk dress standing in a dug-out grave during a rainstorm, a reporter interviewing a car crash victim, and a white-robed immortal steering a small boat on a wide river. Before watching these videos, looped in a random sequence and projected within a structure reminiscent of a bus stop shelter, viewers are guided to a recording booth, complete with microphone. Through the headphones available in the booth, a middle-aged woman is heard retelling her sad life story (presumably recorded in this same booth), in a flat but tender voice. The woman's story is inspired by a documentary entitled *Reindeer, Oh Reindeer* (2007), shot by the Chinese director Sun Zengtian, about an Evenk woman named Liu Ba. Tao's piece combines several elements: the memory of the original film adhering to traditional documentary style, with its dramatic whispered narration, the bus stop shelter and recording booth, together with the seven disparate scenes. The total effect created is one of cognition and expressiveness bigger and more sophisticated than the sum of its parts. Here, narrative is only a part of the story. Viewers need to arrive at their own interpretations, by virtue of their immersion and exploration.

Similarly, creating an immersive experience to spur reflection is one of the motivations behind Tao's *Acting Tutorial* (2014) and *Excessive* (2015), which also address the conflicts of the human predicament from a surreal perspective and the notion of performance under stress. *Acting Tutorial* features a series of increasingly frightening classes in an acting course. The impact of the work is so powerful as it unfolds that viewer discomfort and agitation can be literally breathtaking. *Excessive* tells a family story using a voiceover that compels us to reach an objective viewpoint, to form our own opinion and judgements. In these two pieces, Tao explores to what extent true feelings are conveyed in any performance, but also how our own daily lives are also performances. When these two works were presented in an exhibition at the Ullens Center for Contemporary Art (UCCA) in Beijing in 2015, they were installed in the same room so as to better enhance their combined impact. Thus, "imagined" fantasy and "true" reality rub up against each other in these works and across all of Tao's creations, just as they do in the tales remembered by the artist from his childhood.

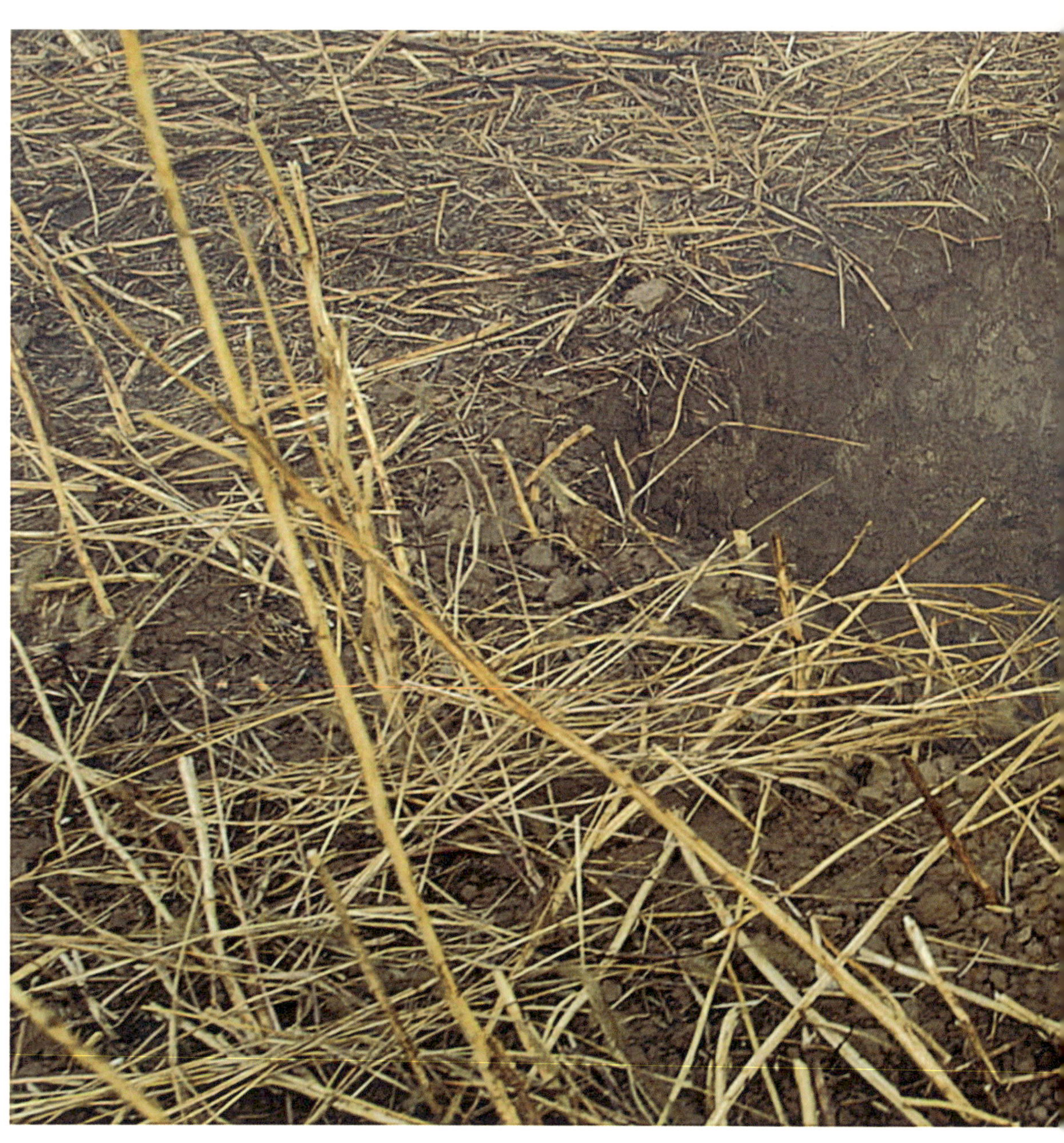

Tao Hui
1 Character & 7 Materials
2015
Sound and video installation
1 Character: sound installation, microphone,
headphones, 13′55′′ (Chinese) and 17′43′′ (English)
7 Materials: HD video, 11′48′′

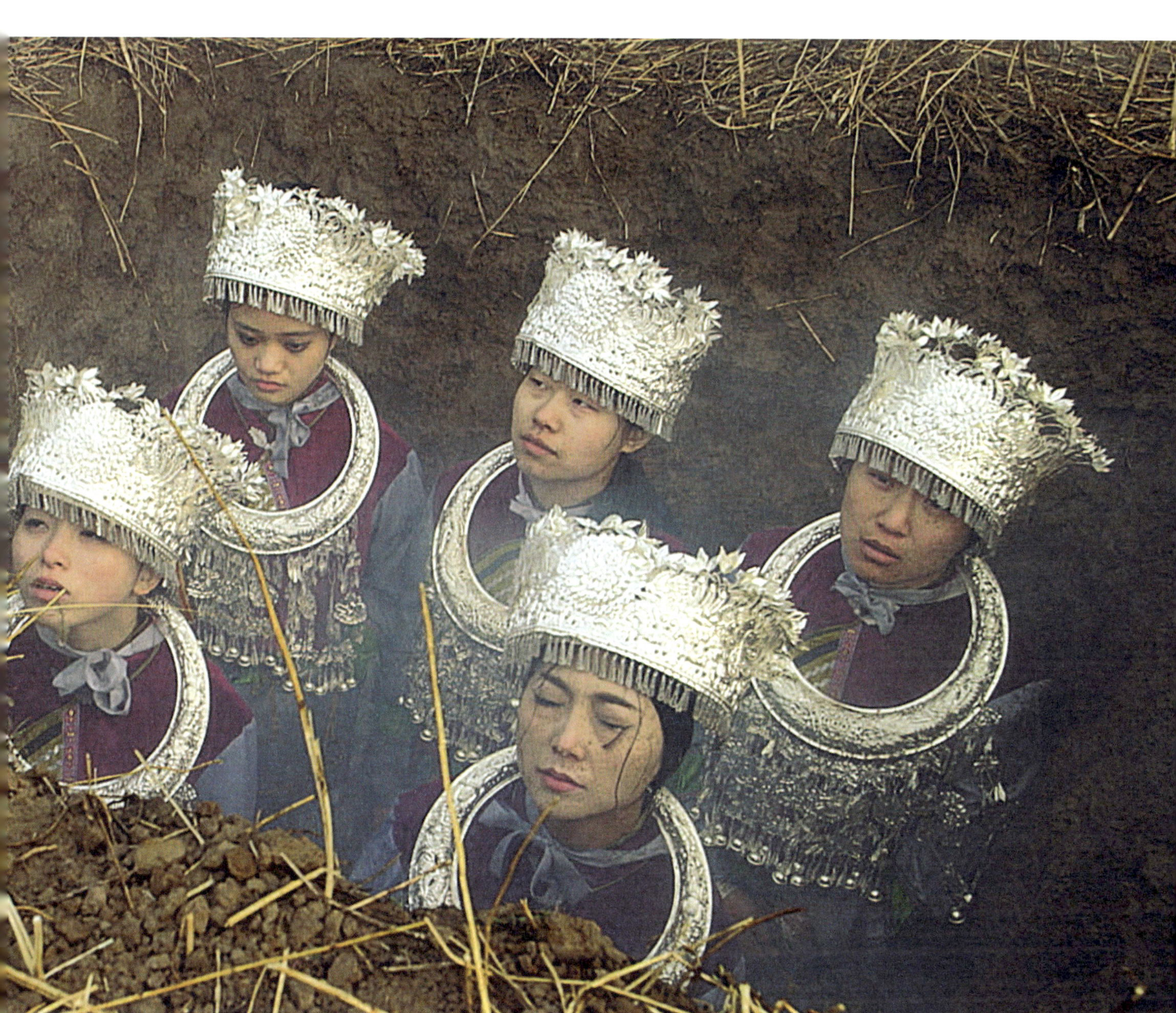

Tao Hui
Installation views of *1 Character & 7 Materials*
2015

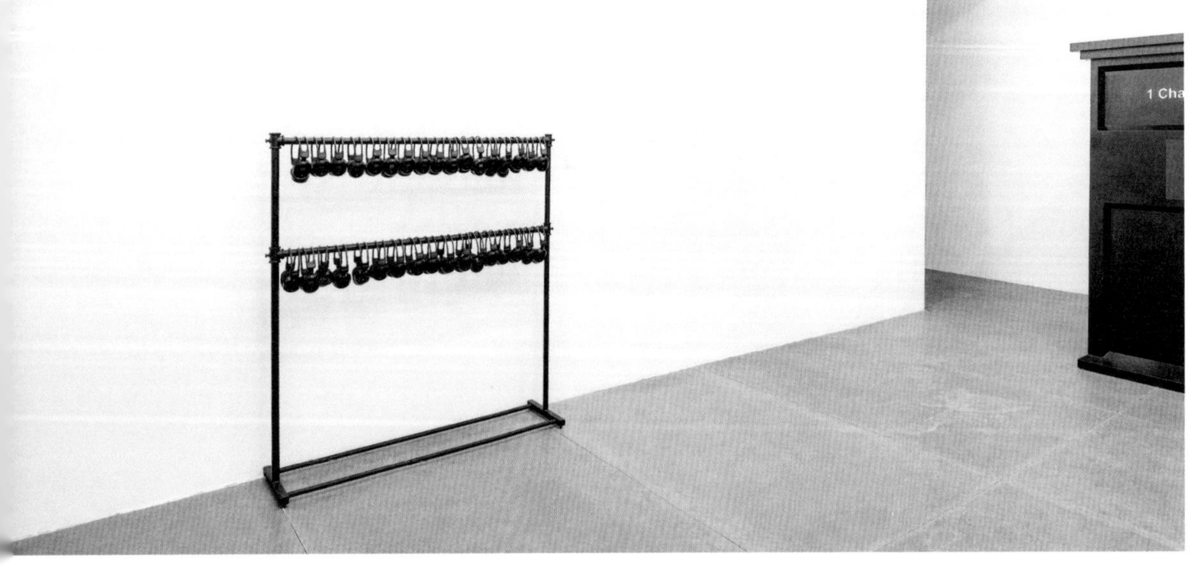

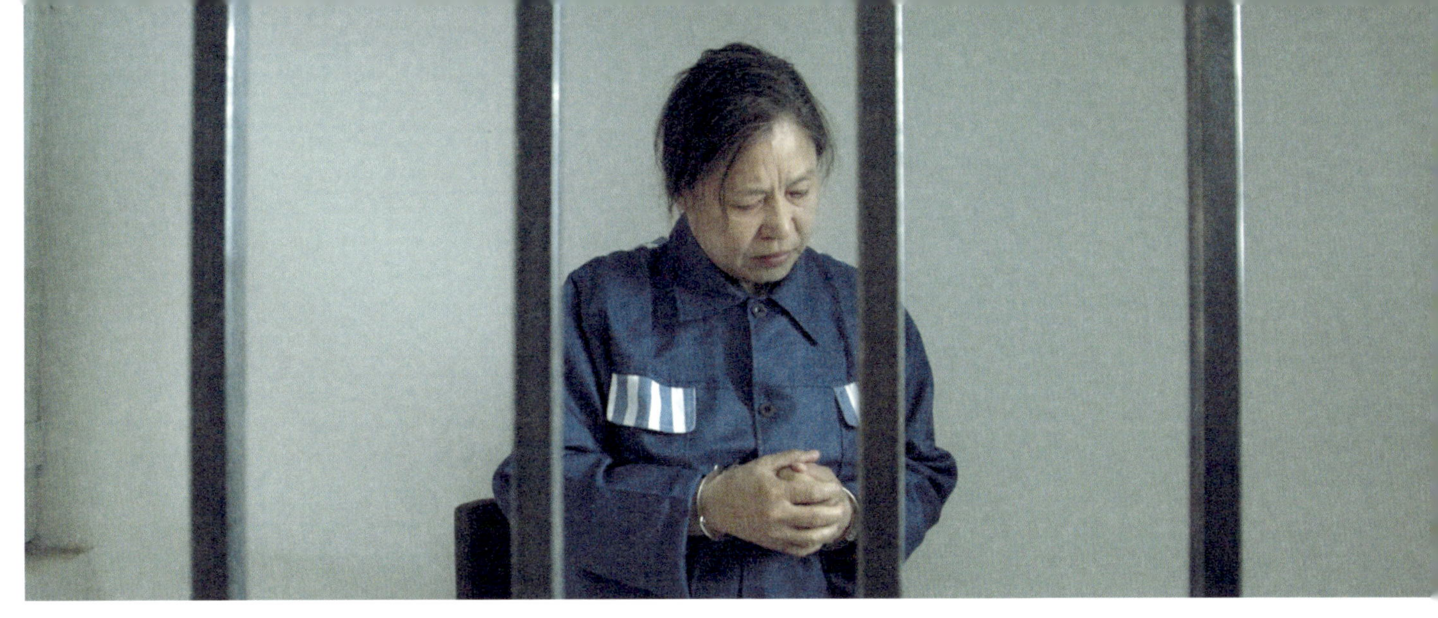

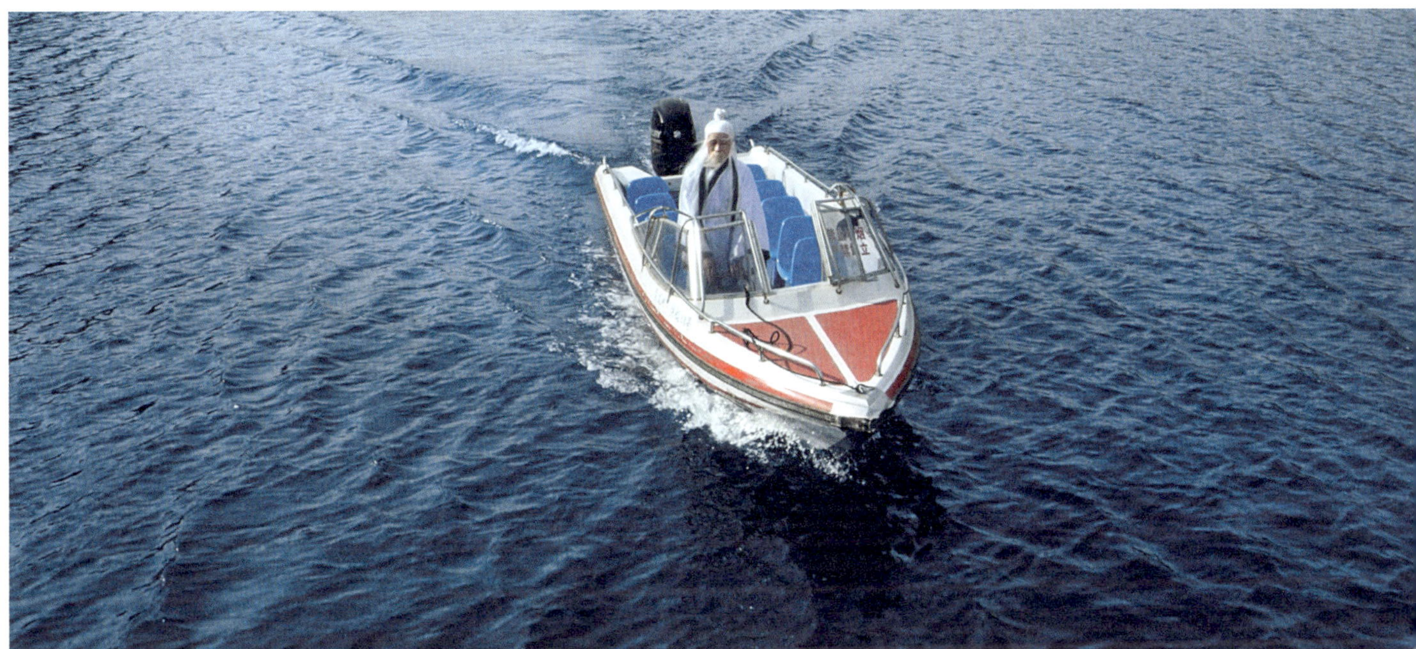

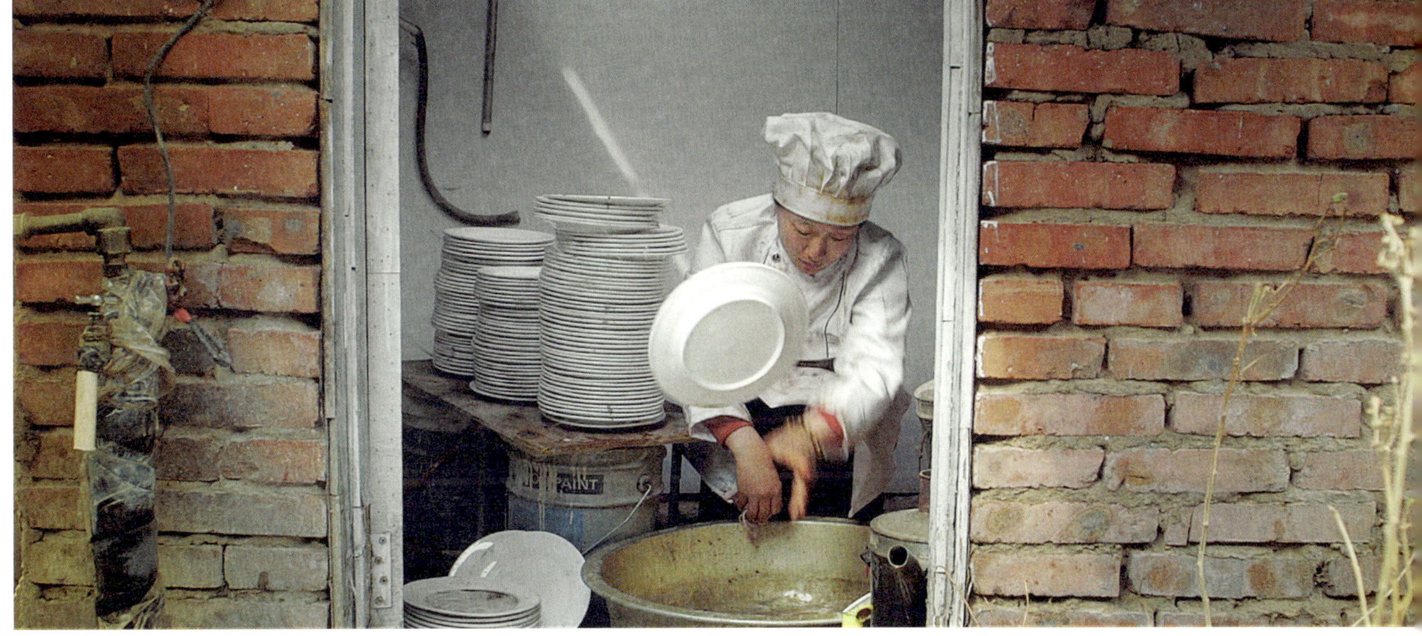

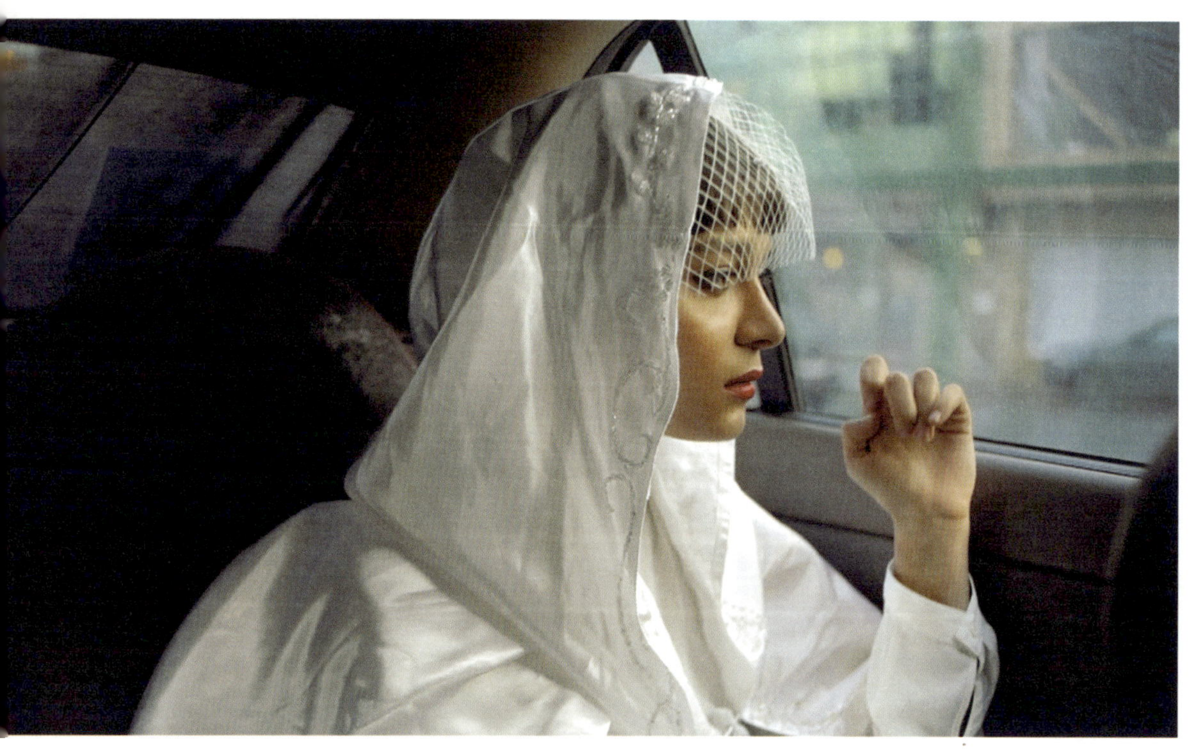

Tao Hui
The Dusk of Teheran
2014
Single-channel HD video
4′

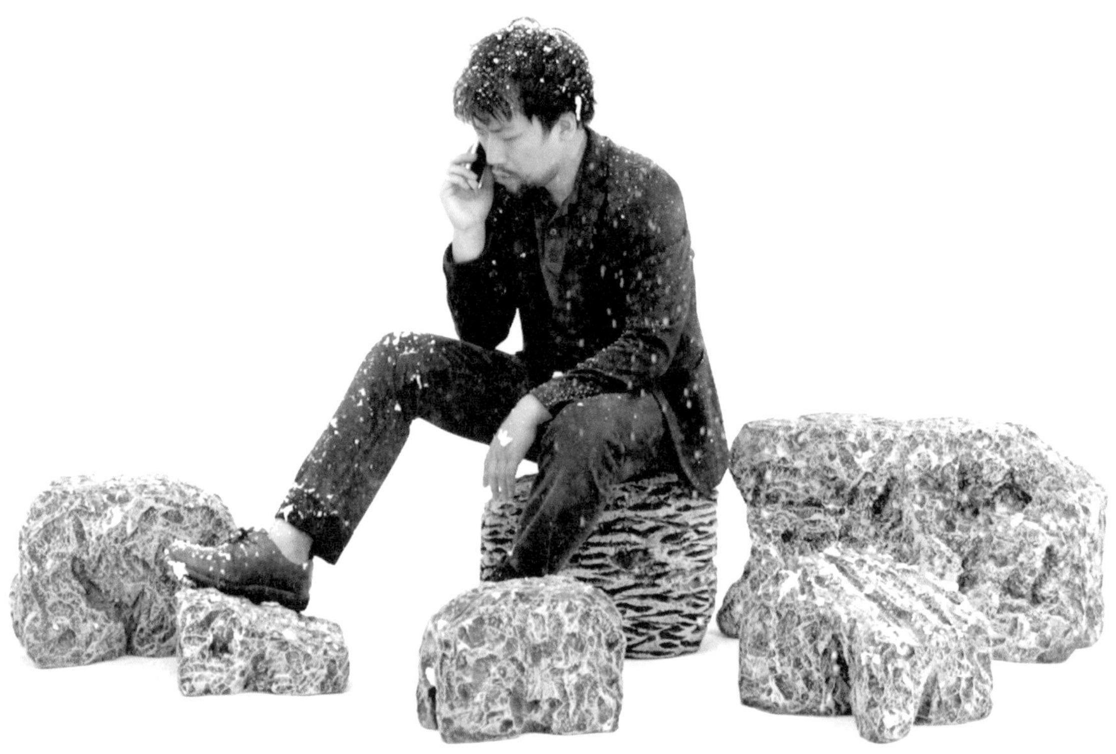

Tao Hui
Excessive
2015
Single–channel HD video
19′32″

XU QU

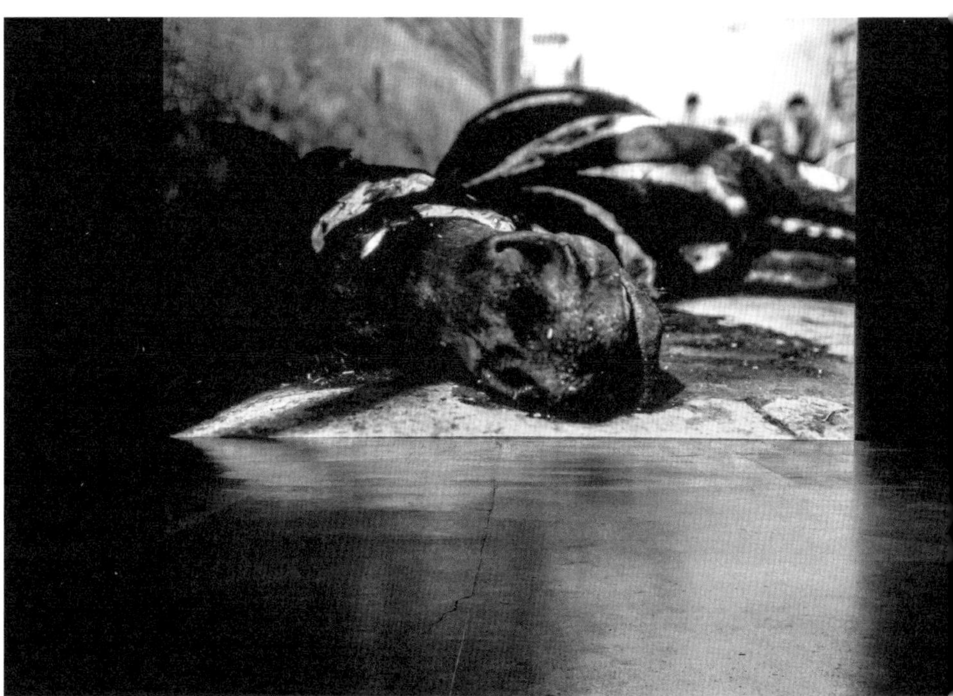

Xu Qu
Zebra
2015
Single-channel HD video
8'32''

THE
SCALE
OF
MISDEEDS

ZHANG XIYUAN

In the summer of 2011, Xu Qu stepped aboard the *Qiongsha III*, a navy resupply ship moored at Yongxing (Woody) Island in the South China Sea. As the ship left the dock, the deep azure blue and endless expanse of the sea made a profound impression on the artist. This breathtaking scene would later loom large as an important theme in Xu's work. The palm trees along the beach at Yongxing, the sailboats and the untroubled horizon inspired a relaxed feeling of contentment. But the scene also brought to mind the false veneer of moderation in political events, from the nine-dash line drawn in the South China Sea and subsequent territorial disputes to the dismissal of Hu Yaobang as Communist Party chairman and the 1989 political crisis. A deceptively mild tone is often employed for political expediency. For example, Hu's ousting was whitewashed as "a very mild measure" by then-party elder Deng Xiaoping during his 1987 meetings with both prime minister Mugabe and secretary of state Schultz. This artistic approach, incorporating an element of deliberate contradiction, together with a reflection on appearances, has been widely adopted by the current crop of Chinese artists, many of whom place great emphasis on social awareness and criticism.

The trip to Yongxing was arranged through family connections, enabling Xu to obtain permission for his visit from the military personnel guarding the base on the island. As an outsider on Yongxing, he found a unique poetic quality in the peaceful coexistence between the local fishermen going about their daily lives honouring centuries-old traditions and the military personnel with their modern equipment and practices. The following year, the Chinese government established the island as a municipality to govern the South China Sea territory, and then opened it up to tourists. The island's poetic contradictions, its peace and tranquillity, are now gone forever.

Many feel that the best way to analyse the creative paths followed by artists is by comparing each artist's body of work with those of his or her contemporaries. Xu's installation entitled *It's Not a Matter of Time* definitely presents an opportunity for this type of analysis. This work was exhibited as part of "ON | OFF: China's Young Artists in Concept and Practice", the 2013 show at the Ullens Center for Contemporary Art (UCCA) in Beijing, co-curated by Bao Dong and Sun Dongdong, which was widely hailed as the most comprehensive survey to date of work by young and mid-career Chinese artists born after the Cultural Revolution. The piece embodies Xu's development as an artist, by turns anachronistic and obscure, seemingly crafting his own stories, with an approach that is slightly off-kilter in comparison with most art the public is accustomed to seeing. *It's Not a Matter of Time*, which was installed

in a corner of UCCA's exhibition hall, is a work in two
parts. A white plaster forearm rested on a black marble
pedestal, pointing to a single white porcelain cup and
saucer at its side, which was refilled every day by the
staff of the Timezone Café across the street from UCCA.
The second part consisted of two large plastic water jugs
mounted at different heights on the wall, held in place
by metal bars reaching up from the floor. The jugs were
replaced each morning by the man who usually delivered
water to the museum, only to be destroyed later in
the day using the fire axe propped at the ready against
the wall. Xu's re-creation of "afternoon coffee" and
"daily water" both paid tribute to the Fluxus movement
and represented a continuation of the creative trajectory
begun by the artist while studying at the Braunschweig
University of Art. The piece poked fun at the occasional
absurdity of art's usual focus. The staff members refilling
the water and the coffee performed their tasks in
complete silence to better reveal the soundscape of the
museum, the visiting public and all of the exhibition's
installations. This juxtaposition was intended to inspire
visitors to question the usual authorities who give
meaning to everyday events in our lives, whether artistic
or otherwise. Apparently, the work had little effect at *ON
| OFF*. The cups of coffee were ignored by most visitors,
though the leaking water almost damaged the museum's
heating system.

Xu's "Currency Wars" (started in 2014) series
shares its title with a recent Chinese bestseller critical
of the developed world's financial hegemony and giving
vent to conspiracy theories. The title comes from an
argument put forward in 2010 by Guido Mantega, Brazil's
finance minister, who used the phrase when noting that
governments across the globe were competing to lower
their exchange rates as a way of lifting their economies
after the financial crisis. Xu uses different watermarks
of banknotes from around the world to create colourful
abstract compositions, a "currency of paintings", thus
expressing the impact of the financial system on the arts
and reflecting on how art often becomes a commodity.
With each work in the series, Xu seems to present
a growing nihilism, manifesting itself not only in
the crudely repeated mosaic, but also by placing the
paintings, when displayed together, on movable stands,
using space models and games of chance to randomly
control their movements. Xu thus simulates the
circulating properties of currencies, while reminding
us that works of art are exchanged for money in the
market and become tokens of wealth. Nevertheless,
in his concept a faint hope remains that aesthetics
is still the highest form of ethics, in a world where
art is often reduced to symbols and transactions.

Zebra is a brown pony that has just been slaughtered
and bled out. Contemplating a photograph of a live

African zebra, the horse butcher is slicing off strips of the animal's hide, exposing the white fat underneath. Soon the dead pony is "sketched" into a zebra. It is a cruel, senseless scene, a seeming waste of life. Using animal carcasses to challenge the limits of public taste is akin to the extreme art of the Post-Sense Sensibility movement from 1999 to 2001 in China, which triggered a media firestorm. This focus on flesh and blood is intended to raise awareness about how society has become numb to violence. The past two decades of economic growth, accompanied by significant social and psychological changes, are intriguing and daunting to comprehend. Society has moved towards an overemphasis on the practical, indifference to others and utter commercialisation. The artist seems to be expressing Chinese society's bewilderment and identity crisis: has China's socialist market economy degenerated into a kind of national socialism?

Situated just outside the eastern 5th Ring Road encircling Beijing, Heiqiao Village is a Chinese-style stronghold of black realism. Built on landfill, it provides abundant low-rent housing for migrant workers, with abandoned pets wandering the streets. Ironically, it is also an enclave of art studios, bringing together the best and worst of contemporary art, from the vulgar to the outstanding. Two years ago, Xu revealed to me that he had devised a prank programme he calls "Festival". On his way to the studio each morning, he buys some meat to feed to the poor stray dogs, and then videotapes them as they eat. Each time one of these videos is selected for an art exhibition, he stops the feedings and only resumes once the exhibition has ended.

In 1998, the Asian financial crisis and the anti-Chinese riots in Indonesia occupied the front pages. Xu Qu had just turned twenty and his rebellious spirit went beyond just wearing odd clothes. As a member of the first generation born after the onset of the economic reform in China, Xu was not surprisingly turning into quite a sceptic. However, his "radical" youth was perhaps driven more by hormones than genuine political awareness. While studying at the Nanjing Institute of Fine Arts, he recruited several students to form the band Rubber Tube. He played bass guitar and also sang lead vocals. This was at a time when underground rock was very popular in China. The group gave performances praised as "ceremonial" and "hard core" among the coterie of rockers in Nanjing.

The artist seems at his best producing works of ridicule and satire. At the same time, he has benefited greatly from the internationalisation of Chinese contemporary art and an artistic scene in China arguably more open than ever before. His future as an artist will hinge upon the identity he commits to, and the ideologies he endorses or criticises.

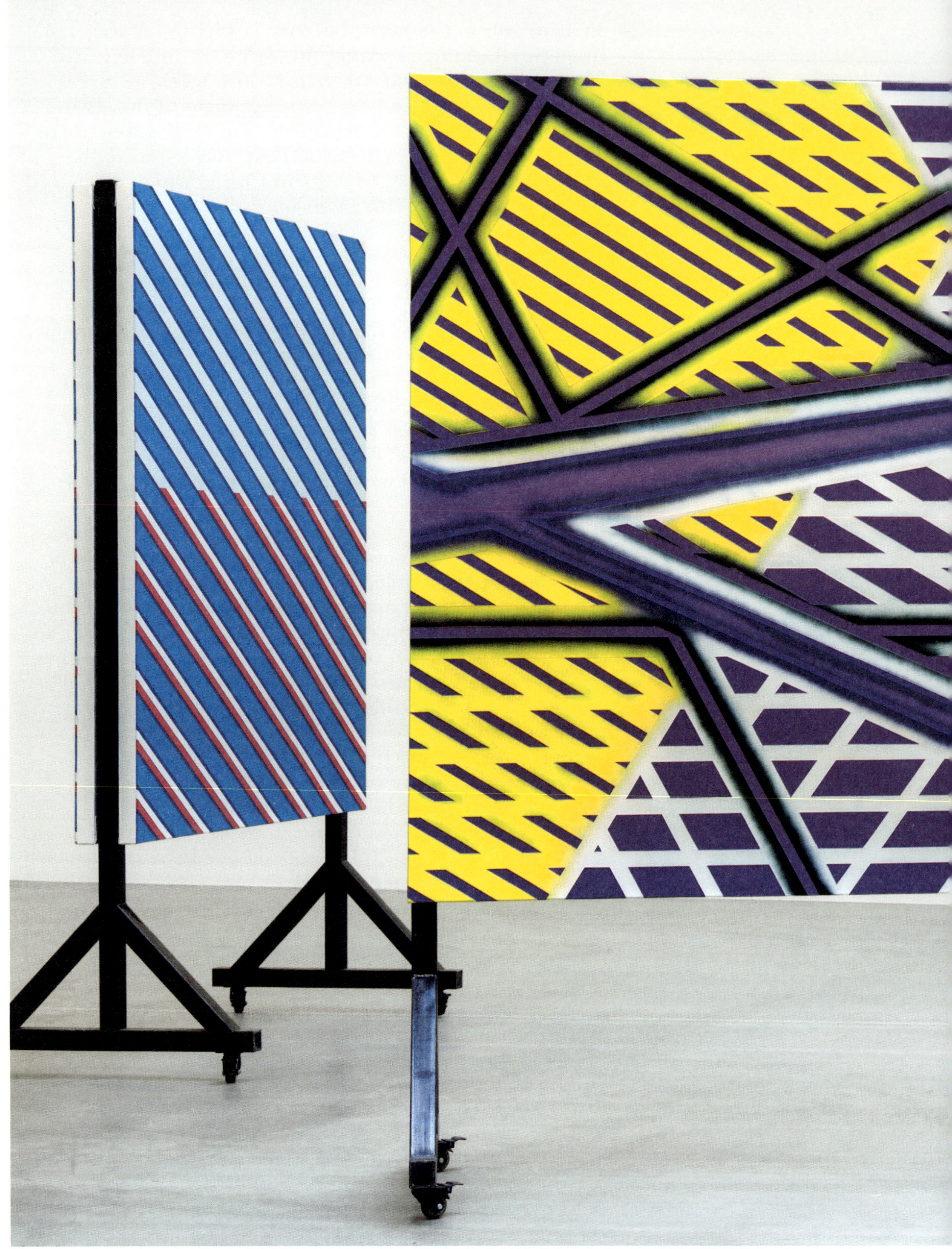

Xu Qu
Currency Wars
2015
Installation view at Almine Rech Gallery, Brussels

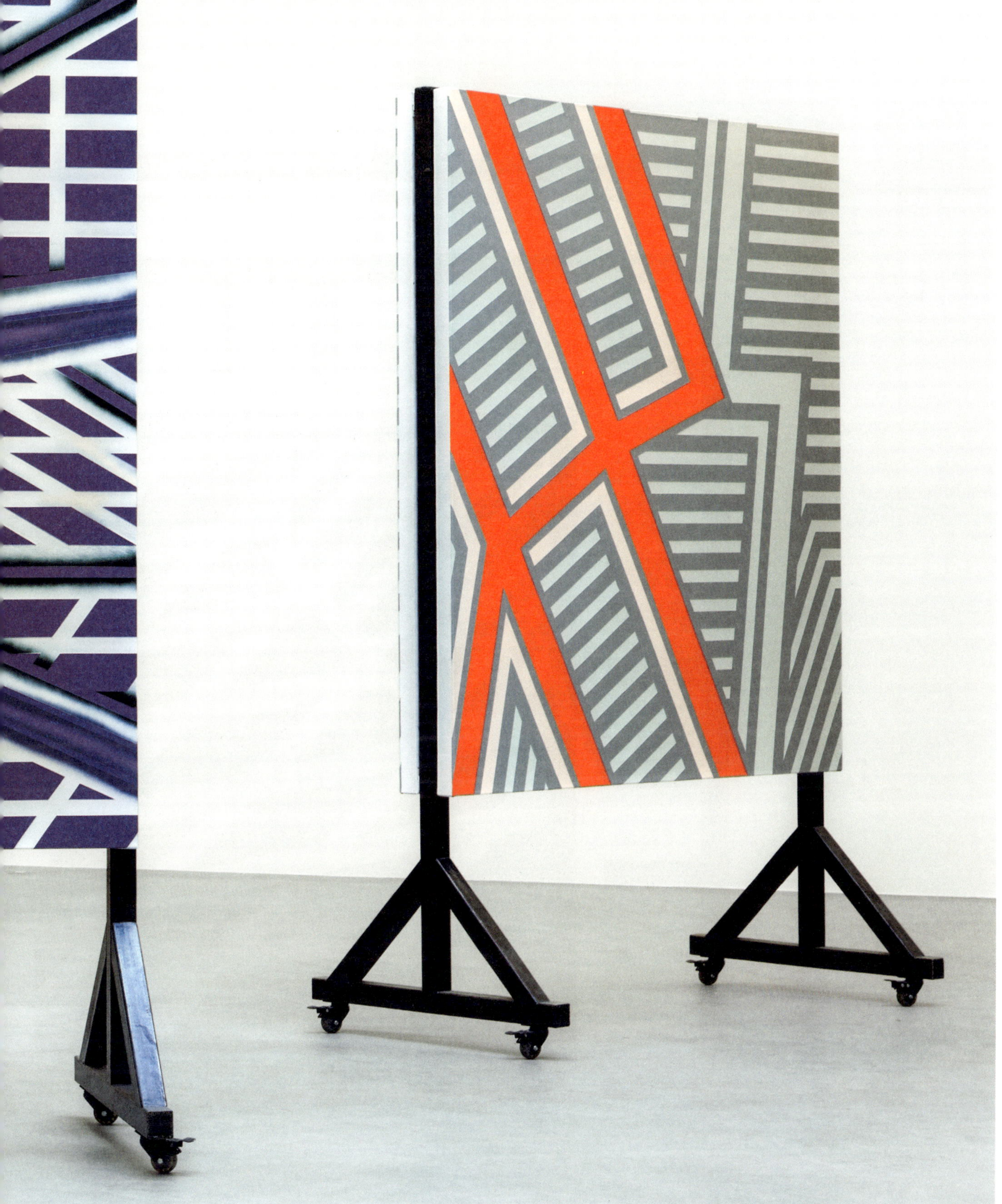

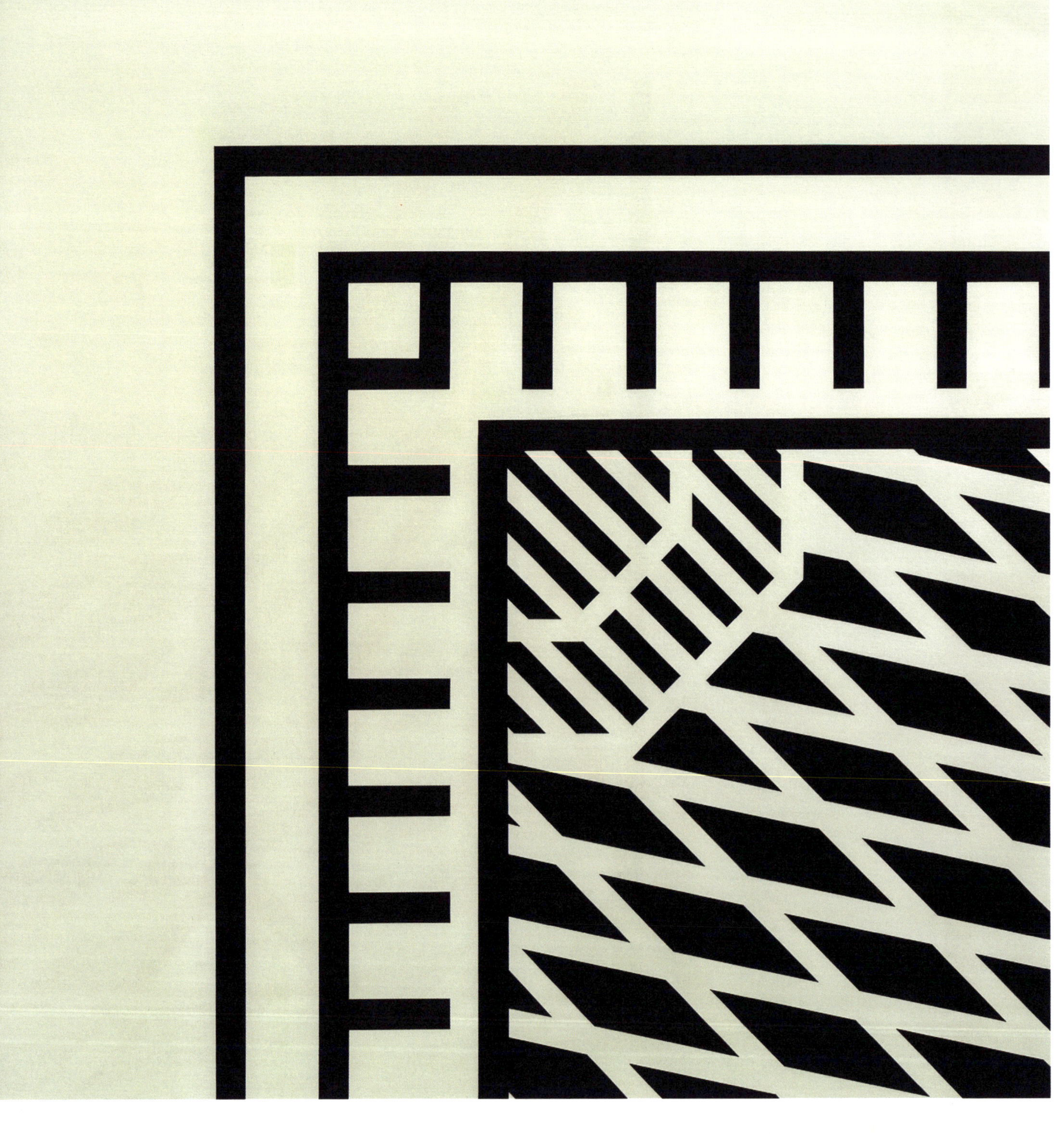

Xu Qu
Currency Wars – Dollar 2, New
2015
Acrylic paint on canvas
150 × 158 cm

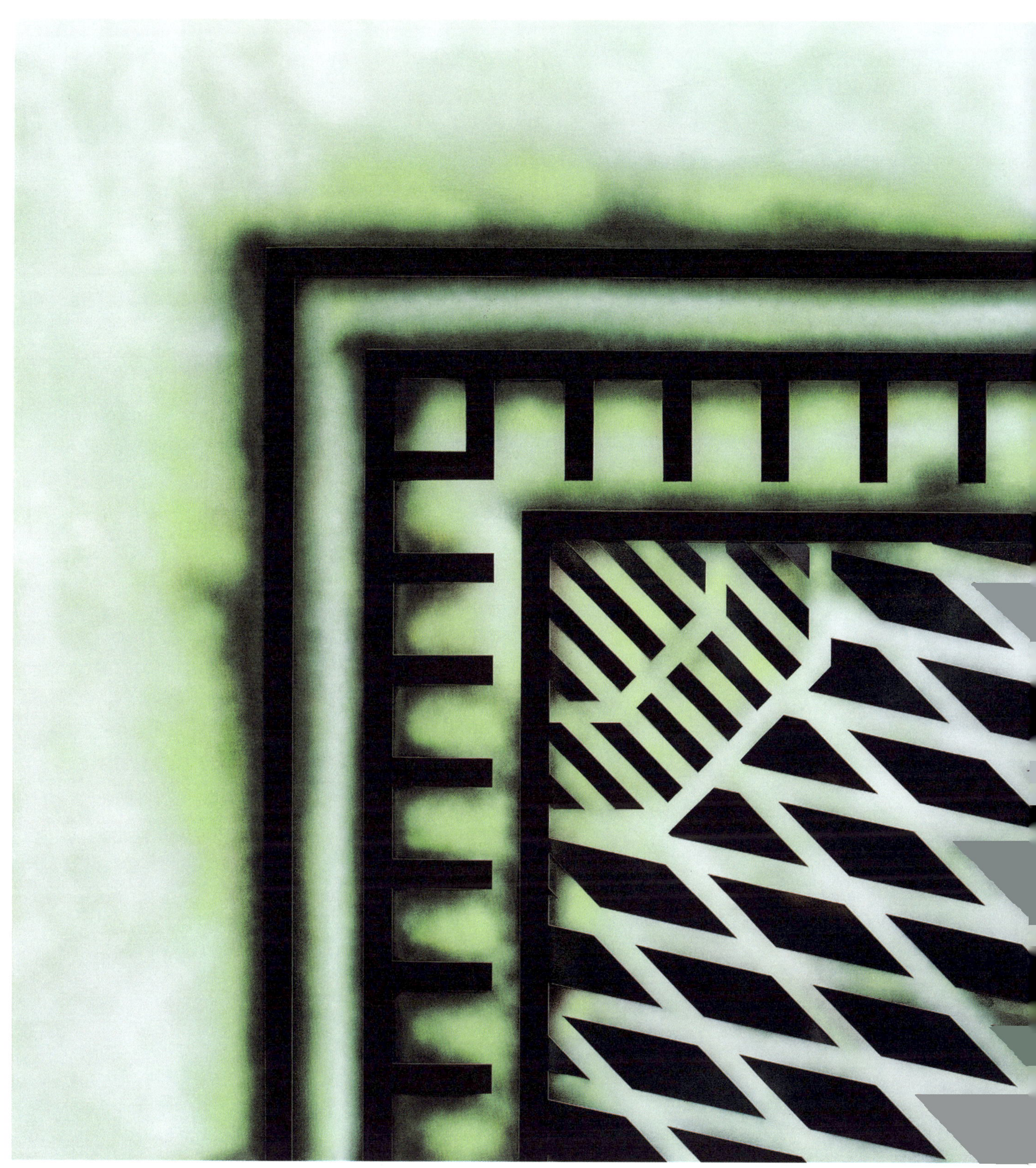

Xu Qu
Currency Wars – Dollar 2, Old
2015
Acrylic and spray paint on canvas
150×158 cm

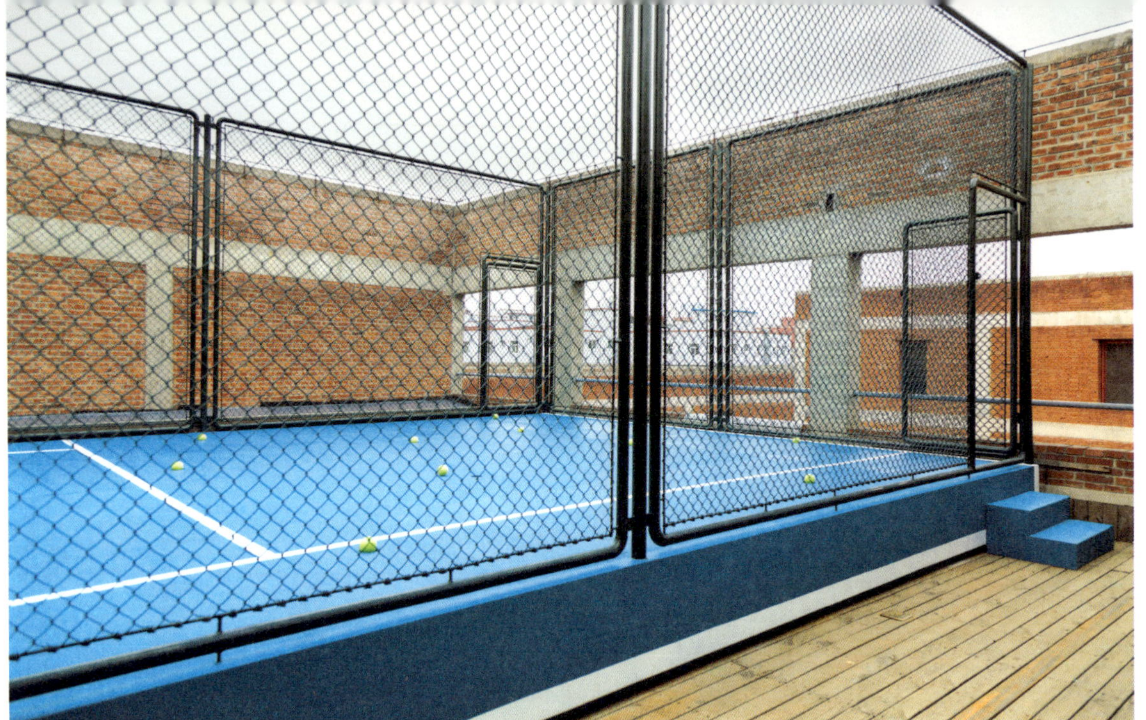

Xu Qu
Tennis Court
Installation view at Taikang
Space, Beijing, 2014

144

XU
QU

Xu Qu
Performance at
"On/Off: China's Young
Artist in Concept
and Practice"
Ullens Center
for Contemporary Art,
Beijing, 2014

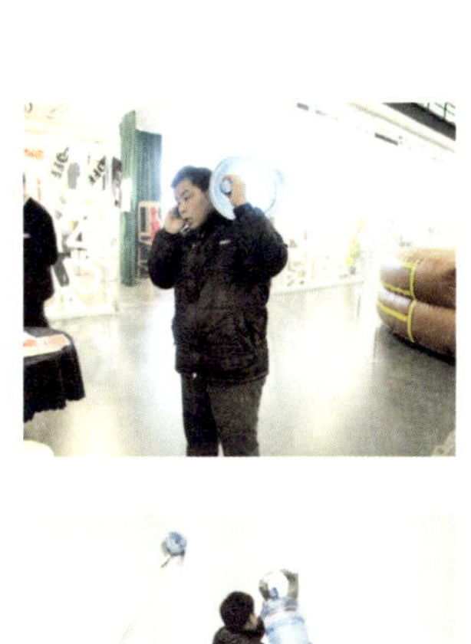

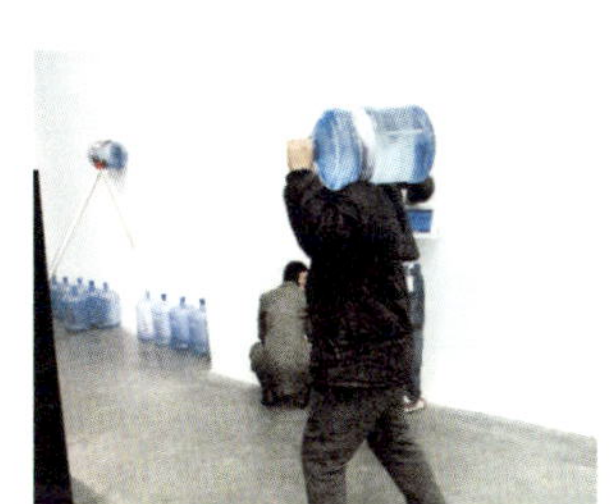

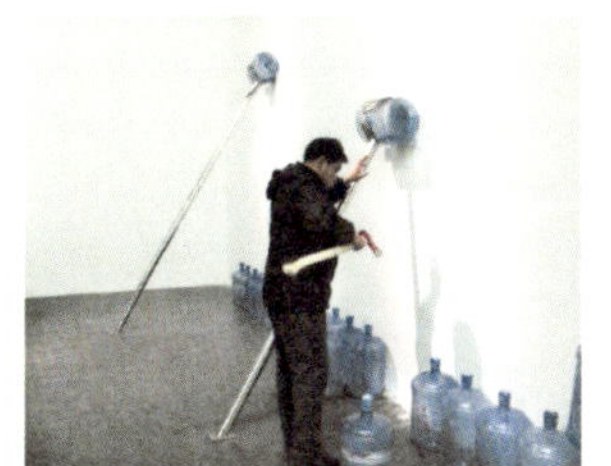

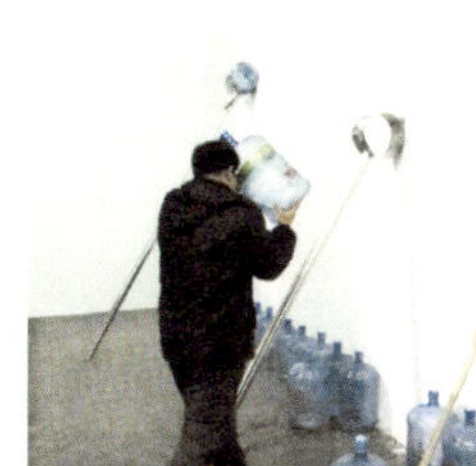

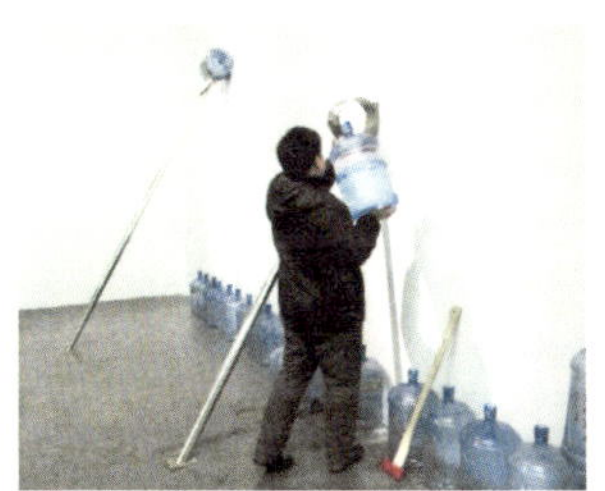

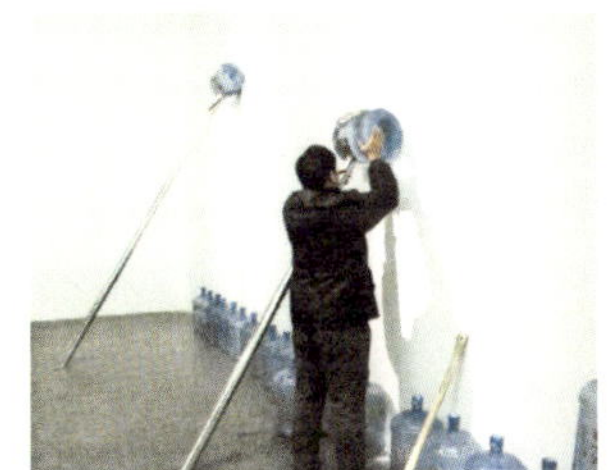

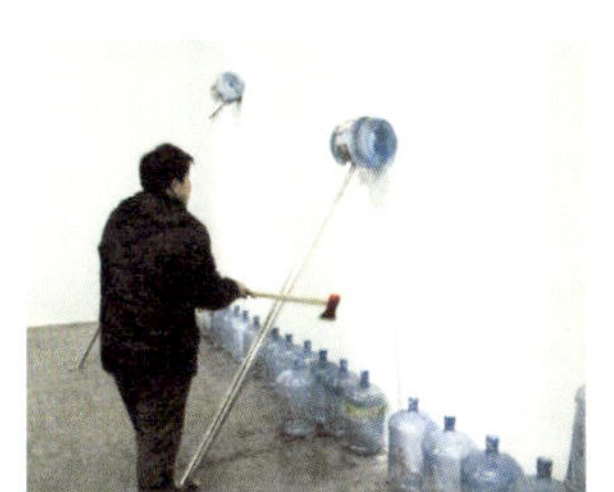

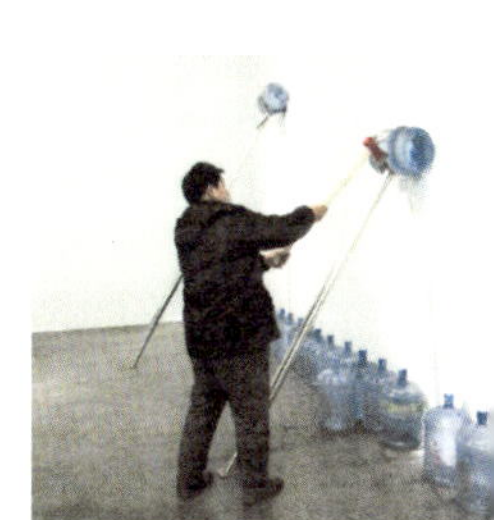

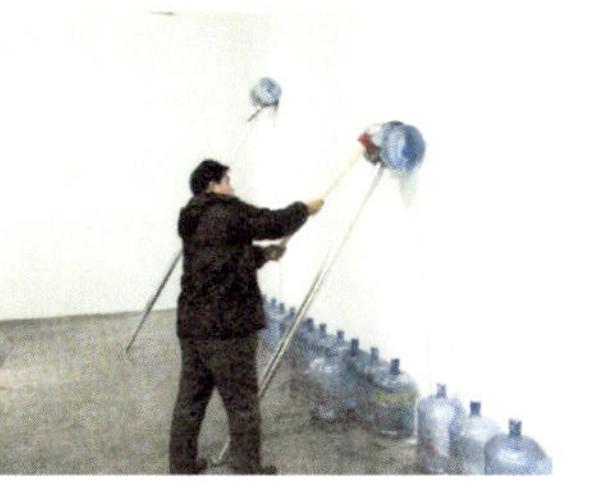

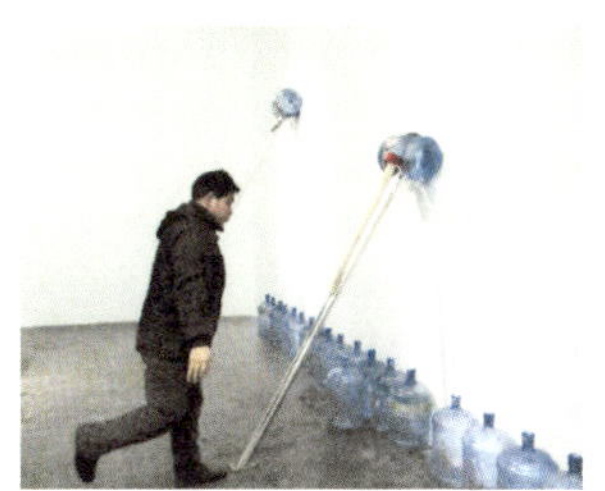

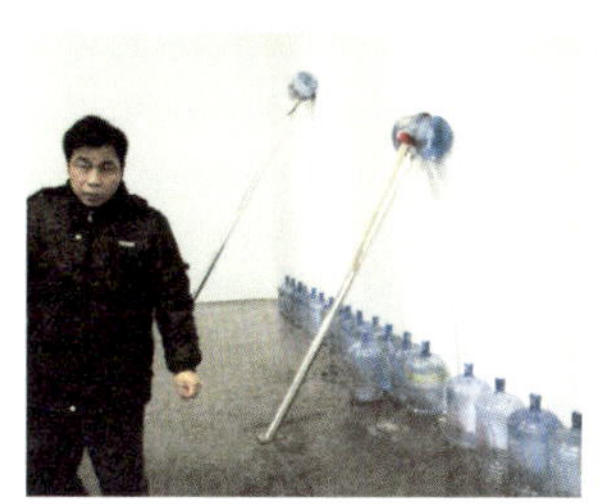

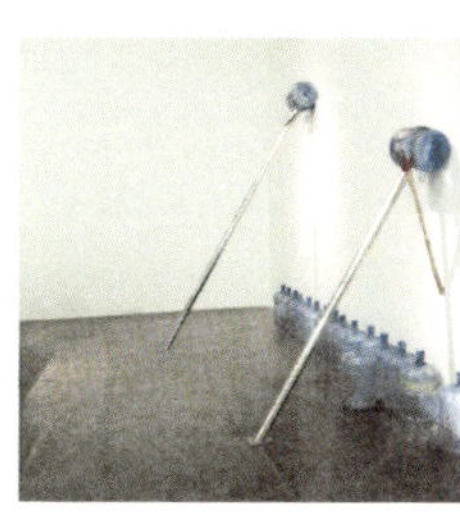

XU ZHEN

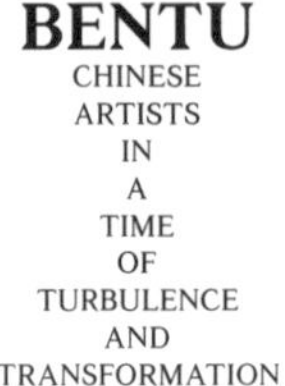

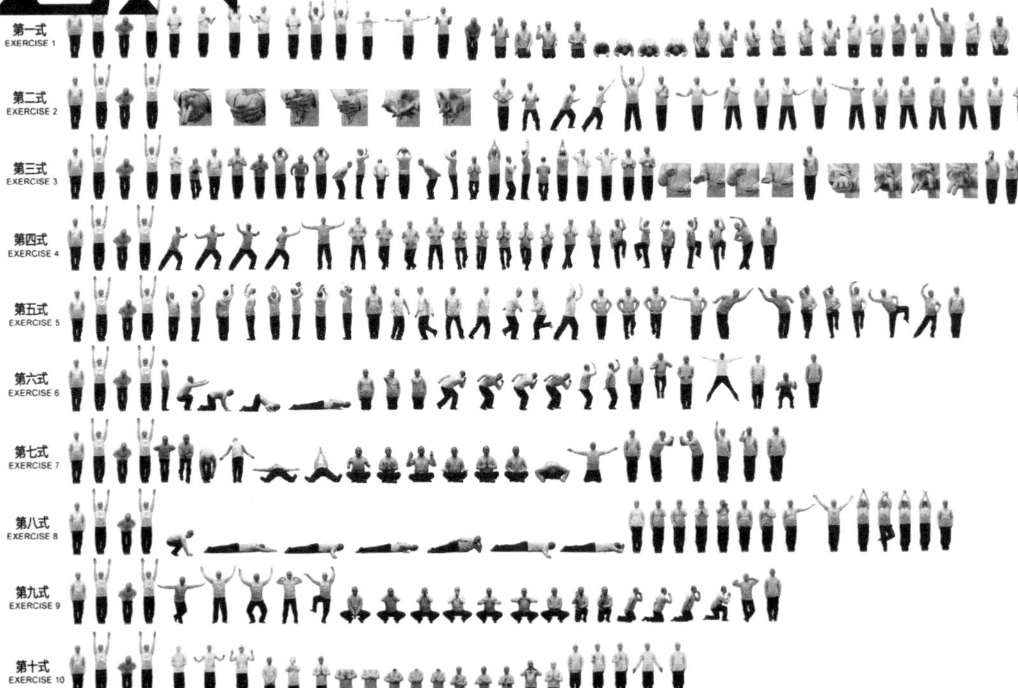

Xu Zhen
Physique of Consciousness
2011
Poster

MADEIN COMPANY AS HALLMARK

PHILIP TINARI

After emerging on the Shanghai scene in the late 1990s, Xu Zhen quickly created a role for himself that was equal parts artist, organizer, entrepreneur and provocateur. His exploits co-curating important underground exhibitions such as "Supermarket: Art for Sale" (April 1999) and "Fan Mingzhen and Fan Mingzhu" (November 2002) are legendary in the history of a Shanghai art world then finding its feet. For his own part, in 2001 he became the youngest Chinese artist to participate in the Venice Biennale, showing his video *Scream*, in which pained cries attract and then quickly lose the attention of passers by in crowded places. He was 24. Xu Zhen's subsequent decision to co-found the non-profit exhibition space and organizing agency BizArt was transformational for many artists in his city. So too was his move in 2005 to launch a bulletin-board-style website for the discussion of exhibitions, artist portfolios and many other topics that remains, a decade later, an important online forum for the field. Throughout this period, Xu Zhen was making works that blurred the boundaries between performance, installation and institutional critique: witness his piece for the 2004 Shanghai Biennale in which he simply sped up the clock atop the Shanghai Art Museum, itself a former colonial horse-racing clubhouse, so that the hours passed in seconds – much to the confusion of people living nearby.

Like a number of other great artists in China, some of his best works turn on a kind of ironic deceit: witness the time in 2006 when he and friends "climbed Mount Everest" to bring back an icy chunk from its summit equal in height to the artist – 1.86 meters – displaying this papier-mâché trophy alongside a documentary film of his adventure with winking assurances that the whole thing was real. More controversially, in 2008 he painstakingly re-created the scene of a Pulitzer-Prize-winning 1993 news photograph of a vulture waiting for a starving Sudanese infant to die, which later drove the photographer Kevin Carter to suicide after harsh criticism of his failure to intervene and save the child. Xu Zhen's tableau vivant, staged in Beijing's Long March Gallery under the title *The Starving of Sudan*, featured a robotic bird and an African toddler set amidst huge quantities of dirt, desert vegetation and hot lights. And yet for as long as he has been active Xu Zhen's artistic oeuvre has been but the most important physical manifestation of his wide-ranging practice as convener, informant and poster child of the Shanghai art scene – roles that he assumed by default under the same name, "Xu Zhen", under which he produced his work.

Seen in this context, his decision in 2009 to consolidate all of these functions under a single moniker other than the one on his national ID card makes a lot of sense. "MadeIn Company" might be read then less as a critique of corporate capitalism than as a "studio name" like those that Chinese painters had assumed for centuries. The initial idea behind MadeIn, aside from housing these many disparate functions and removing them, if only by a step, from the artist's hand and brand, was to transform a team of studio assistants into an enterprise focused on the development of new cultural "product". MadeIn's decision in 2013 to rerelease "Xu Zhen" as a label under which certain product ranges could circulate came as no surprise. The idea of the artist studio run as an entity has precedents throughout recent art history – from the industrial metaphor behind Andy Warhol's Factory, to Jeff Koons's research-and-development heavy operation, to more marketing and merchandising-driven entities like Damien Hirst's Other Criteria and Takashi Murakami's Kaikai Kiki. What distinguishes Xu Zhen is the way he appropriates the notion of the "company" less as an economic actor than a social space. To work for MadeIn Company is an all-encompassing endeavour not unlike working at a Chinese state-owned enterprise under the height of Socialism during the 1950s and 1960s, where the "work unit" mediated one's entire social existence.

What then of the works of "Xu Zhen produced by MadeIn Company", as the labels now insistently read? We might say that they aspire to a kind of sceptical universalism, as most clearly manifested in a piece like the *Physique of Consciousness* (2011). For this, Xu Zhen and the MadeIn team researched gestures, postures and movements that recur across the world's religious and cultural traditions. They then processed them into a set of yoga-like calisthenics, to be practised by curious aspirants. From there they began a sprawling Google-image search for these particular body poses as they appear in archaeological artefacts, museum holdings and news photographs, finally editing these into a "museum" of mounted images in glass vitrines, telling a cross-cultural history based entirely on form. Here he offers, in essence, a humorous recapitulation of recent trends in museology and art history, from the reconceptualization of how to display objects previously considered "primitive" in the opening of the Musée du Quai Branly, to the aesthetic proposition of "migration of form" which underlay Roger Buergel and Ruth Noack's 2007 Documenta XII, to the historiographical shift towards decentring modernism through research into its non-Western genealogies.

It is perhaps from this investigation that the idea for the "Eternity" series of sculptures first arose. Initial manifestations were straightforward, with head-to-head juxtapositions of masterpieces from the Eastern and Western traditions: the Elgin marbles topped with key examples of Northern Sui statuary, or a bodhisattva from the Tianlongshan grotto (now held in a Japanese collection) supporting the *Victory of Samothrace,* complete with its gravity-defying boat-shaped pedestal. These explorations have since evolved to look at more subtle juxtapositions of entirely Western sculptural forms, as in the 2015 piece *Thousand Arms European Classical Sculpture,* in which key specimens from ancient Greece onward are arranged in a line such that their outstretched arms resemble the Buddhist deity Guanyin. The current piece suspends Jean-Pierre Cortot's 1834 *The Soldier of Marathon Announcing Victory* above the first-century Roman *Dying Gaul.* That both pieces come from the collection of the Louvre, and that this appropriation is made by a Chinese artist for a French institution and audience, hints at the playful new cultural possibilities of a moment in which exchange can work in an infinite number of directions, along a wide variety of axes.

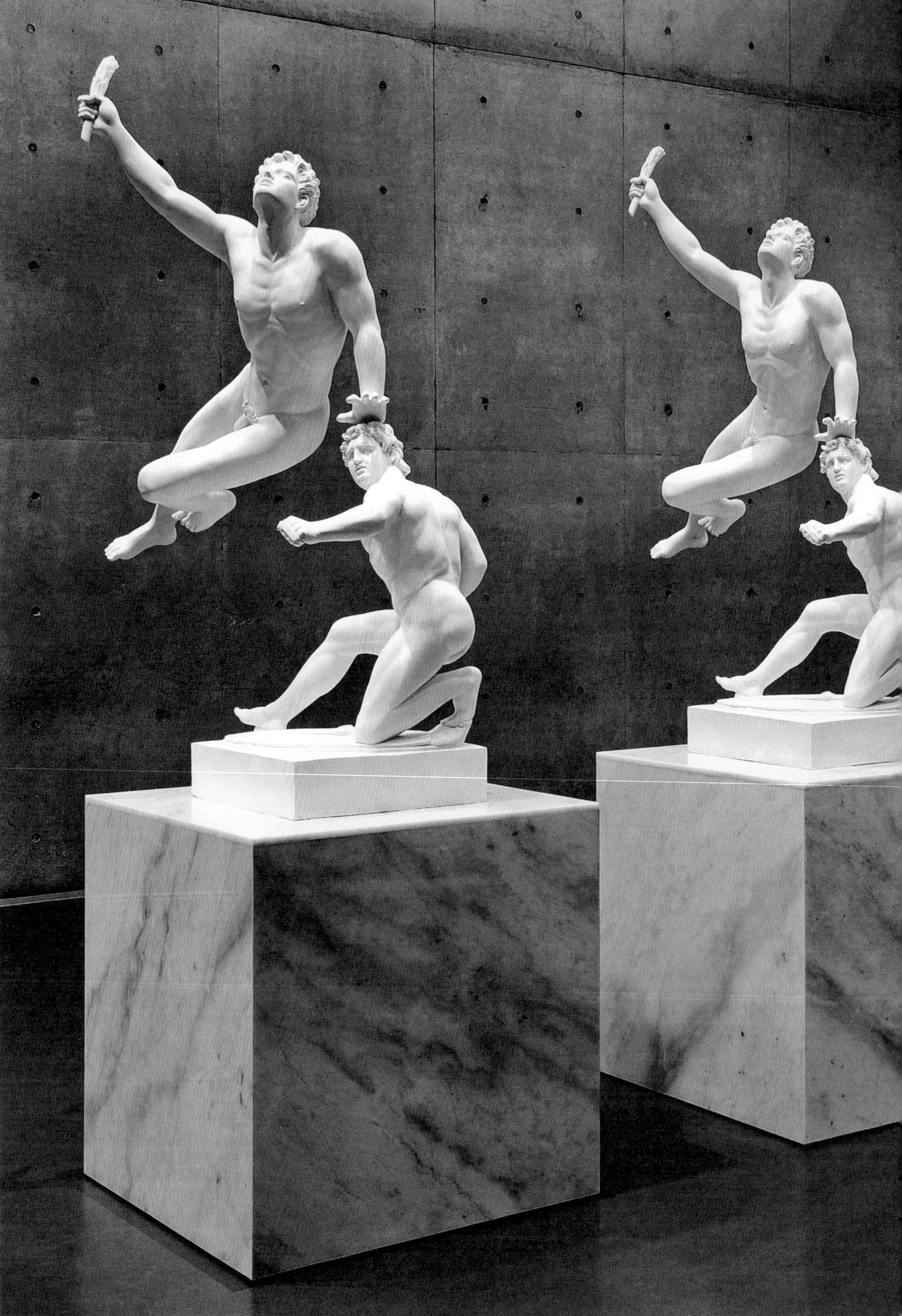

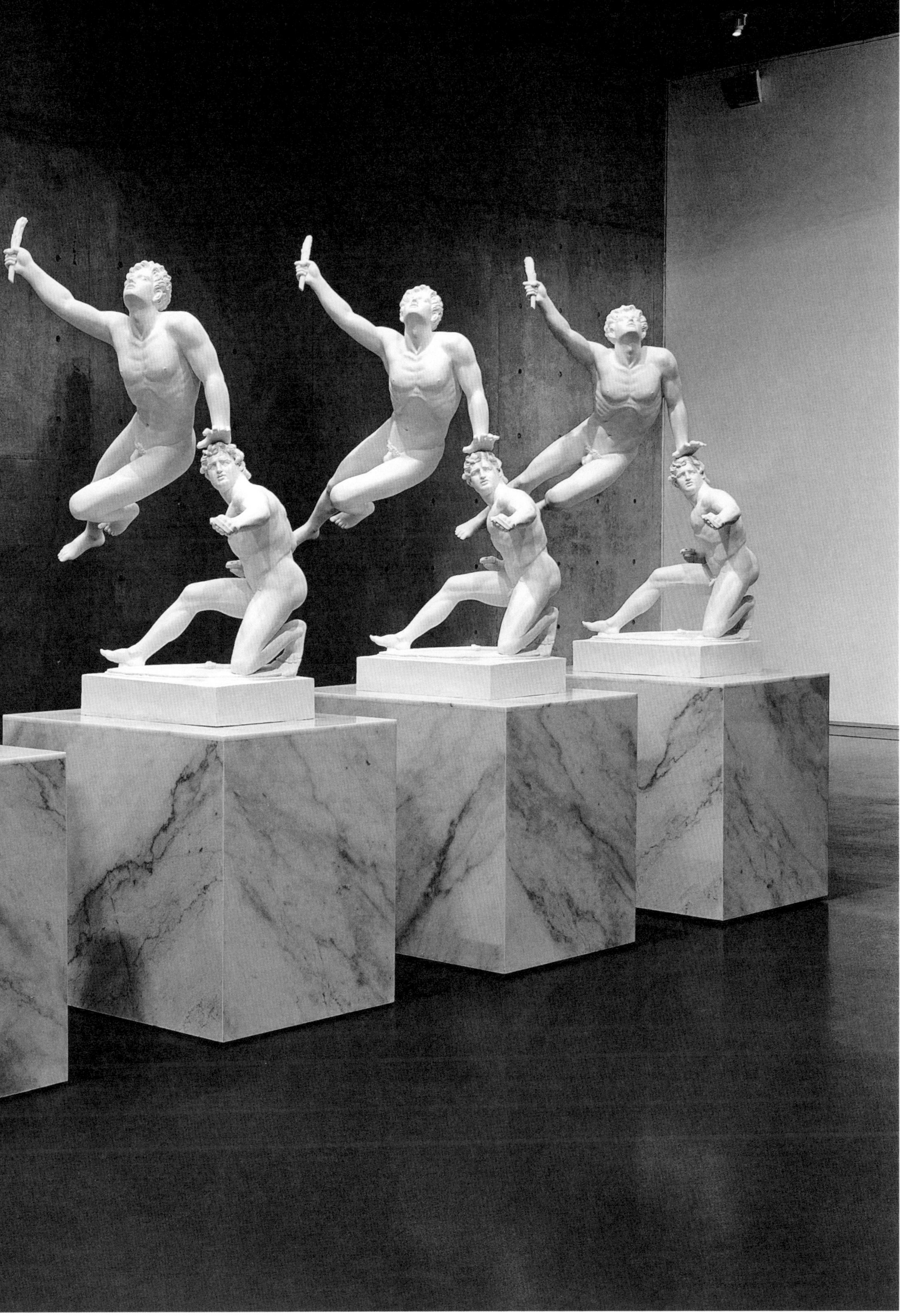

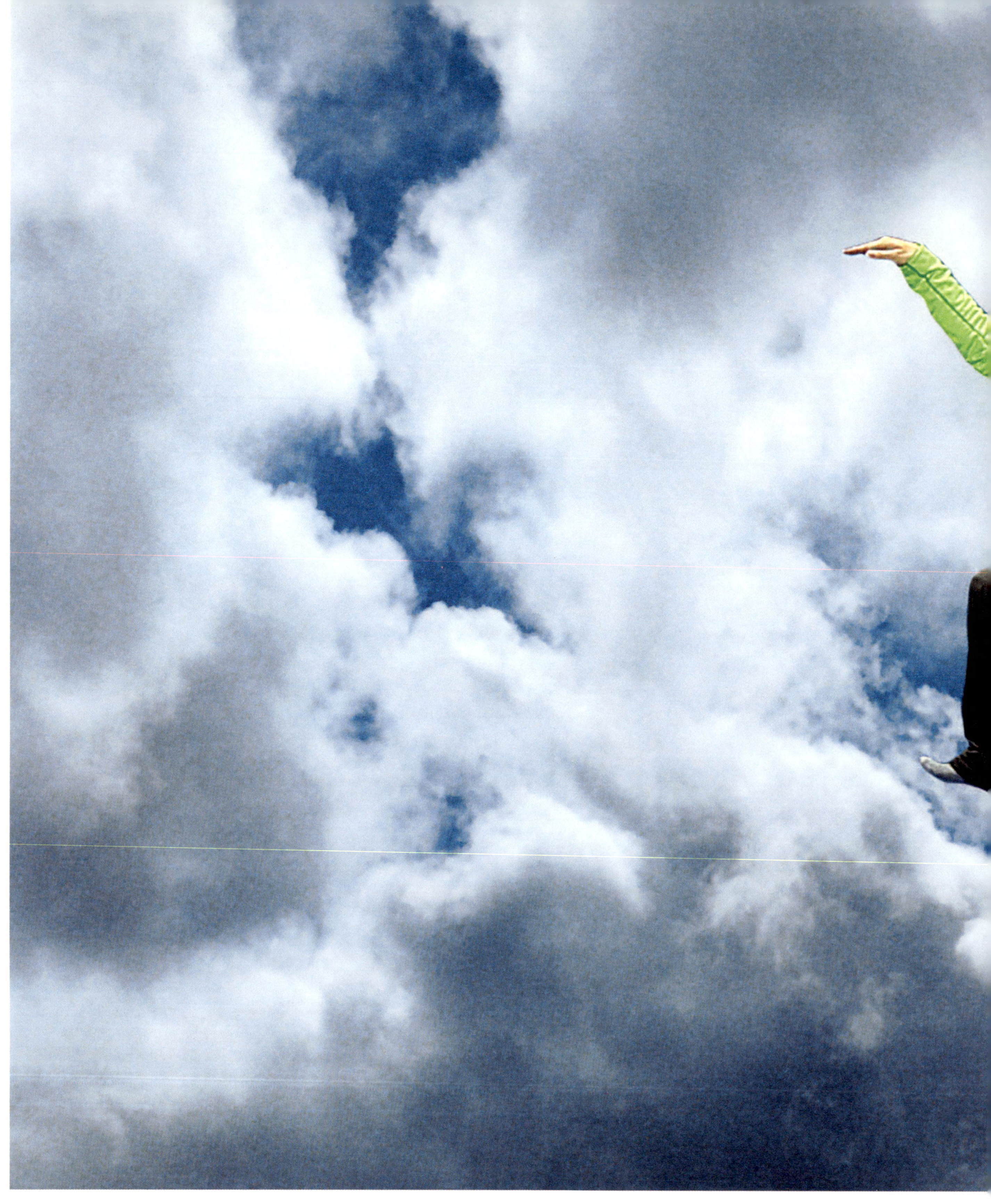

Preceding double page
Xu Zhen
*Eternity – The Soldier of Marathon
Announcing Victory, Dying Gaul*
2014
Glass-fibre-reinforced concrete,
marble grains, marble, metal
157 × 96 × 250 cm

Xu Zhen
Physique of Consciousness
2011
Video

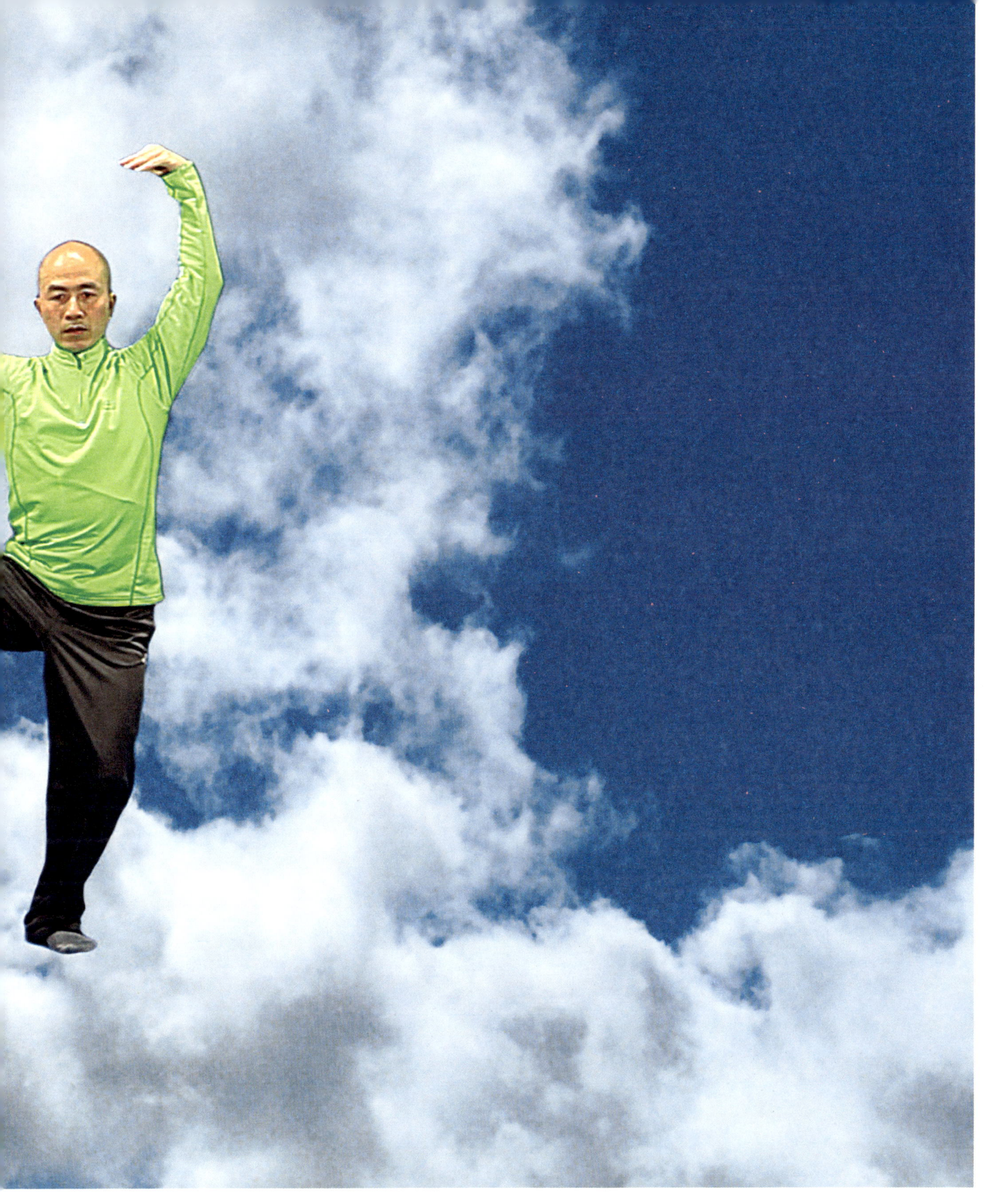

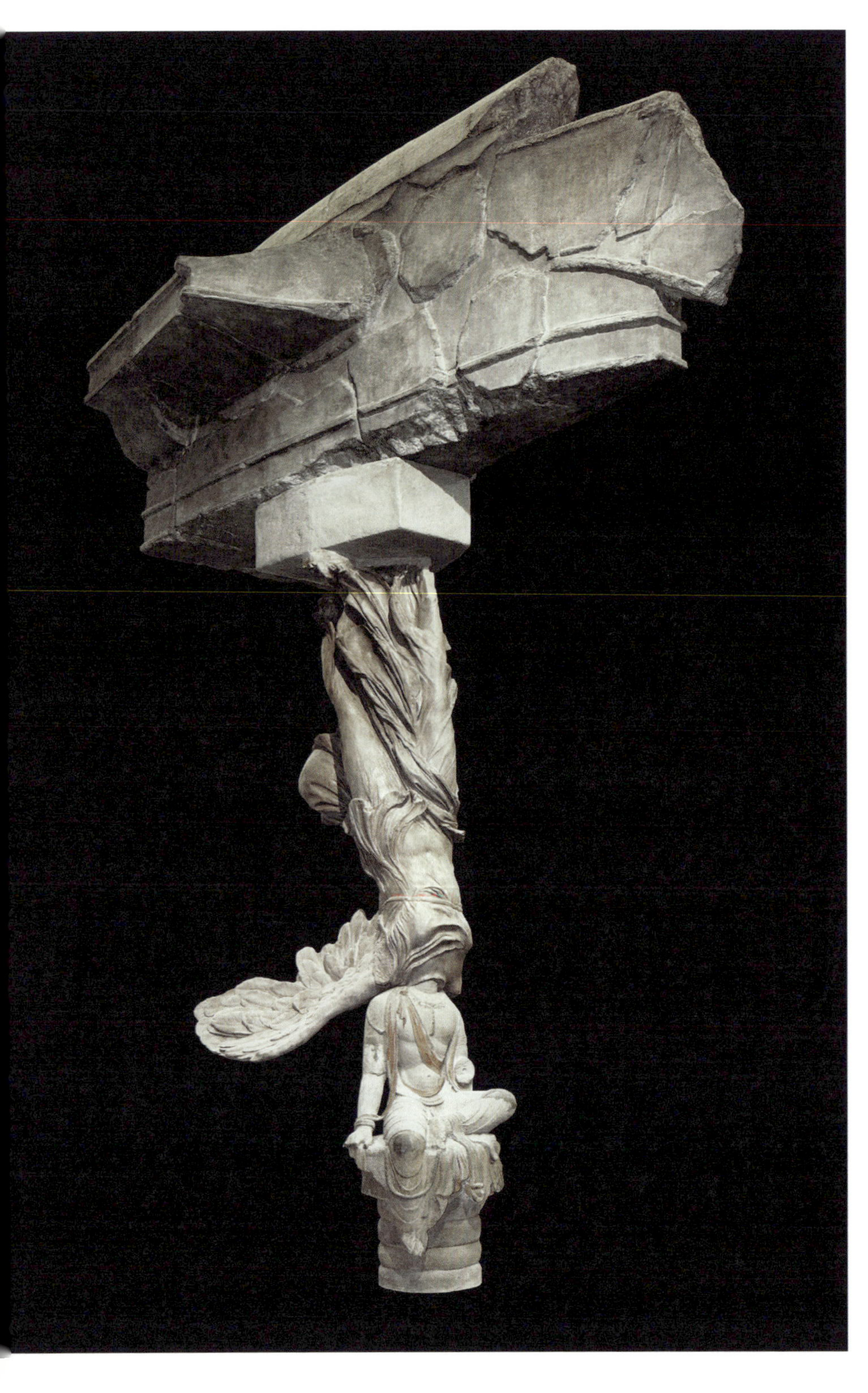

Xu Zhen
Eternity – Winged
Victory of Samothrace,
Tianlongshan Grottoes
Bodhisattva
2013
Glass fibre, steel, concrete
626 × 460 × 230 cm

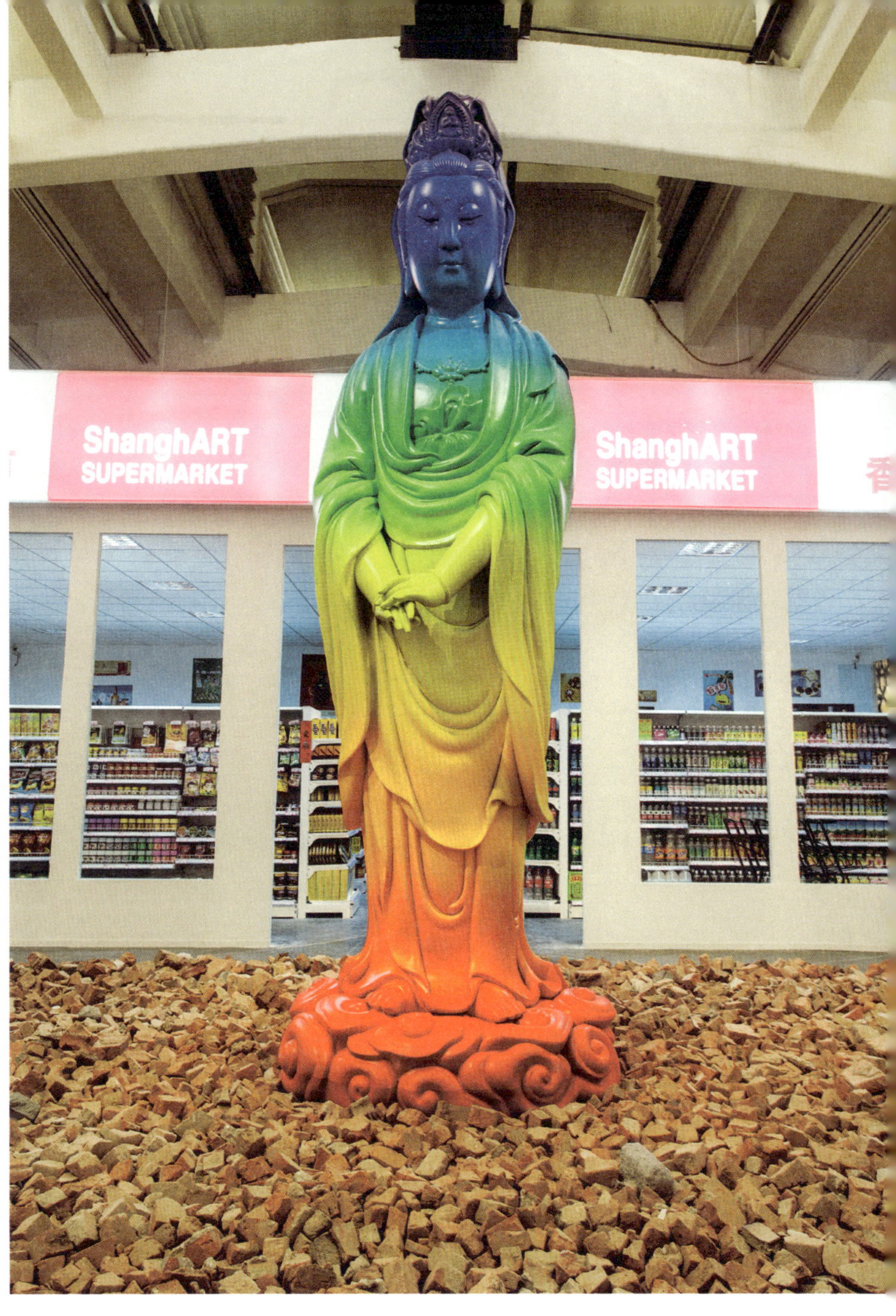

Xu Zhen
New
2013
Stainless steel, paint
130 × 110 × 402 cm

YANG FUDONG

Yang Fudong
*Blue Kylin – A Journal
of Shandong*
2008 – 2015
Video installation

BLUE
KYLIN

AIMEE LIN

Blue Kylin (2008–2015) is one of Yang Fudong's most notable works from his post-2005 period. Prior to this, the artist had been focusing his efforts on the five-part, black-and-white cinematic masterpiece *Seven Intellectuals in the Bamboo Forest* (2003–2007), before returning to his home in order to create a pseudo-documentary entitled *East of Que Village* (2007). Then, in 2006, on his way to Shandong where he was filming *Seven Intellectuals in a Bamboo Forest IV*, he passed through the historic town of Jiaxiang, home to a very particular bluestone. The grand spectacle of the quarries surrounding the town made such a deep impression on him that he was moved to return two years later in order to film *Blue Kylin*.

"Blue" is the colour of the stone; "Kylin", a magical animal in ancient China and a symbol of good luck. Jiaxiang is known as China's "stone town" whose high quality bluestone has been honoured by sculptors since the Han dynasty (206 BC–220 AD). Wu Hung, the eminent art historian of the late Eastern Han dynasty (25–220 AD), cites the funerary monuments of Wu Shi Shrine as the fullest artistic expression of Jiaxiang's stonework. In recent decades, China's explosion of wealth has created a market for traditional stone carvings, such as mythological beasts, *paifang* (street arches) and *huabiao* (ceremonial columns). Today, these objects can be found scattered throughout cities and the countryside, even inside the extravagant "palaces" of China's new rich. Responding to this demand, Jiaxiang and its surroundings have been transformed into a huge quarry site, dedicated to all stages of stone production: quarrying, transportation, processing and carving. For Yang Fudong, however, it is the white dust enveloping the area that reveals something significant about conditions on the bottom rung of the production ladder: how the workers, the artists and creators, really live.

Running like a thread throughout Yang Fudong's work is the question: what is art? As today's art bows to reality, and creativity is subordinated to the production process, artist and audience alike must engage with this question. Yang Fudong's reaction is not a verbal one, but rather an in-depth and in-place act of observation and cinematography. For example, *Seven Intellectuals in the Bamboo Forest* (2003–2007) presents a group of anonymous youths in a utopian spirit world. 2007's pseudo-documentary *East of Que Village*, depicts an ordinary, northern Chinese village's quotidian social structures; and in *Blue Kylin* (2008–2015) we are confronted by the involvement of society's lowest rung in the production of art. Despite their variant forms, these three works deal with artists' distance from reality: *Seven Intellectuals in the Bamboo Forest* tells us that the spiritual has no place in the real world;

East of Que Village shows us that distant reality is unreachable; *Blue Kylin* places the artist at a positional extreme – when confronted by his distance from reality, the artist surrenders any attitude, judgement and conception. He melts into the world under his lens, adopting an attitude of worldly tolerance.

Whenever Yang Fudong conceives a new work, he outlines the several phases the project will undergo over its lifespan. The series called *Blue Kylin* includes several different versions designed for specific exhibitions, each one to be regarded as a distinct chapter. The first, *Blue Kylin I* appeared in the 2008 *Guangzhou Triennial Farewell to Post-Colonialism* in Guangdong Museum of Art and comprises a 20-minute video with a 16-segment video loop and an unfinished bluestone sculpture. In this initial version, the video of the quarry and the loop of mining scenes show the artisanal sculptors starting the process of creating a traditional sculpture from scratch. It ends in front of the final piece: a massive, broken, unfinished *huabiao* sculpture, the manual and mechanical marks traced onto it transforming the exhibition hall into a funerary farewell to a grandiose civilization, amputated from reality, cut off from the "present".

In 2009, Yang Fudong's solo exhibition *Dawn Mist, Separation Faith* at the Zendai Museum of Modern Art in Shanghai included the second chapter of his work, *Blue Kylin II*. This version consists of three large video projections and 29 slide projectors displaying two thousand photos. By using the photographic slideshow, Yang Fudong was experimenting with ideas surrounding stop-frame film-making. Since movies, originally known as motion pictures, are consecutive displays of individual frames, slideshows can be interpreted as slower movies. Yang Fudong would further his reflections and experimentation on the dialectical relationship between photos and cinematography in his later works, such as 2013's *Push The Door Softly And Walk In, Or Just Stay Standing Where You Are* and 2014's *The Light That I Feel*, two examples of the single-frame movie.

The third chapter, *Blue Kylin/A Journal of Shan Dong* (2008), a five-screen video installation, was exhibited twice: in *West Bund 2013: A Biennial of Architecture and Contemporary Art Waterfront*, Xuhui District, and *Twin Tracks*, his solo exhibition at the Yuz Museum in Shanghai. This version included five unsynchronized videos projected onto five huge screens arranged around the hall. The length of each video varies from 19 to 42 minutes. This work is typical of his iconic immersive style that surrounds spectators in a barrage of images.

These three chapters bear witness to Yang Fudong's exploration of various cinematographic forms on the same topic: the first is a mixed installation of sculpture and video; the second a mixed installation of video and photography; the third, in his mature iconic style, a multi-screen video installation. According to Yang Fudong's original conception, *Blue Kylin* will have a final chapter, a return to the black-and-white photographic silent film. Perhaps the format's particular associations with the aesthetic of mourning will become the artist's unique commentary on naked reality.

Yang Fudong was born in Beijing in 1971. Shattered when his dreams of becoming a footballer failed to materialize, he turned to art. On graduating from the Central Academy of Fine Arts High School, he attended the Academy of Fine Arts in Hangzhou, majoring in oil painting. At the Academy, his senior project entitled *Stranger Project* (1993) required him to remain silent for three months. In 1998, he moved to Shanghai to study photography and film. Beginning with photography, *The First Intellectual* (2000) explores the evolution of the intellectual's mind. Yang Fudong's work focuses on the speculative relationships between various media formats: photography, video, cinematography, sculpture and painting. His early work targeted the contradictions within the urban intellectual's mindset when confronted with reality. In the last decade, while continuing to reflect on cinematographic forms, he developed a unique method of video installation in which images touch gently on mental states too elusive to be captured by words.

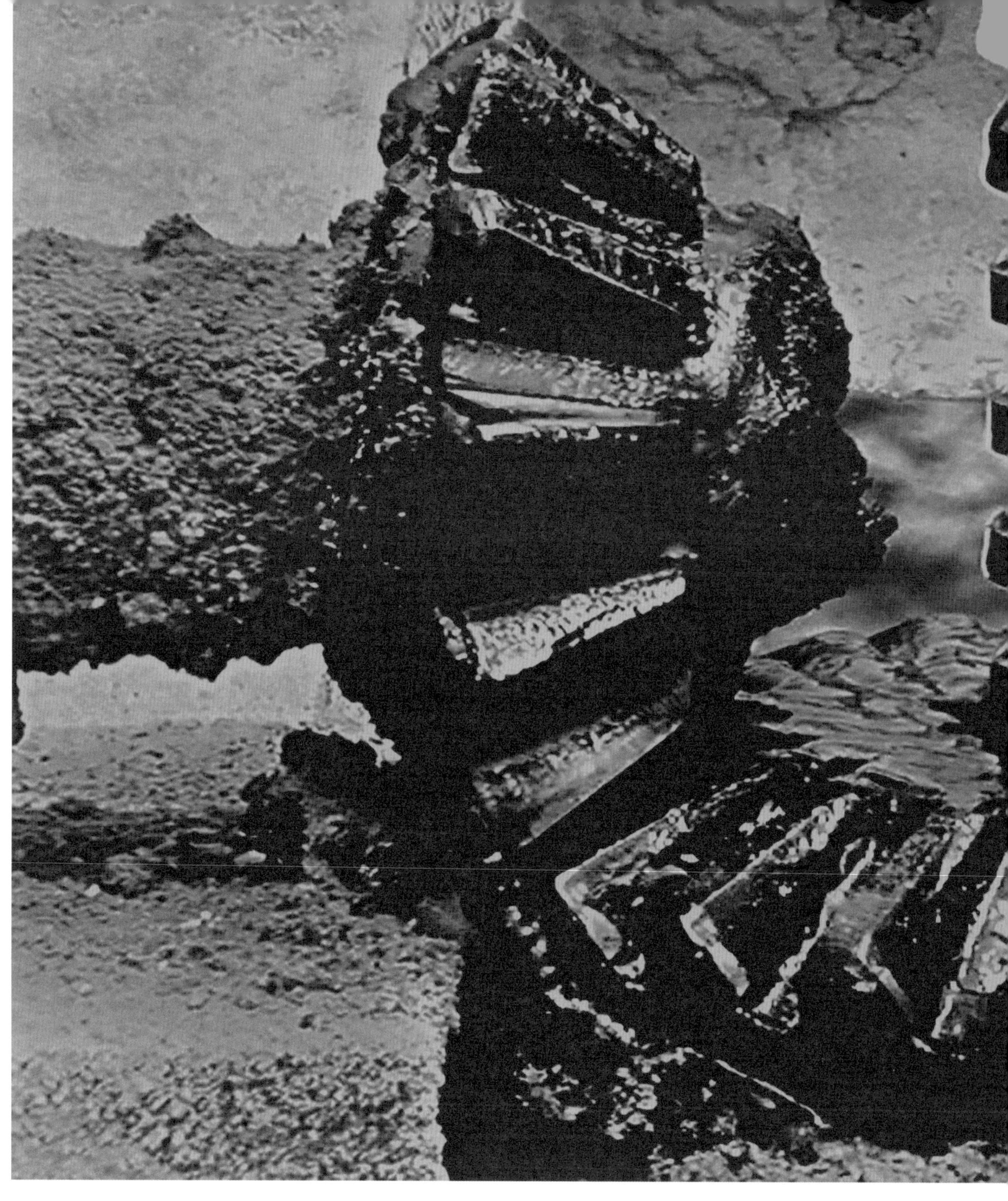

Yang Fudong
Blue Kylin – A Journal of Shandong
2008 – 2015
Video installation

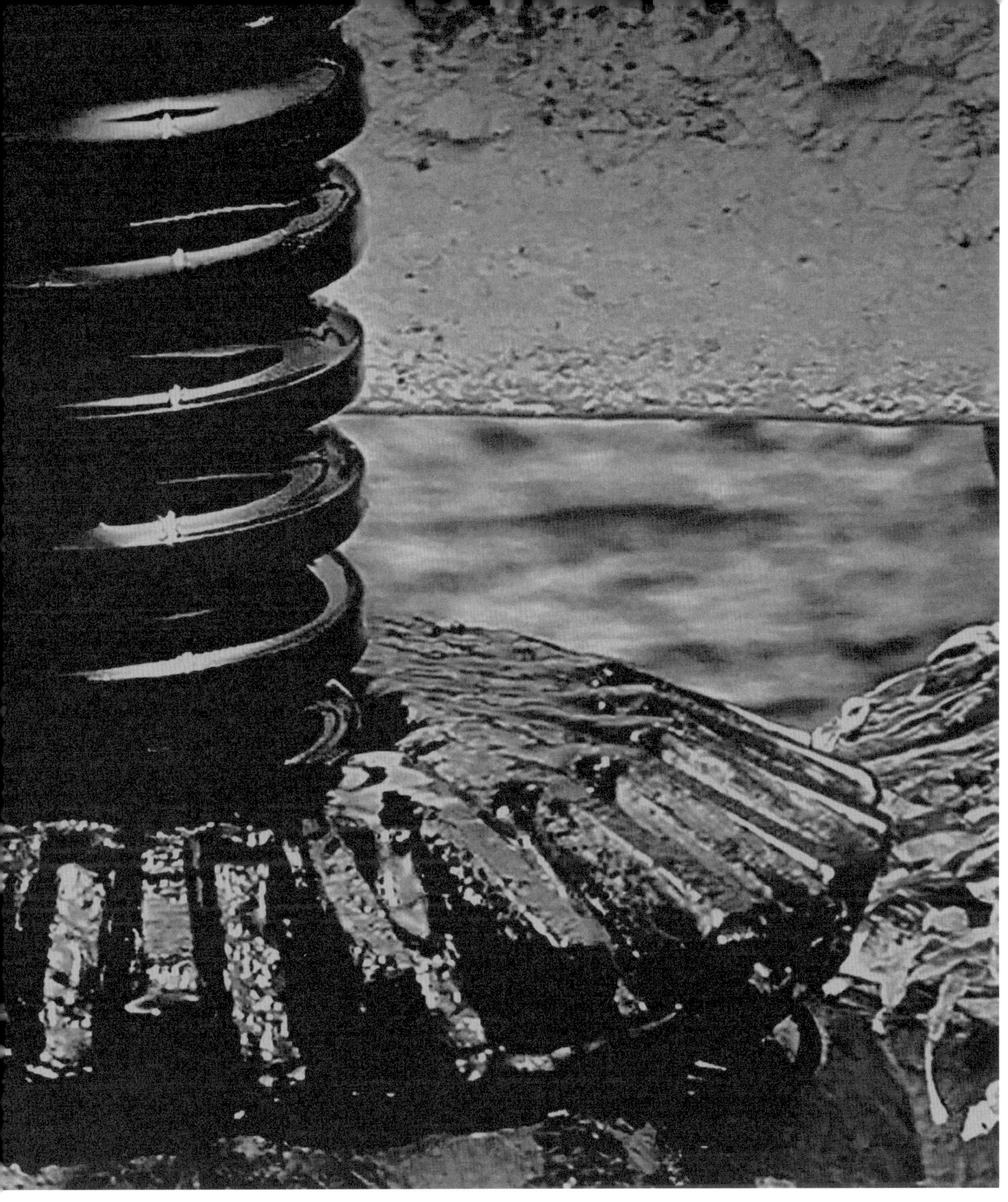

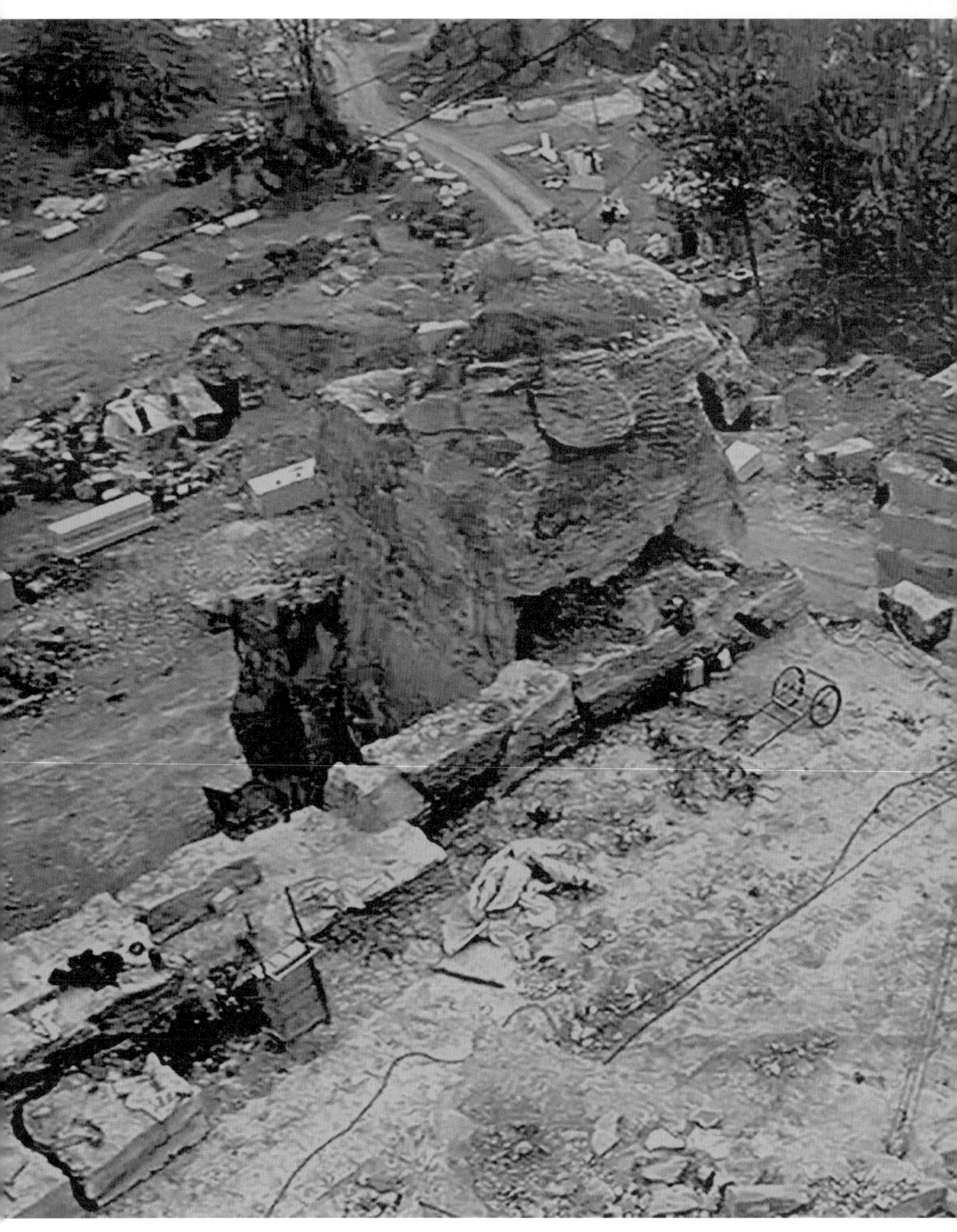

Yang Fudong
Blue Kylin – A Journal of Shandong
2008 – 2015
Video installation

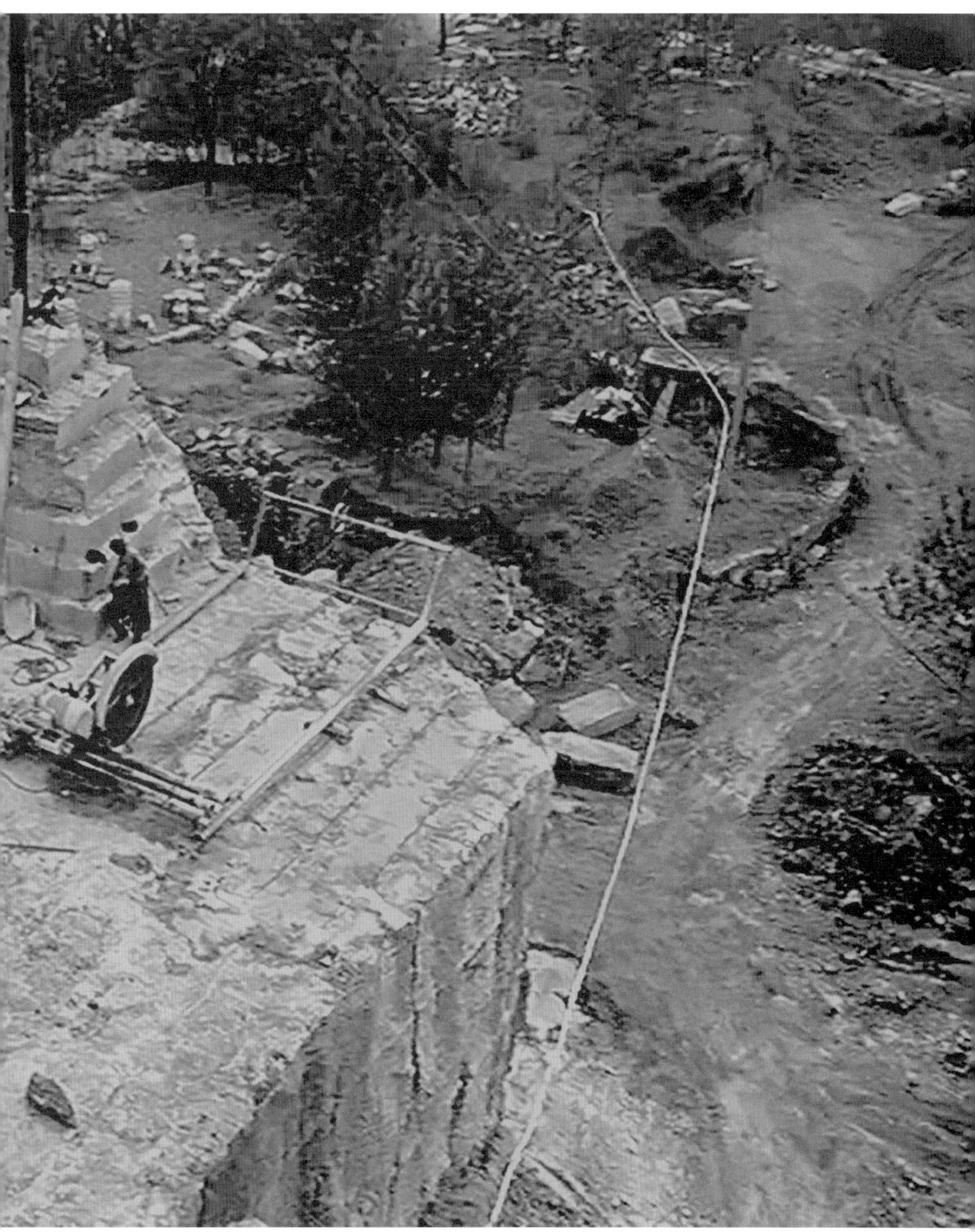

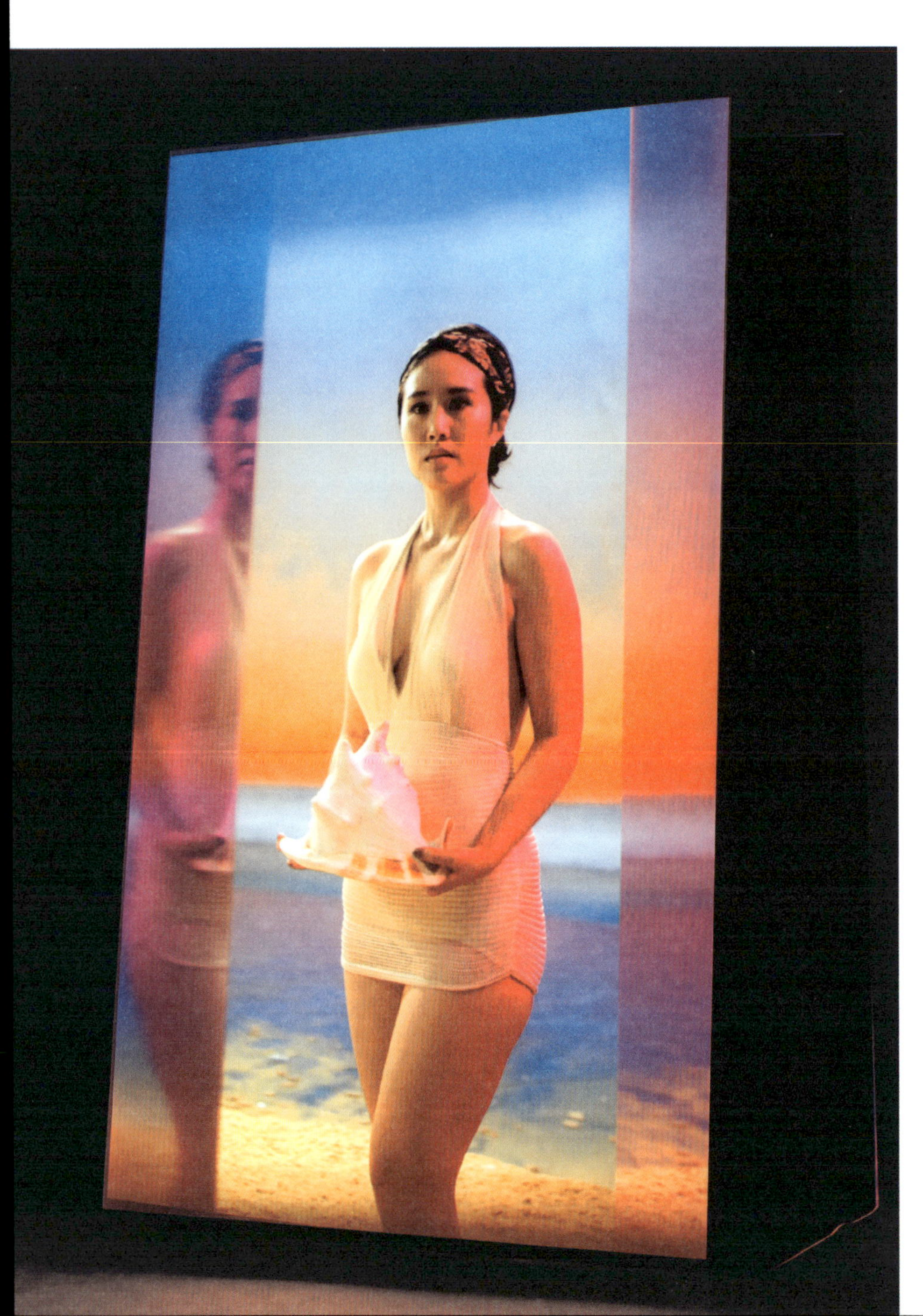

Yang Fudong
*The Coloured Sky:
New Women 2*
2014
HD video installation
15'48''

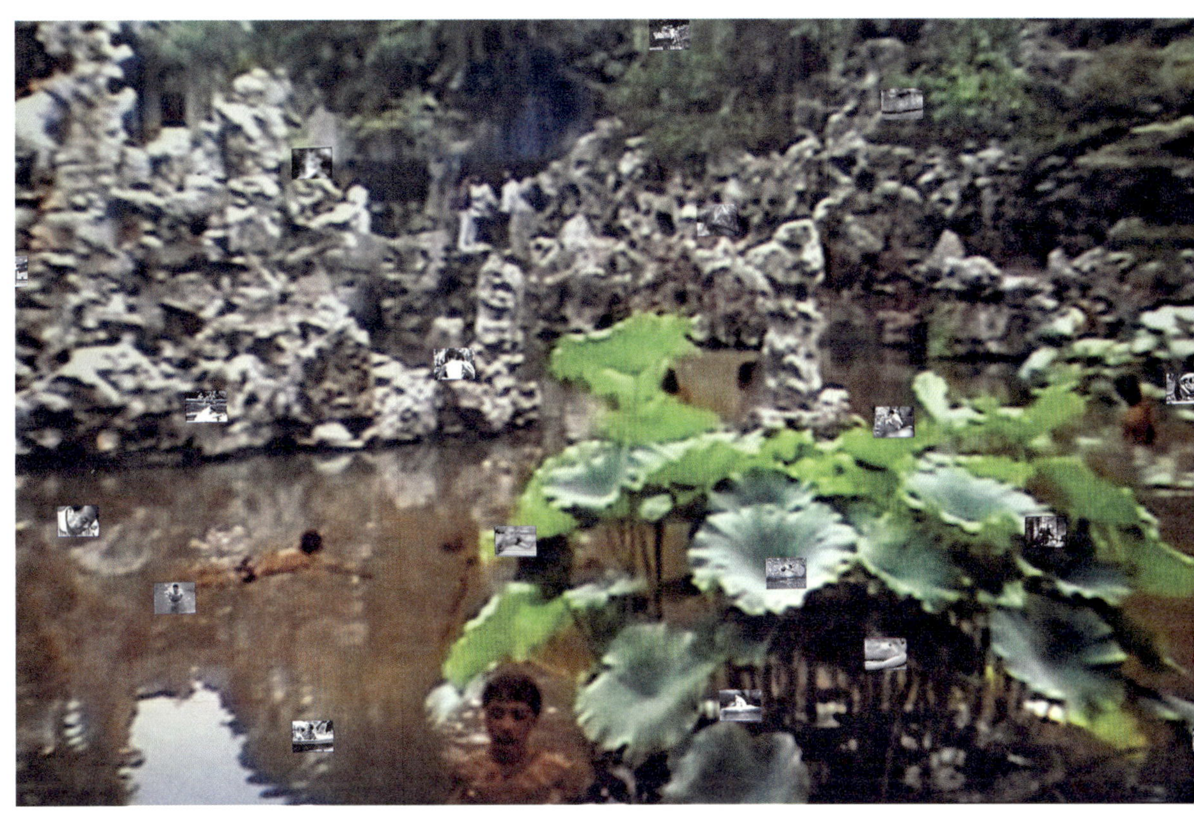

Yang Fudong
Tonight Moon
(Jin Wan De Yue Liang)
2000
Video installation
5'34''

ARTISTS
BIOGRAPHIES

CAO
FEI

Born in 1978 in Guangzhou, China. Currently working and living in Beijing. Graduated in 2001 from the Academy of Fine Arts, Guangzhou. In 2006 she was awarded the China Contemporary Art Award for Best Young Artist and she was a finalist in the 2010 Future Generation Art Prize and the Hugo Boss Prize.

SOLO
EXHIBITIONS

2015

Cao Fei: Shadow Plays, The Mistake Room, Los Angeles
Cao Fei: Splendid River, Secession, Vienna

2014

La Town, Cao Fei's Solo Exhibition, Lombard Freid Gallery, New York
Cao Fei's Theatrical Mirror, OzAsia Festival, Contemporary Art Centre of South Australia, Adelaide

2013

Haze and Fog, Eastside Projects, Birmingham; Centre for Chinese Contemporary Art, Manchester; Tate Modern, Starr Auditorium, London

2011

RMB City Opera, The Nelson-Atkins Museum of Art, Kansas City, MO, USA

SELECTED
GROUP
EXHIBITIONS

2015

15 Rooms, Long Museum, Shanghai
No Longer / Not Yet, Minsheng Art Museum, Shanghai
All the World's Future, 56th Venice Biennial, Arsenal Pavilion, Venice

2014

Whose Utopia?, Poetry and Dream, Tate Modern, London
Haze and Fog Screening, Ullens Center for Contemporary Art, Beijing; Prospectif Cinéma, Centre Pompidou, Paris
Chinese Realities / Documentary Visions, The Museum of Modern Art, New York

HAO
LIANG

Born in 1983 in Chengdu, China. Currently working and living in Beijing. Graduated in 2009, from the Sichuan Fine Arts Institute, Chinese Painting Department, Master of Fine Arts.

SOLO
EXHIBITIONS

2014

Secluded and Infinite Places: Hao Liang Solo Exhibition, Hive Center for Contemporary Art, Beijing

2011

Nest Image – Hao Liang Solo Exhibition, My Humble House Art Gallery, Taipei

SELECTED
GROUP
EXHIBITIONS

2014

Reform Art-system by Ancient Examples – Contemporary Elaborate-style Painting Exhibition, Today Art Museum, Beijing
Devotion to Ink, Hong Kong Maritime Museum & Ora-Ora, Hong Kong
Re-modernization, 3rd Documentary Exhibition of Fine Arts, Hubei Museum of Art, Wuhan

2013

Mind Is Outer Space, Casey Kaplan gallery, New York
ILLUSION/IMAGE Contemporary Chinese Ink Art Series, Hive Center for Contemporary Art, Beijing
The 8th International Ink Art Biennial of Shenzhen, Guan Shanyue Art Museum, OCT Art & Design Gallery, Shenzhen

2012

DARK ENERGY, Today Art Museum, Beijing
Cynical Resistance, Hakgojae Gallery, Seoul
MULTI-LAYERED – 2012 Contemporary Traditional Chinese Elaborate-style Painting Nomination Exhibition, Shanghai Art Museum, Shanghai
Contemplate Shanshui – Sunny after Snow, 43rd Art Basel, Basel

HU
XIANGQIAN

Born in 1983 in Guangdong, China. Currently working and living in Beijing. Graduated in 2007 from the Academy of Fine Arts, Guangzhou. In 2013 he won the Hugo Boss Asia Art Award.

SOLO
EXHIBITIONS

2015

A Performance A Day Keeps the Doctor Away, Long March Space, Beijing

2013

A Looks Like B, Arrow Factory, Beijing

2012

Protagonist, Long March Space, Beijing

2010

Body as a Museum/Sweet and Sweat, 24HR Art, Northern Territory Centre for Contemporary Art, Australia

SELECTED
GROUP
EXHIBITIONS

2015

Artist Making Movement, Asian Art Biennial, National Taiwan Museum of Fine Arts, Taichung
Nocturnal Friendships, Lehmann Maupin, Hong Kong
Essential Matters – Moving Images from China, Borusan Contemporary, Istanbul
The World in 2015, Ullens Center for Contemporary Art, Beijing

2014

Burning Down the House, 10th Gwangju Biennial, Gwangju *Before the Beginning and After the End*, Long March Space, Beijing

2013

West Bund 2013: A Biennial of Architecture and Contemporary Art, Shanghai
Re:emerge – toward a new cultural cartography, Sharjah Biennial, Sharjah Art Foundation, Sharjah
2012 ON | OFF: China's Young Artists in Concept and Practice, Ullens Center for Contemporary Art, Beijing

LIU CHUANG

Born in 1978 in Hubei, China.
Currently working and living
in Beijing. Graduated in 2001 from
Hubei Institute of Fine Arts.

SOLO
EXHIBITIONS

2014
Love Story, Salon 94, Paris
Untitled (Dancing Partners),
Kunsthall Stavanger, Stavanger

2012
Liu Chuang: Works #16–21,
LEO XU PROJECTS, Shanghai

2010
51m 2:13# Liu Chuang,
Taikang Space, Beijing

SELECTED
GROUP
EXHIBITIONS

2015
Social Factory, 10th
Shanghai Biennale, Power Station of
Art, Shanghai

2014
Silence: the 1990s, Galerie
Balice Hertling, Paris
Burning Down the House,
10th Gwangju Biennial, Gwangju
*My Generation: Young Chinese
Artists*, Tampa Museum of Art
& Museum of Fine Arts,
St Petersburg, Florida
The 8 of Paths: Art in Beijing,
Uferhallen, Berlin

2013
28 Chinese, Rubell Family
Collection and Contemporary
Arts Foundation, Miami
*West Bund 2013: A Biennial of
Architecture and Contemporary
Art*, Shanghai
*ON | OFF: China's Young Artists
in Concept and Practice*, Ullens
Center for Contemporary Art,
Beijing

2012
*Artists' Film International:
Liu Chuang, Anetta Mona Chisa
& Lucia Tkácová, Dan Finsel
and Sriwhana Spong*,
Whitechapel Gallery, London
*Sub-phenomena – the first
"CAFA·Future" exhibition*, CAFA
Art Museum, Beijing
Until the End of the World, Tang
Contemporary Art Beijing, Beijing
Boy: A Contemporary Portrait, LEO
XU PROJECTS, Shanghai

LIU SHIYUAN

Born in 1985 in Beijing, China.
Currently working and living
in Beijing and Copenhagen.
Graduated in 2009 from the
Central Academy of Fine Art and in
2012 from The School of Visual
Art, Master of Photography,
Video and Related Media.

SOLO
EXHIBITIONS

2015
As Simple As Clay, YUZ Museum,
Shanghai
From "Happiness" To "Whatever",
Leo Xu Projects, Shanghai
Lost In Export, White Space
Beijing, Beijing

2014
*My Paper Knife, Local Futures,
Alter-Circuit*, Asian Contemporary
Arts Consortium and Et al. gallery,
San Francisco
Beyond The Pale, Andersen's
Contemporary, Copenhagen

2013
*The Edge of Vision, or the Edge
of the Earth*, White Space Beijing,
Beijing

SELECTED
GROUP
EXHIBITIONS

2015
Unordinary Space, Aurora
Museum, Shanghai
Here Out There, Helsinki Festival,
Helsinki
*Moving in time B3+BEIJING
Moving Image Exhibition*,
CAFA Art Museum, Beijing
Second Thought, Flower Gallery,
New York

2014
*A Screening with Christopher
Phillips*, Asia Art Archive
in America, New York
Now You See, Whitebox Art Center,
New York

2013
Difference Engine, Magician Space,
Beijing
Local Futures, He Xiangning
Art Museum, Shenzhen
Finishing School, Dimensions
Variable, Miami

2012
The 7th Shenzhen Sculpture
Biennale, OCT Contemporary
Art Terminal, Shenzhen

LIU WEI

Born in 1972 in Beijing, China.
Currently working and living
in Beijing.
Graduated in 1996 from the
Academy of Fine Arts of China,
Oil Painting Department.
In 2008 he won the Chinese
Contemporary Art Award for
Best Artist. In 2011 he won the
Credit Suisse Today Art Award
and in 2012 the Martell Artist
of the Year Award.

SOLO
EXHIBITIONS

2015
Silver, White Cube, Hong Kong
Liu Wei: Colors, Ullens Center
for Contemporary Art, Beijing

2014
Sensory Spaces 4, Museum
Boijmans Van Bueningen,
Rotterdam
Density, White Cube, London

2013
Void, Arrow Factory, Beijing
Liu Wei, Lehman Maupin Gallery,
New York

2012
Liu Wei: Foreign, Almine Rech
Gallery, Paris

SELECTED
GROUP
EXHIBITIONS

2015
La Vie moderne, 13th Biennale
de Lyon, Lyon
The Civil Power, Minsheng Art
Museum, Beijing
*Adventures of the Black Square
Abstract Art and Society
1915-2015*, Whitechapel Gallery,
London

2014
Bringing the World Into the World,
Queens Museum, New York
*Criss-Cross: Artworks of Young
Chinese Contemporary Artists
from Long Collection*, Long
Museum West Bund, Shanghai

2013
*West Bund 2013: A Biennial of
Architecture and Contemporary
Art*, Shanghai
*Re:emerge – towards a new cultural
cartography*, 11th Sharjah Biennial,
Sharjah Art Foundation, Sharjah

LIU XIAODONG

Born in 1963 in Liaoning, China.
Currently working and living
in Beijing.
Graduated in 1995 from Central
Academy of Fine Arts, Oil Painting
Department, Master of Fine Arts. In
1998–1999 he studied at the
Academy of Fine Art, Complutense
University of Madrid. He is
currently a professor at the Central
Academy of Fine Arts, Beijing.

FILMOGRAPHY

2006
Conceived concept for Jia Zhangke's
film, *Dong*
Conceived concept for Jia Zhangke's
film, *Still Life*

1993
Artistic Director for Zhang Yuan's
Beijing Bastard

1992
Acted in Wang Xiaoshuai's
The Days

SOLO
EXHIBITIONS

2015
Painting as Shooting,
Fondazione Giorgio Cini, Venice

2014
*Childhood Friends Getting Fat:
Moving Image of Liu Xiaodong*,
Minsheng Art Museum, Shanghai

2013
Liu Xiaodong: Hometown Boy,
Seattle Art Museum, Seattle
*Liu Xiaodong: In Between Israel
and Palestine*, Mary Boone Gallery,
New York

SELECTED
GROUP
EXHIBITIONS

2014
10th Annual Gwangju Biennial,
Gwangju

2013
*From Beijing: Works by the Faculty
of China Central Academy of Fine
Arts*, New York Academy of Art,
New York
Host & Guest, Tel Aviv Museum
of Art, Tel Aviv

2012
*Encounter: The Royal Academy
in Asia*, Institute of Contemporary
Arts Singapore, Singapore

QIU ZHIJIE

Born in 1969 in Fujian, China.
Currently working and living
in Beijing and Hangzhou. Graduated
in 1992 from the China National
Academy of Fine Art, he is
an Associate Professor in the Mixed
Media Art Department and
Co-Director of the Visual Culture
Center of CAA in Hangzhou.

SOLO
EXHIBITIONS

2015
*Qiu Zhijie: Qiu's Annotation
of the Lantern Festival Plan*,
Museum of Contemporary Art
of CAAM, Hangzhou

2014
*A Suicidology of the Nanjing
Yangtze River Bridge – On Leveling
All Things*, Art Museum of Nanjing
University of the Arts, Nanjing

2013
The Unicorn and the Dragon,
Fondazione Querini Stampalia,
Venice

2012
Blue Prints, Witte de With
Art Center, Rotterdam
Tathagata, Tian Ren He Ye
Museum, Hangzhou

SELECTED
GROUP
EXHIBITIONS

2015
All the World's Future, 56th Venice
Bienniale, Arsenale Corderie,
Venice

2014
The 31th Sao Paulo Art Biennial,
Sao Paulo
*On site: Cross Contextual Ink Art
Experience*, Himalayas Museum,
Shanghai

2013
*Ink Art: Past as Present
in Contemporary China*,
Metropolitan Museum of Art,
New York
*The Origin of Dao: New Dimensions
in Chinese Contemporary Art*,
Hong Kong Museum of Art,
Hong Kong
55th Venice Biennial, Museo
Diocesano d'Art Sacra, Venice

2012
*Guanxi: Contemporary Chinese
Art*, Guangdong Museum of Art,
Guangzhou

TAO HUI

Born in 1987 in Chongqing, China.
Currently working and living
in Beijing.
Graduated in 2010 from
the Sichuan Fine Arts Institute,
Oil Painting Department.
In 2015, he won the Grand Prize
at the 19th Contemporary Art
Festival Sesc_VideoBrasil: Southern
Panoramas, São Paolo.

SOLO
EXHIBITIONS

2015
1 Character & 7 Materials,
AIKE-DELLARCO, Shanghai
New Directions: Tao Hui, Ullens
Center for Contemporary Art,
Beijing

2013
Sightseers, Space Space, Chengdu

SELECTED
GROUP
EXHIBITIONS

2015
*Sesc_VideoBrasil: Southern
Panoramas*, 19th Contemporary
Art Festival, São Paolo
*Essential Matters – Moving Images
from China*, Borusan
Contemporary, Istanbul
Perched in the Eye of a Tornado,
Ying Space, Beijing
*Sunlight – between Tehran
and Chongqing*, LP Art Space,
Chongqing

2014
Positive Space, Times Museum,
Guangzhou
*UP-YOUTH, China Young Artists
Exhibition*, Times Art Museum,
Beijing
*How do we become a part
of the world?*, Landing Museum,
Chengdu; DAC Art Center,
Chongqing
Iran to China, Darbast Platform,
Mohsen Gallery, Tehran

2013
Be Conscious of Yourself,
Suzhou Museum, Suzhou
Art Basel Leap Video Project, Hong
Kong
*Sesc_Videobrasil: Southern
Panoramas*, 18th Contemporary
Art Festival São Paulo

XU
QU

Born in 1978 in Nanjing, China.
Currently working and living
in Beijing. Graduated in 2002
from Nanjing Art Institute.
From 2005 to 2008 he studied
at the Braunschweig University
of Art, Germany, under John
M. Armleder and Birgit Hein.

SOLO
EXHIBITIONS

2015
Currency Wars, Almine Rech
Gallery, Brussels
Intercourse, Antenna Space,
Shanghai

2014
A Hit, Tang Contemporary Art
Beijing, Beijing
Tennis Court, Taikang Space,
Beijing

2013
*Mutable Forms and Immutable
Consciousness*, Bangkok Tang
Contemporary Art Bangkok,
Bangkok, Thailand

SELECTED
GROUP
EXHIBITIONS

2015
Mobilization, 3rd Ural Industrial
Biennial of Contemporary Art
Stereognosis Zone, Redtory
Museum of Contemporary Art,
Guangzhou
Vapor and Dust, Yallay Gallery,
Hong Kong

2014
COSMOS, 21st Century Minsheng
Art Museum, Shanghai
Nihilistic Belief, ANTENNA
SPACE, Shanghai

2013
The Sun, V Arts Centre (Space 1),
Shanghai
Pessimism or Resistance, Taikang
Space, Beijing
ON | OFF: China's Young Artists in
Concept and Practice, UCCA,
Beijing

2012
*GUEST: Standing on the Shoulders
of Little Clowns*, UCCA, Beijing
Light Bending Onto the Retina, 18
Gallery, Shanghai

XU
ZHEN

Born in 1977 in Shanghai, China.
Currently working and living
in Shanghai.
Graduated in 1996 from the
Shanghai School of Arts and Crafts.
In 2004 he won the
China Contemporary Art Award
for Best Artist. In 2014 he was
selected to be the Commissioned
Artist for The Armory Show.

SOLO
EXHIBITIONS

2015
*Corporate – Xu Zhen (Produced by
MadeIn Company) Solo Exhibition*,
Graz Kunsthaus, Graz
Movement Field, Walburdger
Wouters, Brussels
In Light of 25 Years, Xu Zhen,
MadeIn Company Solo Exhibition,
Witte de With, Rotterdam

2014
*Xu Zhen: A MadeIn Company
Production*, Ullens Center for
Contemporary Art, Beijing
*Blissful As Gods – Xu Zhen Solo
Exhibition Produced by MadeIn
Company*, ShanghART, Shanghai

2013
Light Source, Tian Ren He Yi Art
Center, Hangzhou, China

2012
Sleeping Life Away, Galerie Nathalie
Obadia, Paris
Inside the White Cube, White Cube,
London

SELECTED
GROUP
EXHIBITIONS

2015
15 Rooms, Long Museum West
Bund, Shanghai
How to Gather?, 6th Moscow
Biennial, Moscow
*Essential Matters – Moving Images
from China*, Borusan
Contemporary, Istanbul

2014
*Myth / History: Yuz Collection of
Contemporary Art*, Yuz Museum,
Shanghai
Do It Moscow, Garage – Museum of
Contemporary Art, Moscow

YANG
FUDONG

Born in 1971 in Beijing, China.
Currently working and living
in Shanghai. Graduated in 1995
from the China Academy of Art,
Oil Painting Department.
In 2004 he was a finalist in
the Hugo Boss Prize.

SOLO
EXHIBITIONS

2015
The Colored Sky: New Women II,
Marian Goodman Gallery, Paris

2014
Yang Fudong: Incidental Scripts,
CCA Singapore, Singapore
Yang Fudong: Filmscapes,
Australian Centre for the Moving
Image, Melbourne
The Light That I Feel, SALT
outdoor video installation,
Sandhornøya, Norway

2013
*Yang Fudong: Estranged Paradise,
Works 1993–2013*, The Kunsthalle
Zurich, Switzerland
Yejiang / The Night Cometh,
ShanghART Singapore, Singapore

2012
Quote Out of Context, Solo
Exhibition of Yang Fudong, OCT
Contemporary Art Terminal,
Shanghai

SELECTED
GROUP
EXHIBITIONS

2014
Tales from the Taiping Era,
Redbrick Art Museum, Beijing

2013
*West Bund 2013: A Biennial of
Architecture and Contemporary
Art*, Shanghai
12th La Biennale de Lyon, Lyon
*Re: emerge – towards a new
cultural cartography*, 11th Sharjah
Biennial, Sharjah Art Foundation,
Sharjah

2012
*The Best of Times, The Worst of
Times: Rebirth and Apocalypse in
Contemporary Art*, The First Kyiv
International Biennial of
Contemporary Art ARSENALE
2012, Mystetskyi Arsenal, Kiev

AUTHORS
BIOGRAPHIES

SUN DONGDONG

Sun Dongdong, born in 1977 in Nanjing, China, is a curator, critic and freelance writer. He graduated in 2001 from the Nanjing University of the Arts with a degree in Fine Arts. In 2005, he received his MFA in Art History from the Nanjing University of the Arts. Since 2005, he has been involved in writing about and curating Chinese contemporary art. In 2009, he began working at *LEAP* magazine as a senior editor, covering scholarship and exhibition reviews. In 2014, he was chosen to be one of seven members of the Pinchuk Art Foundation's Future Generation Art Prize selection committee. Sun Dongdong currently lives and works in Beijing.

Notable curatorial ventures include *ON | OFF: China's Young Artists in Concept & Practice* at the Ullens Center for Contemporary Art (2013), *Wormhole —Geo-Attraction* at the Lin & Lin Gallery in Taipei (2014), *No Express: Hu Weiyi* at the Ullens Center for Contemporary Art, Pavilion (2015), and the *Shi Qing: Hinterland Project* at the Time Museum in Guangzhou (2015)

PIERRE HASKI

Pierre Haski is a journalist, co-founder of the Rue 89 website and regular international columnist for *L'Obs*. He was a special correspondant for *Libération* in Beijing (2000, 2006) and is the author of *Journal de Ma Yan* (Ramsay, 2002) and *Cinq ans en Chine* (Les Arènes, 2006).

VENUS LAU

Venus Lau is a curator and writer based in Shenzhen, where she is artistic director of OCT Contemporary Art Terminal, and Beijing. She is the curator of the Secret Timezones Trilogy at UCCA, an exhibition series comprised of solo presentations by Korakrit Arunanondchai, Ming Wong and Haegue Yang, exploring alternative temporalities. Lau also co-curated "rites, thoughts, notes, sparks, swings, strikes. a hong kong spring" with Cosmin Costinas at Para Site, Hong Kong. She is the editor of publications including *Cao Fei: Splendid River* and *Certain Pleasures: A Zheng Peili Retrospective*.

AIMEE LIN

Aimee Lin is a writer and art critic based in Shanghai. Since she joined *ArtReview* in 2013, she has co-founded its sibling magazine *ArtReview Asia*, a critical quarterly distributed in the pan-Asia area. From 2009 to 2012, she was the founding editor of LEAP. She often contributes to publications and catalogues as a writer and an editor; she sometimes curates.

LU MINGJUN

Lu Mingjun has a PhD in History from Sichuan University (2011). He is currently Associate Professor of Art History at Art College, Sichuan University. Lu's research interests include the history of modern and contemporary Chinese art, and art historiography in Europe and America since the 1960s. His recent books include *Writing and Narrating of Vision: The Vision of History and Theory* (2013), *Visual Cognition and Art History: Michel Foucault, Hubery Damisch, Jonathan Crary* (2014), and *On Meta-Painting: An Art Institution and Cognition of Universality* (2015). In 2015, he was the recipient of the Robert H. N. Ho Family Foundation Greater China Research Grant.

ROBIN PECKHAM

Robin Peckham is a curator and editor living in Beijing. Currently editor-in-chief of *LEAP*, the international magazine devoted to contemporary art in China, he previously founded and operated the independent space Saamlung. He has organized exhibitions including *Dali and Chinese Contemporary Art* at K11 Art Foundation; *Peril and Weirdness: Painting as a Universalism* at M Woods Museum; *Art Post-Internet* at Ullens Center for Contemporary Art, *The Burning Edge* at City University of Hong Kong, and *The Border Show*. His writings are published regularly in *Artforum*, *Yishu* and *Broadsheet*, and he has had books published by the Minsheng Art Museum, Para Site Art Space and Timezone8.

JÉRÔME SANS

Jérôme Sans is a curator, art critic, artistic director and director of internationally renowned institutions. From 1999 to 2006 he was the co-founder and co-director of the acclaimed Palais de Tokyo in Paris. He then moved to the UK, where he became director of programmes at the BALTIC Center for Contemporary Art in Newcastle. From 2008 to 2012, he was the director of the ground-breaking Ullens Center for Contemporary Art in Beijing (UCCA).

Jérôme Sans has curated numerous major exhibitions around the world, including the Taipei Biennial (2000), the Lyon Biennial (2005) and the Nuit Blanche in Paris (2006). He is currently artistic director of one of the most important urban development projects in Europe, the Lyon Rives de Saône-River Movie, and has been named recently as co-artistic director to the Grand Paris Express project. Jérôme Sans is also co-founder of Perfect Crossovers Ltd., a Beijing-based consultancy for specific cultural projects between China and the rest of the world. He has contributed to various art publications, and between 2012 and 2014 was creative director and editor-in-chief of the French cultural magazine *L'Officiel Art*. He is the author of several books, including *Au Sujet de/ About Daniel Buren* (Flammarion, 1998), *Araki* (Taschen, 2001), *China Talks* (Timezone 8, 2009) and *China: The New Generation* (Skira, 2014), both compilations of interviews with leading and young Chinese contemporary artists. He has also written a series of pocket books for publisher Blue Kingfisher, including *Ma Yansong, Bright City* (2012), *Jannis Kounellis, Smoke Shadows* (2012) and *Kendell Geers, Hand Grenade from my Heart* (2012).

CLAIRE STAEBLER

Claire Staebler is associate curator at the Louis Vuitton Fondation.

LIU TIAN

Liu Tian researches topics relating to artistic creation, curating, writing and visual culture. Since 2006, he has curated exhibitions, including *Ash/ Blade/ Frame/ Ocean: Four Images about Photograph* (2015), *VOID: There's Nothing More Left, But A Little Trace From Human Beings* (2015), *Memorandum for Gaia– The 1st PSA Emerging Curators Program* (2014), *Idiosyncrasies: Hanart 100* (2014), *West Bund 2013: A Biennial of Architecture and Contemporary Art* (2013), *What A Form: A Reportage-Wu Shanzhuan and Inga Svala Thórsdóttir* (2013). He is currently preparing a PhD at the Institute of Contemporary Art and Social Thoughts, School of Inter-Media Art, China Academy of Art, and his current area of research is media reality.

PHILIP TINARI

Philip Tinari was appointed director of the Ullens Center for Contemporary Art in 2011. In this capacity, he organizes a programme of exhibitions devoted to established figures and rising talents both Chinese and international, as well as a wide range of public and educational programmes and development activities aimed at UCCA's annual public of nearly a million visitors. Over the past four years at UCCA, he has curated exhibitions of work by such artists as William Kentridge, Liu Wei, Sterling Ruby, Matthew Monahan, Kaari Upson, Alex Israel, Pawel Althamer, Xu Zhen/MadeIn Company, Ji Dachun, Tino Sehgal, Taryn Simon, Wang Keping, Teppei Kaneuji, Tehching Hsieh, Wang Xingwei, Kan Xuan, Yung Ho Chang, Yun Fei-Ji and Gu Dexin. Prior to joining UCCA he was founding editor of the bilingual art magazine *LEAP*, published by the leading Chinese publishing group Modern Media. He speaks and writes Mandarin fluently, and has written and lectured around the world on contemporary art in China. Tinari currently serves on advisory boards to institutions including the Guggenheim, the Asia Society and NTU Center for Contemporary Art Singapore, and was recently named a Young Global Leader by the World Economic Forum. He holds a BA from the Program in Literature at Duke, an AM in East Asian Studies from Harvard, and was a Fulbright scholar at Peking University. He is currently pursuing a DPhil in art history at the University of Oxford.

NIKITA YINGQIAN CAI

Nikita Yingqian Cai lives and works in Guangzhou, where she is currently Associate Director and Chief Curator at Guangdong Times Museum. She has curated such exhibitions as *A Museum That is Not* (2011), *Jiang Zhi: If This is a Man* (2012), *You Can Only Think about Something if You Think of Something Else* (2014) and *Roman Ondák: Storyboard* (2015). She is also organizing the para-curatorial series at Guangdong Times Museum, which features an annual seminar and a related publication. These seminars have included "No Ground Underneath: Curating on the Nexus of Changes" (co-organized with Carol Yinghua Lu, 2012), "Active Withdrawal: Weak Institutionalism and the Institutionalization of Art Practice", (co-organized with Biljana Ciric, 2013), "Cultivate or Revolutionize? Life between Apartment and Farmland" (co-organized with Binna Choi, 2014) and "Between Knowing and Unknowing: Research in-and-through Art" (2015). Her writings have appeared in a number of publications and magazines, and she is a contributing writer to *LEAP*, *Artforum.com.cn*, *Arttime* and the *Yishu Journal of Contemporary Chinese Art*.

ZHANG XIYUAN

Zhang Xiyuan is an art writer and critic. Born in 1987, he lives and works in Beijing. He is co-founder of THE OFFICE project/alternative space and received a grant from the China National Arts Fund in 2015 for writing. Between 2012 and 2015, he worked as PR editor and programme manager of the Public Programme department at the Ullens Center for Contemporary Art. In 2011, he won the first Artforum.com.cn Award for Art Criticism. He has a BA and MA in the Arts from Beijing Normal University in 2010.

SASHA ZHAO

Sasha Zhao is a writer, editor, curator and musician based in Beijing. A *LEAP* veteran of over four years, she came to the magazine with a background in industrial design and online publishing. Her work centres primarily on exhibitions and publications devoted to young Chinese artists.

YANG ZI

Yang Zi, a critic and curator, graduated from Nanjing University with a degree in religious studies. He is the Publications and Exhibitions Coordinator at the Ullens Center for Contemporary Art (UCCA), Beijing. Prior to joining UCCA, he used to write for *LEAP*, *Artforum China* and *Art Newspaper*.

CREDITS & COPYRIGHTS

AI WEIWEI
Tree
2010
Tree sections
530 × 560 × 660 cm
COLLECTION FONDATION
LOUIS VUITTON
© AI WEIWEI, 2016
COURTESY OF THE ARTIST
AND LISSON GALLERY

HUANG YONG PING
L'Arc de Saint-Gilles
2015
Wood, iron,
fiberglass, dog hair,
gold leaf
156 × 448 × 70 cm
COLLECTION FONDATION
LOUIS VUITTON
© ADAGP, PARIS 2016
COURTESY OF THE ARTIST
AND KAMEL MENNOUR
GALLERY, PARIS
PHOTO: FABRICE SEIXAS

HUANG YONG PING
*Cinquante bras
de Bouddha*
1997–2013
Metal, plastic, polyester,
various objects
477 × 404 × 415 cm
COLLECTION FONDATION
LOUIS VUITTON
© ADAGP, PARIS 2016
COURTESY OF THE ARTIST
AND KAMEL MENNOUR
GALLERY, PARIS
PHOTO: FABRICE SEIXAS

ZHANG HUAN
Long Island Buddha
2010–2011
Copper
172 × 277 × 177 cm
COLLECTION FONDATION
LOUIS VUITTON
©ZHANG HUAN STUDIO, 2016
COURTESY OF THE ARTIST
AND PACE GALLERY

ZHANG HUAN
Great Leap Forward
2007
Ash on linen
286 × 1080 cm
COLLECTION FONDATION
LOUIS VUITTON
©ZHANG HUAN STUDIO, 2016
COURTESY OF THE ARTIST
AND PACE GALLERY

ZHANG HUAN
Sudden Awakening
2006
Ash and steel
70 × 78 × 100 cm
COLLECTION FONDATION
LOUIS VUITTON
©ZHANG HUAN STUDIO, 2016
COURTESY OF THE ARTIST
AND PACE GALLERY

XU ZHEN
*Eternity – Material:
Winged Victory
of Samothrace,
Tianlongshan Grottoes
Bodhisattva*
2013
Fiberglass, steel,
concrete
626 × 460 × 230 cm
PRODUCTION:
MADEIN COMPANY
COLLECTION FONDATION
LOUIS VUITTON
© XU ZHEN, 2016
COURTESY OF THE
ARTIST AND SHANGHART
GALLERY, SHANGHAI
PHOTO: MADEIN COMPANY

YAN PEI-MING
*All Crows Under
the Sun Are Black!*
2012
Oil on canvas
280 × 400 cm
PHOTOGRAPHIE:
ANDRÉ MORIN
COURTESY DE L'ARTISTE
ET MASSIMO DE CARLO,
MILANO/LONDON

YAN PEI-MING
Les Temps Modernes
2015
Oil on canvas
Diptych: 280 × 400 cm
(each panel)
COLLECTION FONDATION
LOUIS VUITTON
©ADAGP, PARIS 2016
COURTESY OF THE ARTIST AND
THADDEUS ROPAC GALLERY

XU ZHEN
New
2014
Painted stainless steel
130 × 110 × 402 cm
COLLECTION FONDATION
LOUIS VUITTON
PRODUCTION MADEIN GALLERY
© XU ZHEN, 2016
COURTESY OF THE ARTIST
AND SHANGHART GALLERY,
SHANGHAI
PHOTO: MADEIN GALLERY

YANG FUDONG
*Tonight Moon
(Jin Wan De Yue Liang)*
2000
Video installation,
colour, black
and white, sound
5'34''
COLLECTION FONDATION
LOUIS VUITTON
©YANG FUDONG, 2016
PHOTO: YANG FUDONG:
ESTRANGED PARADISE,
WORKS 19932013, AUGUST
21, 2013 – DECEMBER
8, 2013 (INSTALLATION
VIEW); COURTESY OF
THE BERKELEY ART MUSEUM
AND PACIFIC FILM ARCHIVE.
PHOTO: SIBILA SAVAGE.

YANG FUDONG
*The Coloured Sky:
New Women II*
2014
Video installation, colour,
sound
15'48''
COLLECTION FONDATION
LOUIS VUITTON
©YANG FUDONG, 2016
CO-PRODUCED BY ACMI
MELBOURNE AND AUCKLAND
ART GALLERY TOI O TAMAKI
COURTESY OF THE ARTIST;
GALERIE MARIAN GOODMAN;
ACMI MELBOURNE
ET AUCKLAND ART GALLERY
TOI O TAMAKI
PHOTO: AURÉLIEN MOLE

CAO FEI
*RMB CITY Second Life
city planning*
2009
Video
24'50''
COLLECTION FONDATION
LOUIS VUITTON
© CAO FEI, 2016
COURTESY OF THE ARTIST
AND VITAMIN CREATIVE SPACE,
GUANGZHOU

ZHANG XIAOGANG
My Ideal, 2008
Bronze, variable
dimensions
My Ideal
2003–2008
Oil on canvas
279 × 500 cm
COLLECTION FONDATION
LOUIS VUITTON
©ZHANG XIAOGANG, 2016
COURTESY OF THE ARTIST
PHOTO: PRIMAE

TAO HUI
The Dusk of Teheran
2014
Video, colour, sound
4'
COLLECTION FONDATION
LOUIS VUITTON
© TAO HUI, 2016
COURTESY OF THE ARTIST AND
AIKE DELLARCO, SHANGHAI

ZHOU TAO
One Two Three Four
2008
Video, colour, sound
3'33''

ZHOU TAO
*Chick speaks to duck,
pig speaks to dog*
2005
Video, colour, sound
6'
COLLECTION FONDATION
LOUIS VUITTON
© ZHOU TAO, 2016
COURTESY OF THE ARTIST AND
VITAMIN CREATIVE SPACE,
GUANGZHOU

ISAAC JULIEN
Ten Thousand Waves
2010
Video installation,
colour, sound
49'42''
COLLECTION FONDATION
LOUIS VUITTON
© ISAAC JULIEN, 2015
COURTESY ISAAC JULIEN;
VICTORIA MIRO GALLERY,
LONDRES

YANG FUDONG
*Seven Intellectuals
in the Bamboo Forest,*
Parts I–V
5 films (35 mm)
transferred to DVD,
black and white, sound
Variable duration
MUSIC: JIN WANG (PARTIE II)
COLLECTION FONDATION
LOUIS VUITTON
©YANG FUDONG, 2016
COURTESY OF THE ARTIST,
GALERIE MARIAN GOODMAN;
SHANGHART GALLERY

CAO FEI
*Storyboard
of "Chain Reaction"*
2000
Sketch
COURTESY OF ARTIST
AND VITAMIN CREATIVE SPACE

CAO FEI
Strangers: City
2015
Video
4'18''
COURTESY OF THE ARTIST,
VITAMIN CREATIVE SPACE
AND OMEGLE.COM

CAO FEI
Installation view
of *Strangers: City*
2015
Video
4'18''
COURTESY OF THE ARTIST,
VITAMIN CREATIVE SPACE
AND OMEGLE.COM

CAO FEI
*RMB City: A Second Life
City Planning*
2007
Digital print
120 × 160 cm
COLLECTION FONDATION
LOUIS VUITTON
COURTESY OF THE ARTIST
AND VITAMIN CREATIVE SPACE

CAO FEI
*Whose Utopia:
My Future is Not a Dream*
2006
C-print
120 × 150 cm
COLLECTION FONDATION
LOUIS VUITTON
COURTESY OF THE ARTIST
AND VITAMIN CREATIVE SPACE

HAO LIANG
Yanshan Garden
2015
Photograph
12.4 × 18.8 cm
COURTESY OF THE ARTIST

HAO LIANG
The Virtuous Being
2015
Ink and colour
on silk hand scroll
Hand scroll size:
40 × 1312 cm
COURTESY OF THE ARTIST

BENTU
CHINESE
ARTISTS
IN
A
TIME
OF
TURBULENCE
AND
TRANSFORMATION

HAO LIANG
The Virtuous Being
(detail)
2015
Ink and colour
on silk hand scroll
COURTESY OF THE ARTIST

HAO LIANG
*Passage from Xian
to Ghost – Portrait
of Wang Shizen*
2014
Ink and colour
on silk hand scroll
37 × 75 cm
COURTESY OF THE ARTIST

HAO LIANG
*Passage from Xian
to Ghost – The Legendary
Land Penglai*
2014
Ink and colour
on silk hand scroll
62 × 180 cm
COURTESY OF THE ARTIST

HAO LIANG
*Passage from Xian
to Ghost – Portrait
of Virtuoso*
2014
Ink and colour
on silk hand scroll
28 × 47 cm
COURTESY OF THE ARTIST

HAO LIANG
Two Sculptures
3 × 3 × 33 cm (x 3)

HU XIANGQIAN
Sketch for *Speech
at the Edge of the World*
2013
25 × 17 cm
COURTESY OF THE ARTIST

HU XIANGQIAN
Sketch for *Speech
at the Edge of the World*
2013
25 × 17 cm
COURTESY OF THE ARTIST

HU XIANGQIAN
*The Woman in Front
of the Camera*
2015
HD video
2′53″
COURTESY OF THE ARTIST

HU XIANGQIAN
*Speech at the Edge
of the World*
2013
Single channel
HD video
12′23″
COURTESY OF THE ARTIST

HU XIANGQIAN
*Reconstructing
Michelangelo – Sketch
I & Reconstructing
Michelangelo – Threshold*
2015 HD video, wood
56′24″ and 11′19″
COURTESY OF THE ARTIST
AND LONG MARCH SPACE

HU XIANGQIAN
The Secret Mission
2015
HD video
38′06″
COURTESY OF THE ARTIST
AND LONG MARCH SPACE

LIU CHUANG
Untitled (Unknown River)
2014
Drawing on paper
19 × 20 cm
COURTESY OF THE ARTIST

LIU CHUANG
*BBR1 (No. 1 of Blossom
Bud Restrainer)*
2015
Video
4′56″
COURTESY OF THE ARTIST

LIU CHUANG
*BBR1 (No. 1 of Blossom
Bud Restrainer)*
2015
Video
4′56″
COURTESY OF THE ARTIST

LIU CHUANG
*Untitled
(The Dancing Partner)*
2010
Video
5′15″
COURTESY OF ARTIST

LIU CHUANG
*Buying Everything on You
(Li Shuanghu)*
2006
Mixed media
120 × 240 × 20 cm
COURTESY OF THE ARTIST

LIU SHIYUAN
Sketch for
"*From Happiness
to Whatever*"
2015
24 × 36 cm
COURTESY OF THE ARTIST

LIU SHIYUAN
*From Happiness
to Whatever*
2015
Carpets, speakers, iPod
Variable dimensions
Installation view
at Leo Xu Projects gallery,
Shanghai
COURTESY OF LEO XU
PROJECTS, SHANGHAI

LIU SHIYUAN
*From Happiness
to Whatever* (detail)
2015
COURTESY OF LEO XU
PROJECTS, SHANGHAI

LIU SHIYUAN
As Simple as Clay
2013
Installation view at
Leo Xu Projects gallery,
Shanghai, 2015
Variable dimensions
(each unit: 15.2 × 10.2 cm)
COURTESY OF LEO XU
PROJECTS, SHANGHAI

LIU SHIYUAN
Video stills
from *Lost in Export*
2014
Video, stereo sound
33′34″
Music composed by
Kristian Mondrup Nielsen

LIU WEI
Project for
the installation
at the Fondation
Louis Vuitton, Paris
2015
Sketch
COURTESY OF THE ARTIST

LIU WEI
Liberation No. 16
2014
Oil on canvas
400 × 720 cm
COURTESY LIU WEI STUDIO

LIU WEI
Untitled (project
for the Fondation
Louis Vuitton, Paris)
2015
COURTESY OF THE ARTIST

LIU WEI
Don't touch
2011
Oxhide, wood, steel
Variable dimensions
COURTESY LIU WEI STUDIO

LIU WEI
Enigma
2014
Variable dimensions
Mixed media
COURTESY LIU WEI STUDIO

LIU WEI
Look! Book
2014
Variable dimensions
Books, wood, steel
COURTESY LIU WEI STUDIO

LIU XIAODONG
Jincheng Airport
2010
Oil on canvas
300 × 400 cm
COURTESY OF THE ARTIST

LIU XIAODONG
*Li Wu works the
nightshift and still
cannot sleep by day*
2010
Oil on canvas
150 × 140 cm
COURTESY OF THE ARTIST

LIU XIAODONG
Bent Rib
2010
Oil on canvas
150 × 140 cm
COURTESY OF THE ARTIST

LIU XIAODONG
Into Taihu
2010
Oil on canvas
300 × 400 cm
COURTESY OF THE ARTIST

LIU XIAODONG
Out of Beichuan
2010
Oil on canvas
300 × 400 cm
COURTESY OF THE ARTIST

QIU ZHIJIE
Map of the Third World
2015
Ink mural (for the 6th
Moscow Biennial)
70 × 1400 cm
COURTESY OF THE ARTIST

QIU ZHIJIE
*Memory about the
Post-Sense Sensibility*
2014
Ink on paper
70 × 140 cm
COURTESY OF THE ARTIST

QIU ZHIJIE
The Storm is coming
2007
Performance
at PERFORMA 2007
DR

QIU ZHIJIE
*When love is dead –
where is the capital
of Madagascar?*
2008
Photograph
11 × 17 cm
(Work from *A Suicidology
of the Nanjing Yangtze
River Bridge Project*)
COURTESY OF THE ARTIST

TAO HUI
Photo shoot,
The Acting Tutorial
2014
DR

TAO HUI
1 Character & 7 Materials
2015
Sound and video
installation
1 Character: sound
installation, microphone,
headphones, 13′55″
(Chinese) and 17′43″
(English)
7 Materials: HD video,
11′48″
COURTESY OF THE ARTIST
AND AIKE DELLARCO GALLERY,
SHANGHAÏ

TAO HUI
Installation views
of *1 Character
& 7 Materials*
2015
COURTESY OF THE ARTIST

TAO HUI
The Dusk of Teheran
2014
Single-channel HD video
4′
COLLECTION FONDATION
LOUIS VUITTON
COURTESY OF ARTIST

TAO HUI
Excessive
2015
Single-channel HD video
19′32″
COURTESY OF THE ARTIST

XU QU
Zebra
2015
Single-channel HD video
8′32″

XU QU
Currency Wars
2015
Installation view
at Almine Rech Gallery,
Brussels
RIGHT AND LEFT: COLLECTION
FONDATION LOUIS VUITTON
COURTESY OF THE ARTIST
AND ALMINE RECH GALLERY

XU QU
*Currency Wars –
Dollar 2, New*
2015
Acrylic paint on canvas
150 × 158 cm
COURTESY OF THE ARTIST
AND ALMINE RECH GALLERY

XU QU
*Currency Wars –
Dollar 2, Old*
2015
Acrylic and spray
paint on canvas
150 × 158 cm
COURTESY OF THE ARTIST
AND ALMINE RECH GALLERY

XU QU
Tennis Court
Installation view at Taikang
Space, Beijing, 2014
COURTESY OF THE ARTIST

XU QU
Performance
at "On/Off: China's Young
Artist in Concept and
Practice"
Ullens Center for
Contemporary Art,
Beijing, 2014
COURTESY OF THE ARTIST

XU ZHEN
Physique of Consciousness
2011
Poster
PRODUCED BY MADEIN
COMPANY
CREDIT MADIN COMPANY

XU ZHEN
*Eternity – The Soldier
of Marathon Announcing
Victory, Dying Gaul*
2014
Glass-fibre-reinforced
concrete, marble grains,
marble, metal
157 × 96 × 250 cm
PRODUCED BY MADEIN
COMPANY
PHOTO THOMAS FUESSER

XU ZHEN
Physique of Consciousness
2011
Video
PRODUCTION MADEIN COMPANY
PHOTO XU ZHEN /
MADEIN COMPANY

XU ZHEN
*Eternity – Winged
Victory of Samothrace,
Tianlongshan Grottoes
Bodhisattva*
2013
Glass fibre, steel, concrete
626 × 460 × 230 cm
COLLECTION FONDATION
LOUIS VUITTON
PRODUCTION MADEIN COMPANY
PHOTO XU ZHEN /
MADEIN COMPANY

XU ZHEN
New
2013
Stainless steel, paint
130 × 110 × 402 cm
COLLECTION FONDATION
LOUIS VUITTON
PRODUCTION MADEIN COMPANY
PHOTO XU ZHEN /
MADEIN COMPANY

YANG FUDONG
*Blue Kylin – A Journal
of Shandong*
2008
Video installation

YANG FUDONG
*Blue Kylin – A Journal
of Shandong*
2008
Video installation

YANG FUDONG
*Blue Kylin – A Journal
of Shandong*
2008
Video installation

YANG FUDONG
*The Coloured Sky:
New Women 2*
2014
HD video installation
14′48″
COLLECTION FONDATION
LOUIS VUITTON
CO-PRODUCED BY ACMI
MELBOURNE AND AUCKLAND
ART GALLERY TOI O TAMAKI
COURTESY OF THE ARTIST;
GALERIE MARIAN GOODMAN
ACMI MELBOURNE ET
AUCKLAND ART GALLERY TOI
O TAMAKI
PHOTO AURÉLIEN MOLE

YANG FUDONG
*Tonight Moon
(Jin Wan De Yue Liang)*
2000
Video installation
5′34′
COLLECTION FONDATION
LOUIS VUITTON
PHOTO: YANG FUDONG:
ESTRANGED PARADISE,
WORKS 19932003, AUGUST
21, 2013 – DECEMBER 8,
2013 (INSTALLATION VIEW);
COURTESY OF THE BERKELEY
ART MUSEUM AND PACIFIC
FILM ARCHIVE.
PHOTO: SIBILLA SAVAGE

EXHIBITED WORKS

CAO FEI
Strangers
2015
Video
4'18''

HAO LIANG
The Virtuous Being
2015
Ink and color on silk
Hand scroll, painting size:
40×927cm
Hand scroll size:
40×1312cm

HAO LIANG
Research for
The Virtuous Being
1–Postcard of Chinese
Garden
19th century
Photograph
9×14cm

2–Rubbings
of *Wangchuan Villa*
19th century
Paper and ink
33×38.5cm×6

3–Manuscript
of *The Virtuous Being*
2015
Pencil and color on paper
10×70cm

4–Yanshan Garden
2015
Photograph
7×10.5cm

5–A Letter to Hangzhou
Weaving From Wang Shizhen
16th century
Xerox copy
36.8×45.8cm

6–*Yanshan Garden* 2015
Watercolor, photograph
7×10.5cm×4

7–Wangchuan Villa
(Guo Zhongshu's Version)
19th century
Collotype print
21.5×31.5cm×2

8–Yanshan Garden
2015
Photograph
12.4×18.8cm

HU XIANGQIAN
*Speech at the Edge
of the World*
2013
Video
12'23''

HU XIANGQIAN
*The Woman in Front
of the Camera*
2015
Video
2'33''

LIU CHUANG
*BBR1 (No.1 of Blossom
Bud Restrainer)*
2015
Video
4'56''

LIU SHIYUAN
*From Happiness
to Whatever*
2015
Carpets, speakers,
iPod player
Variable dimensions

LIU WEI
LIBERATION NO.16
2014
Oil on canvas
400×720cm
Untitled
2015
Installation (plexiglas,
glass, mirror, metal)

LIU XIAODONG
Jincheng Airport
2010
Oil on canvas
300×400cm

LIU XIAODONG
My Egypt
2010
Oil on canvas
300×400cm

LIU XIAODONG
*Chengzi Standing
on the West Bridge*
2010
Oil on canvas
150×140cm.

LIU XIAODONG
*Chengzi Shows up
at the Wrong Door*
2010
Oil on canvas
150×140cm

LIU XIAODONG
*Xiao on Duty at the
Police Station*
2010
Oil on canvas
150×140cm

LIU XIAODONG
*Li Wu works the nightshift
and still can not sleep by
Dday*
2010
Oil on canvas
150×140cm

LIU XIAODONG
Han Shengzi buys land
2010
Oil on canvas
150×140cm

LIU XIAODONG
Xuzi at home
2010
Oil on canvas
150×140cm

LIU XIAODONG
Bent rib
2010
Oil on canvas
150×140cm

QIU ZHIJIE
From Huaxia to China
2015

QIU ZHIJIE
Ink on paper
6 rolls
370×120cm each

TAO HUI
1 Character & 7 Materials,
2015
Sound and video
installation
1 Character : sound
installation, microphone,
headphones, 13'55''
(Chinese) and 17'43''
(English)
7 Materials : HD video,
1 channel, 11'48''
Steel stand (with
headphones),
146.5×130×40cm
Bus Station (steel, glass,
rear-projection screen),
248×364.5×70cm
Bench (steel),
35×80×30cm

XU QU
Currency Wars
2015
Acrylic and spray paint
on canvas
12×2 paintings 150 x158cm

XU ZHEN
Physique of Consciousness
2011
Video

XU ZHEN
*Eternity – The Soldier
of Marathon Announcing
Victory, A Wounded
Galatian*
2014
Glass fiber reinforced
concrete, marble grains,
marble, metal
157×96×250cm

YANG FUDONG
*Blue Kylin – A Journal
of Shan Dong*
2008–2015
Video installation,
10 screens

BENTU
CHINESE
ARTISTS
IN
A
TIME
OF
TURBULENCE
AND
TRANSFORMATION

WE WOULD LIKE TO EXPRESS
OUR WARM GRATITUDE TO:
Bérénice Angrémy
Léo de Boisgisson
Patricia Brunerie
Cao Dan
Marie-Monique Couvegnes
Jean-Marc Decrop
Alexia Dehaene
Ludovic Delalande
Aike Dellarco Shanghai China
Laurence de Failly
Jens Faurschou
Larys Frogier
Luz Gyalui
Hou Hanru
Hu Fang
Kit Huen
Gunnar Kvaran
Sylvain et Dominique Lévy
Li Bowen
Long March Space
Nielsen Kristian Mondrup
Alexandra Munroe
Hans Ulrich Obrist
Jeanette Pacher
Peter Pakesch
Pi Li
Jeffrey Sequeira
Almine Rech Gallery, Brussels
Shanghart Gallery
Angeline Scherf
Budi Tek
Vitamin Creative Space
White Cube London
Xie Jinbiao
Zhang Lulu

Printed in Italy by Stamperia Artistica,
Trofarello, January 2016
Image reproductions
Litho Art New, Turin, Italy

Library of Congress Control
Number: 2015958381
A catalogue record for this book
is available from The British Library